# GROUP CHILD CARE
## as a Family Service

# GROUP CHILD CARE
## as a Family Service

by Alan Keith-Lucas
and Clifford W. Sanford

**The University of North Carolina Press**
**Chapel Hill**

Copyright © 1977 by
The University of North Carolina Press
All rights reserved
Manufactured in the United States of America
ISBN 0-8078-1303-6
Library of Congress Catalog Card Number 76-40411

Library of Congress Cataloging in Publication Data

Main entry under title:

Group child care as a family service.

  Bibliography: p.
  Includes index.
   1.  Children—Institutional care—United States—
Addresses, essays, lectures. 2. Social work with
children—United States—Addresses, essays, lectures.
3. Family social work—United States—Addresses, essays,
lectures. 4. Foster home care—United States—Addresses,
essays, lectures. I. Keith-Lucas, Alan. II. Sanford,
Clifford W.
HV741.G74       362.7'32'0973       76-40411
ISBN 0-8078-1303-6

# Contents

# Introduction

America is, for the second time in forty years, in the throes of a revulsion against anything that can be even vaguely thought of as institutional. But there is a difference. The type of Children's Home against which social workers and much of the public were reacting in the 1930s and 1940s was in general the church-sponsored orphanage, and many people saw the foster family home as an alternative. The reaction in the 1970s is principally directed against the state-operated institution for the mentally ill, the physically and mentally handicapped, and the delinquent child, and the most favored alternative is the small, community-centered group home. Inevitably, however, the larger, campus-based Children's Home has been called into question again. Many churches and other organizations are seriously considering whether such Homes are needed. Would it not be better to decentralize them all into smaller group homes? Do we need Children's Homes, if at all, only as short-time residential treatment centers where resources can be concentrated on overcoming disturbed children's emotional or behavioral problems?

It is no denigration of either the group home, long recognized as the probable "wave of the future" in child care, nor of the much-needed residential treatment center, to suggest that certain children in certain situations need the services of the less specialized Children's Home. But it would be foolish to predict that this role will be accorded to the Home unless it makes very clear whom it is equipped to serve, and how. This role will be found, we suggest, only as the Home can free itself from the past, making clear that it does not exist to take charge of children whose parents have failed them, but rather serving families threatened by breakdown by offering them a period of separation, planning together, modification of attitudes, and consideration of alternatives. It can bring to bear on these problems all the strength of its stability, its physical compactness, and the experience of a closely knit staff acting as a team.

The authors' experience with such Homes spans more than twenty years of direct practice and consultation in this country and abroad. Out of the reciprocity of learning that naturally develops in consultation, certain convictions and theories develop, relating for the most part to Children's Homes which have been called upon to care for children who for family-related reasons cannot live at home. Many such Homes, no longer content to be little better than custodial facilities, are developing well-thought-out professional services. Many have developed a particular philosophy and skills and have become quite sophisticated services to families in danger of disintegration. The emphasis of this book is, therefore, on the agency as a whole in its work with the whole family. The concept and methods of working with the entire family are seen as basic to all other services—of which residential treatment is one among many.

The consultation in which the authors have been involved has chiefly been rendered through Group Child Care Consultant Services, or its predecessor, the Group Child Care Project, of the School of Social Work of the University of North Carolina. This unique organization, of which one author was the first director and the other has been a staff member since 1966, was established in 1956 at the request of twenty children's institutions in the Southeast, and now serves annually more than two hundred agencies in a majority of the states and in some foreign countries through workshops, consultation, staff training, and a limited program of research. The authors acknowledge their tremendous debt to their colleagues, past and present, in this organization and to the organization itself for permission to use its published material. The service has provided a cross-fertilization of ideas as well as a structure that has enabled the authors to draw from publications of the agency, such as the annual *Chapel Hill Workshop Reports* and the *Proceedings of the Winter Seminar for Social Workers*, and to engage in workshops, consultation, training, and studies with a great variety of Homes. All the contributors to Part Two of the book have, in fact, some connection with Group Child Care Consultant Services, as staff member, staff of a member agency, or speaker at one of its meetings. The authors do not claim in any way, however, to represent the official thinking of that agency or to speak for its staff. This book represents the authors' own thinking, with which other staff members may or may not fully concur.

The book consists of three parts. In the first part the principal authors consider the basic theory and methods of the family-centered Children's Home, its history, structure, staffing, and relationships. Much of this material is based on the practice of progressive agencies which the authors have attempted to present conceptually. The second part consists of papers on particular aspects of the work, either given at conferences or especially written for this book. Most of these have been edited in minor ways, mainly to remove topical allusions to the meeting at which they were given, or to avoid repetition of material in Part One. In a short third part more than a hundred books and articles are suggested for further readings and study.

The authors have been particularly beset by the problem of sex-linked pronouns. At length, after much deliberation, the rule was adopted that the sex most often represented in the role being discussed should rule, with no implication that the other sex was not included, or that the job could not be filled by either men or women. Thus, executives are referred to as "he"—there are more men executives than women. Child care workers and parents are referred to as "she"—more mothers than fathers work directly with Children's Homes. The two exceptions to this rule are social workers, referred to as "he" to help distinguish them from child care workers in discussion of their relationships, and children, who are referred to as either "he" or "she" as the author of the piece preferred.

ALAN KEITH-LUCAS                    CLIFFORD W. SANFORD
              *Chapel Hill, North Carolina*    *1976*

# PART ONE
# The Family-Centered Children's Home

# ❧❧ I

# The Development
# of the Children's Home

Children's Homes, as a way of caring for children who cannot live at home, have existed for the better part of two centuries but did not become common until after the Civil War. Since the 1920s rather few have been built, although there has been recently a proliferation of small "group homes," either self-contained or sponsored by a larger agency.

The majority of Children's Homes, except those for delinquents and the handicapped, have been and are church-sponsored, although some have been created by fraternal or civic organizations, a few are funded through community chests, and a very few are maintained by states, counties, or cities.

Although the basic form of the Children's Home has not changed very much during the period of its existence, except for the gradual abandonment of the congregate, one-building institution in favor of a cottage plan—and many venerable Children's Homes have been of the cottage type from the beginning[1]—Children's Homes have changed radically in purpose and in the methods used to implement their goals. This change has partly

1. Connie Maxwell Children's Home, in Greenwood, South Carolina, a charter member of Group Child Care Consultant Services, was the first, in 1891, to build entirely self-contained cottages.

been due to shifts in the needs and circumstances of those served and partly to the development of alternative methods of care. Perhaps this change is due in largest measure to changing concepts about the family, the rearing of children, and the kind of results that the institution hoped for—what in fact constituted a good life for children and adults.

Yet nothing ever completely outgrows its past. Tradition, particularly where policy is made by those who have previously worked under very different conditions, often controls the way people act long after circumstances call for a new approach. It takes time for new concepts to permeate an organization, so that newer ideas may operate in one part of it while another part may reflect the thinking of ten, twenty, or fifty years ago. Thus, an understanding of the historical development of the Children's Home can serve as background for evaluation of a Home's practices in the present, helping in identification of areas that may need revision or updating.

This is not intended to be a detailed history of the Children's Home. It deals rather with the general phases through which the Children's Home has gone, particularly in relation to purpose and clientele served. Certain specific issues pertinent to that development, such as decentralization, payment for care, licensing, and church-state relationships are reserved for future discussion.

There are roughly three stages through which Homes have passed. No firm dates can be given to each stage. Some Homes are even today in the first of these stages and some began to enter the third a number of years ago. Nor do Homes move abruptly from one stage to another. Even a new executive with more progressive views than his predecessor will affect only parts of the system at first. Change may also be slowed down by a board or a constituency used to one way of doing things or by staff members who continue to operate out of their familiar perception of goals and methods long after the official viewpoint has changed. It is not at all uncommon, for instance, to find staff members enforcing rules the origin of which no one can recall and which are directly contrary to a Home's present philosophy.

# Development of the Children's Home

The first stage could be described as *institutionally oriented*, or that of the *orphanage*. Homes were founded to take care of orphan children or those whose parents were too poor to support them. The philosophy of child rearing in these Homes was essentially that of the mid-nineteenth century. Children were seen on the one hand as innocent creatures who needed sheltering from the wickedness of the world, and on the other as having a will of their own that needed to be subdued or broken. In addition, the children of the poor were seen, not unrealistically in those times, to be in great need of instruction in three areas—academic, moral or spiritual, and vocational, or more properly to need training in their capacity to work, for they would be destined to work in generally rather lowly occupations upon "graduation," unless they could show themselves to be intellectually inclined, in which case they could become pastors or missionaries. Moral and vocational training were almost synonymous, since work was considered a moral duty of the poor, not only as adults but as children, and it was thought only proper that poor children should do all they could to support themselves both as part of their moral training and in gratitude to their benefactors.

This last factor was quite important. The alternative to the orphanage was, for most children a hundred or so years ago, abject poverty, the workhouse, or a hand-to-mouth existence as a wanderer or a waif. One of Great Britain's best-known Children's Homes was known as "The Waifs and Strays" up until World War II; one of America's still retains, for historical reasons, its original name, "The New England Home for Little Wanderers." Wandering was, however, often preferable to the workhouse or almshouse, and many institutions today include the word "haven" in their title.

In early times the Home became the child's sole guardian and custodian. One of the less explicit motives for its founding was, in most cases, a desire for a monument to the church's or the fraternal or other organization's charity and responsibility (and therefore to its pride). Most of its managers and constituency felt their way of life or their doctrine to be greatly superior to that from which the child had come, or would experience if he were not in the Home. Poor children were regarded not as individuals with widely differing social and emotional needs, but rather as a group to be reared, protected, and trained. Docility was seen as a most desirable attribute in children, in the poor, and in recipients of charity. Consequently, high priority was given to conformity, obedience for obedience's sake, and a regimented and adult-directed routine. Successful and smooth operation of the institution became more important to many Homes than the needs of the residents. The child was valued more for his contribution to the institution, as a worker, interpreter of the "work"—many children were shamelessly exploited as objects of pity or examples of piety or gratitude—good influence on others, or successful product of the Home, than for himself or for what the Home could do to help him.

Such institutions were usually large, to take care of a maximum number of children, were impressive in their architecture, and were either walled or isolated from their surrounding community both socially and psychologically. Frequently, they became almost the personal domain of a superintendent whose word was law and who made virtually all the decisions both in the Home and in a child's life. He often was referred to, or assumed, such nicknames as "Father," "Daddy," or "Pop." Child care was generally the responsibility of elderly women who were often objects of charity themselves and were given little opportunity to do more than monitor the children and report infractions to the superintendent or to a disciplinarian. Minor infractions of rules were punished by restrictions from the few recreational activities provided after work was done; moderate ones, and in general any impertinence, disobedience, or lesser rebelliousness were followed by corporal punishment, for both boys and girls of any age. More serious rebelling and immoral behavior, particularly in the areas of sex or alcohol, usually met with instant dismissal.

The orphanage had as one of its primary purposes the saving of children from both physical and moral degradation. Since it could not possibly serve all those who were subject to these threats—and family life at home in extreme poverty, with

6

little schooling and almost no religious intruction, was seen as degrading—the Home tended to select "worthy" or promising children and to dismiss them if they proved to be idle, ill-behaved, or ungrateful. The threat of dismissal was a powerful one, in view of the alternatives. The philosophy of saving the child from degradation also accounted for the almost universal practice of cutting the child off irrevocably from any family that he had, particularly if the family were judged to be immoral, ignorant, or irresponsible.

While this picture may seem to be overdrawn, many of these practices and attitudes are to be found in Homes today, and have only recently been abandoned in others. Even Homes with social-work staffs operate sometimes, in their child-rearing practices, largely in terms of control of the group and the keeping of rules, with a strong emphasis on obedience and respect for adult authority. Children are still dismissed for immoral behavior and indeed sometimes deliberately behave in ways that will ensure their discharge.

The second stage can be called that of *child-centered individualization*. Many factors helped to bring it about. Perhaps two of the most potent were the challenge of the foster family home and the concurrent criticism of the institution as impersonal, rigid, and likely to produce shallow, conforming characters incapable of engaging in deep personal relationships. The work of Anna Freud and others[2] emphasized the importance of family life. More and more, children were seen as individuals, each with his own problems. Child rearing had become less autocratic as a result of the work of such educational reformers as Dewey and Froebel. The circumstances of children referred for care to Children's Homes changed radically. The 1909 White House Conference on Children had enunciated the principle that no child should be removed from his family for reasons of poverty alone, and by 1936 the new federal-state program of Aid to Dependent Children, despite its inadequacies, was beginning to keep many poor families together.

2. See, in particular, Anna Freud and Dorothy Burlingham, *Infants without Families: The Case for and against Residential Nurseries* (New York: International University Press, 1944).

# Group Child Care as a Family Service

At the same time the number of orphans was dropping.[3] Medical care was keeping many more parents alive through their child-rearing years, although not always restoring them to effective health. The orphans remaining were being routed by newly created welfare departments to foster family homes. Yet children were still in need of care. Industrialization, mobility, and general unrest were not only destroying the old-time extended family, where uncles, aunts, cousins, and grandparents could come to the rescue of many a child whose parents were dead, absent, or sick, but were also seriously threatening the intensely vulnerable "nuclear family" that was all that was left to the child.

The child in need of care was no longer the orphan or child of the very poor. He was the victim of family breakdown. He was a far more difficult child to care for than the orphan. In the first place, he had often been subject to neglect and abuse in his own home. He was frequently cut off from his kin, other than his immediate family, and from a stable community life. At the same time, his only identity was with his parents. He resented being removed from them while they were still alive and yet was angry with them for their inability and unwillingness to care for him. He would not give up hope that they might care for him again. He had no reason to be grateful to the institution, which was no longer a haven from the rigors of the workhouse but a supplanter of the care that his parents owed him. Such children were at the very least confused, and as interest in mental health developed, they were frequently labeled as disturbed and in need of psychotherapy.

Institutions adapted both in diverse ways and at different speeds to these new concepts and circumstances. Some Children's Homes, particularly in the North, Midwest, and Far West, where public foster family agencies grew rapidly, turned their attention to the more disturbed child and became residential treatment centers for those children who were psychically the most damaged.

3. According to Child Welfare League of America statistics the percentage of full orphans in children's homes was 75 percent in 1923, 27 percent in 1941, and 8 percent in 1957. In one home the proportion of children with both parents living has risen from 33 percent to 76 percent in the last thirty years.

8

# Development of the Children's Home

Some Children's Homes, particularly those with a religious orientation, rejected the findings of the predominant analytical psychology with its emphasis on the sexual impulse and, at that time at least, a philosophy of permissiveness in this area. Others, principally in the South, were still being relied on to serve a substantial proportion of the dependent and neglected child population and could not envisage themselves as caring for a specialized group. Some were discouraged by the high per-capita costs and the problems of finding the highly professional staffs required for residential treatment. A few such Homes clung desperately to the philosophy of the orphanage, but many made less radical but still progressive changes and moved principally in four directions: toward the establishment of much smaller and more homelike living units, toward the creation of an "open" rather than a "closed" campus, toward the employment of social workers, and toward more work with the child's family.

All four were movements toward greater individualization of the child. The number of children in one living unit fell from 30–40 to 20–25 in many Homes by about 1950, to 15–18 by the early 1960s, to a maximum of 12 and a norm in some institutions of 8–10 by the end of the decade. At the same time, new patterns of groupings emerged. By the end of the 1950s a number of Homes had abandoned strict peer-grouping by age and sex and were experimenting with family cottages where brothers and sisters could live together.

Closer living with a smaller number of children enhanced the position of the houseparent. Curiously, perhaps, the fewer children she—or he, for more men and more married couples were entering the field—cared for, the more was demanded of her. She could no longer rely on invigilation and simple house-keeping skills to enable her to control a large number of children. In the more individualized atmosphere of the small living group she was expected to become counselor, substitute parent, and disciplinarian. Yet in many Homes this last function was still considered the most important and a houseparent's ability to "keep control" and produce a smoothly running cottage was given priority. Even when the training of houseparents became increasingly available and began to be used by the more progressive institutions, a large part of the material discussed had to do with "handling" various forms of child behavior and with disciplinary methods. Even today, getting the work done in the cottage appears to be the focus of many a houseparent's concern.

The movement toward the more open institution came about with some relaxation of the need to protect children from outside influences and the growth of public schools and churches in local communities. The old-time orphanage had been a self-contained society, in which children not only lived and worked but went to church and school as well. As such it was easier to control. But increasingly Homes began to recognize that children needed some contact with life outside the Home and gradually gave up their campus-based schools and often their campus-based churches as well. Some institutions also began to see the value of work experiences outside the Home. The reverse phenomenon, opening the campus to the community, was somewhat slower in developing, although there were a number of experiments of this nature. Increasingly, new Children's Homes were built without fences and even as integral parts of their community. Yet many Homes remain today essentially closed societies, whose children are bused to community schools and back again and are denied full participation in extracurricular activities, sometimes for largely logistical reasons, but sometimes also from a desire to keep the children on the campus, where they can be more easily supervised.

Social workers were first employed by Children's Homes in the 1920s. Their primary role was the screening of children referred for care. Homes were beginning to realize that not all children needed group care or could indeed be cared for in it. The social worker saw himself, also, as the child's confidante, therapist, and advocate against the often authoritarian handling of the institution. Usually younger and more highly educated than either the child care staff or the administration, he thought of himself as representing the unrecognized, but rightful, core discipline which should prescribe all that happens to every child in the Home, as well as the Home's policies and priorities. In the clinical residential center where the Home's chief helping method was therapy, generally under the direction of a psychiatrist, such a claim was at least defensible, but in the Home caring for children because of the breakdown of their families, the social worker's services to children in care were generally used only in times of crisis or where a child's behavior was outside the range of the house-parent's or the administrator's experience or ability to handle. Social work service was considered for the most part an additive to the program rather than an integral part of it.

The social worker was, however, the link between the child and his family. It was social work which began to recognize that a child's individual condition could not be handled by the institution if he were cut off completely from the source of so many of his problems. Loyalties to his family often interfered with his adjustment in the institution. Thus the family had to be worked with and encouraged to visit, if at all suitable, in the interests of the child. Many such institutions also tried to return the child to his own family home as soon as possible, and the average length of stay did fall in many such institutions from five or six years to something more like two or three. Older children also began to be accepted. The orphanage, intent on producing a child of whom it could be proud, usually felt that children over twelve years old would not be susceptible to retraining and there-fore denied them admission. It had little hesitation, however, in accepting children at a very young age, even sometimes almost at birth, despite growing evidence that very young children needed much more individual attention than an institution could provide. The child-oriented institution of the 1950s and 1960s generally did not accept children under school age and began to accept youngsters at fifteen, sixteen, or even seventeen if they needed care. In the late 1960s an increasing number of applications con-cerned teenagers who had become alienated from living with the family.

In this stage, which is quite frankly where the majority of so-called progressive Children's Homes are today, and to which the less developed and more traditional Homes are gradually moving, children are certainly treated in a much more humane and imaginative way than they were in the old-time orphanage. Yet many Children's Homes of this kind retain some of the traditions and attitudes of the past, such as dismissing children for bad behavior, an excessive reliance on punishment (and even corporal punishment) as a method of control, and a subordinate position and low salary for the houseparent. As these relics of the past are recognized and re-evaluated, however, many of them are disappearing. The major problems with such Homes is not the persistence of such practices, important as it is to eliminate them, as much as it is a basic lack of clarity as to goals and the process by which these goals may be attained. Many Homes are still not sure what should be their relationship with the child and his family. They recognize the importance of the family to the child yet continue to treat the child as if the institution had become to all intents and purposes his family. Such Homes still think of themselves as supplanting rather than supplementing family life. This ambivalence is illustrated by the classification often applied to the Children's Home that is not designed to treat children with specific psychiatric or behavior dysfunctions and yet has social workers on its staff. These Homes accept children, not because they are disturbed or are in need of re-education, although some of them may be so, but because of family breakdown or alienation. Yet these Homes are often inadequately classified in social work literature and thinking as "treatment-oriented," to distinguish them on the one hand from the true "residential treatment center" and from the poorly regarded "custodial" facility, or the one caring for "dependent and neglected" children on the other.

But to be "treatment-oriented" is to be nothing. It clearly falls short of any true goal and indicates a half-way stage toward a goal which the Home may not have in mind. While there is obvious need for residential treatment centers in our society, there is also need for organizations to deal with problems of family breakdown, alienation, and even normal development, providing as a part of their service a period of care away from home. For many children, particularly those who have problems of relationship with their families and are confused rather than clinically disturbed, and for much family planning, a group-care situation may be the most constructive resource. This care does not necessarily involve intensive psychotherapy or behavior modification; it may do so, but the Home's helping process is not centered on the child's dysfunction. The child is accepted because of the family breakdown, not because of his personal problems. Any disturbance he may show is, in fact, likely to be a result of the breakdown. Indeed, even clinical facilities are paying a great deal more attention both to planning with families and to the quality of day-to-day living that accompanies their primary function. A better definition for Homes which have social work staff but are not residential treatment centers would be "family-oriented" rather than "treatment-oriented."

An initial move toward something different and more purposeful on the part of the Children's Home came in the mid-1960s with the development of the concept of co-planning. Indeed, the era to which the Children's Home is now moving might be called the *family-oriented* or *co-planning* phase. The Home is not viewed as an organization that takes over when the family has failed but is regarded as a resource for a family with difficulties to overcome or needing for its development a period of separation of parent and child. Of course, in some situations the family's problems have resulted in neglect and abuse of the child, or unacceptable behavior on his part, so that society through its courts has intervened and made mandatory a period of care away from home for the child, but this intervention only makes co-planning with the family more necessary in order to forestall, if possible, total family disintegration.

✳✳✳ Placement, then, of a child in a Home is not an end in itself, but is an element of a plan in which the family is given opportunity to make a new start in its relationships. Placement of the child for a limited period of time may relieve pressures in the family and allow parents to get hold of themselves. More and more, social problems, even child abuse itself, are being understood as due as much to pressures occasioned by overcrowding, financial worries, and alienation from resources formerly found in the community or the extended family group, as they are to a personal psychopathology. Or short-term care may be designed to modify a child's behavior that has caused alienation from his family or to provide him with psychotherapy that may overcome a dysfunction or change basic attitudes. The whole family may be worked with in an attempt to clarify, discuss, and promote constructive intrafamily relationships. The parents may be helped to overcome specific problems through counseling, group engagement, or psychotherapy offered either by the Children's Home or in the community. But one of the strongest factors in helping the family to decide on and carry out a plan is the help the Home can give them in coping with the requirements of the new role they have assumed—that of part-time or "living-apart" parents. At a time when we are conscious that the traditional family system has moved from the so-called extended multigenerational family of the past to the "nuclear" family of today—a mother, a father, and one or two children—even the nuclear family is in a process of change. Instead of one model, there are many: the one-parent family, the family with children of three different parentages— what has been described as "his'n, her'n and our'n"—the multiracial adoptive family, the commune. To this might be added the supportive, part-time parent, existing in upper-class Britain for a long time through its use of boarding schools, and now becoming quite common in America in a slightly different way in the extensive use of day care, but not yet generally accepted as legitimate and workable in relation to Children's Homes. Visiting, correspondence, participation in regularly scheduled family conferences, being available for consultation, the providing of vacations, financial responsibility to whatever extent is practical, and the keeping of agreements are the touchstones against which the parent, with the Home's help, can discover for himself how much and what kind of a parent he is willing and able to be. What makes it possible for the parent to use these requirements are the interest and support of the Home, its recognition of the family's right to make its own decisions, and the willingness of the Home not only to accept the parent as a full partner in what happens to the child while he is in the agency's care, but to insist that in fact the parent must accept the Home as his partner in working out his family plans.

Such co-planning may result in the child's return to the family after some period of care. It may result in plans for him with one or the other parent, perhaps with a stepmother or stepfather—curiously, it not infrequently happens that the parent who was absent from the family home at the time placement took place comes back to assume responsibility for his children. If parents can be helped to see that their desire or capability for parenthood is minimal, and to accept this, plans may involve the transfer of responsibility to a relative who cares about the child but who often does not want to become involved until the parents' plans are determined. Adoption, the creation of an entirely new family, may be a responsible option. So may long-term care away from home, in group care, foster family care, a group home, or some other arrangement, with the parent or some other personal guardian providing the sense of family identity that children away from home always need. No one plan is necessarily superior to any other. One might look to a return to a reunited family as the most desirable outcome, but this is true only if it is what the family wants and can support.

There is, however, one option which the Children's Home should try hard to avoid, and that is the disintegration of the family in an unplanned way—the gradual drifting apart of its members or the maintenance of purely nominal, occasional, or irresponsible relationships which offer the child no security, little identity, and no real point of reference outside the Children's Home. Tragically, too many children live this way today, and it is not always the fault of the family. Too many Homes, meeting the family at the point of its greatest weakness, reinforce this weakness by their own vagueness in considering options, their subtle discouragement of the parent, or even the patronizing way in which they "permit" a parent to exercise impulsively rights which are naturally his.

Another characteristic of the Children's Home of the family-oriented, co-planning era is that the Home develops a consistent process for planning with and for children and their families to provide a continuum of experiences through which the child and his family move. This is a carefully structured process which will be examined in more detail later. Its essential concept is that there are times at which children and their parents need to look at some piece of reality with the Home's help before they can go on to make use of the next step in the process of formulating or moving toward their ultimate goals.

Such a structured process carries with it an important corollary. It cannot be carried out without the involvement and cooperation of all the Home's staff. It is not something that administrators or social workers can ordain and carry out by themselves. A process involving the total way a family makes use of the services of a Home must take into account what is happening to the child in his living unit, his school, his recreation, his sessions with a therapist, his contacts with his family, his church attendance, and his work, and it must integrate all these influences. In order to act responsibly, the Home must also gather information from all these sources and bring the person responsible for each into the decision-making process. If each is to play his part in the process, each one's knowledge, experience, and opinions must be respected and become part of any plan that results.

The need for such comprehensive planning has placed even greater demands than heretofore on those persons who have been thought of in the past as the lower echelons and those whose functions were peripheral. Training or further education for these workers is imperative. The child care worker has, for instance, progressed from being a "matron," whose primary responsibilities were physical care and monitoring behavior, to being a "houseparent" in charge of a small group to which she was counselor, disciplinarian, and substitute parent, to being truly a "child care worker" with definite professional responsibilities as a member of the institution's team. Indeed, the latest move in the field, learned for the most part from Europe, is the development of a generalized child-welfare person who can specialize as child care worker, social worker, director of activities, or administrator—almost anything, that is, other than the highly specialized roles of psychiatrist, psychologist, physician, or, perhaps, minister.[4]

4. See, for instance, Jeannine Guindon, "The Educateurs," *Chapel Hill Workshop Reports*, week 2, 1973, pp. 47–53.

# Development of the Children's Home

While this particular development is still in the future for most Children's Homes in the United States, there is growing a greater democracy among all disciplines contributing to the helping process of the Home. In the next chapter we will explore to some extent the helping methods of a Home, to see how these can be brought together into a process.

# 米米II

# The Seven Helping Methods of the Children's Home

A Children's Home can be said to employ seven more or less distinct helping methods in serving the family and the child. Each method can be explained in terms of a response to a particular question that a child or a family needs to have answered. Each one, too, can be distinguished in terms of the person or persons whose primary responsibility it is to provide the service, although the entire staff in a Home is responsible for supporting what is done, with the administrator responsible in general for all services, seeing that they are balanced and consistent.

The seven helping methods—some of which are directed to the family as a whole, and some more specifically to the child's experience in care—can be listed as follows:

1. Planning, or co-planning, responsive in general to the question: "What has happened, is happening, and is going to happen to me (us)?"

2. Care, or nurturing, which answers for the child, "How are my daily needs to be met?"

3. Education, or "What will I need to know?" and perhaps, "How will I learn it?"

4. Group living, or "How do I work out my relationships with others?"

5. Counseling, or "How do I (we) find ways of solving my (our) problems?"

6. Therapy, or "How do I (we) overcome handicaps, either physical or emotional?"

7. Advocacy, "How do I (we) obtain and implement my (our) rights?"

Of these, numbers 1, 5, 6, and 7 are directed to both parent and child, or to the family as a whole, and numbers 2, 3, and 4 relate more specifically to the child.

There may be some overlaps between these methods, yet they serve as a useful way of conceptualizing both the total service of the Home and the part that each staff member accepts as his primary responsibility.

In the various phases of the development of Children's Homes, and in determining the direction of a Home in the present, there may be greater emphasis on various of the helping methods, depending on their usefulness for the Home's purposes. Thus the orphanage stressed education (with training as its primary helping method), was rather minimally concerned with care except in the physical sense, and did very little about planning, group living, counseling, therapy, and advocacy. The child-oriented institution of the 1950s and 1960s placed strongest emphasis on care, particularly in its nurturing aspect, was still much concerned with education, largely in the form of training and discipline, had some concept of counseling and therapy, but tended to isolate these as the province of the social work department. That department in turn claimed advocacy as its special function. Some lip service was given to both planning and group living, but this was for the most part somewhat rudimentary.

The residential treatment center, on the other hand, regards therapy as its primary method. Only fairly recently, with the publication of books such as Polsky's and Claster's *Dynamics of Residential Treatment*[5] and Treischman, Whittaker, and Brendtro's *The Other 23 Hours*[6] has the more clinical center paid much atten-

5. Howard W. Polsky and Daniel S. Claster, *The Dynamics of Residential Treatment* (Chapel Hill: University of North Carolina Press, 1968).

6. Albert E. Treischman, James K. Whittaker, and Larry K. Brendtro, *The Other 23 Hours* (Chicago: Adline Publishing Company, 1969).

tion to care or nurturing. Education has come to the fore lately, however, in the form of behavior modification and in some ways has transformed the child care role into an almost purely educational one. At the same time, residential centers are paying more attention to planning with families than was true in the past.

A new development in the late 1960s and early 1970s has been the group home or camp where the primary helping method is the group experience, often combined with adult expectations for behavior modification.

The family-oriented Children's Home, and more particularly the church-sponsored Home that is the lineal descendant of the orphanage and of the child-oriented "living experience" institution, makes use of all of the helping methods. The name that we gave to it, the co-planning Home, implies that planning is its primary thrust, with all other methods forming part of any good plan in which the child's living in group care for a time is an element.

The remainder of this chapter treats particulars of each of the seven methods and who should be responsible for each. Actual methods are, however, left for more specific discussion later. Planning, which coordinates the whole and creates the process by which the family and the child are assured appropriate service, is the basis of Chapter III, and will be dealt with rather lightly here to avoid repetition.

*Planning* is the primary responsibility of the social work staff. "Primary" here has two senses. The social worker is the primary, but not the sole, planner. He helps the family come to terms initially with the need to plan and aids them in taking the first step toward goals and commitment to such goals. Yet the plan is not solely a social work plan. It is the plan of the whole Home, and everyone in the Home who has any significant part to play in it must be aware of the plan and support it.

The social worker is also the primary planning person because planning, or co-planning, is the primary part of his job. He may have a role to play in group living, counseling, advocacy, in arranging for or even providing therapy, and to a limited extent in child care and education, yet the social worker's first responsibility is for planning with the whole family.

Plans made by Homes are often maintained on two levels, although these are sometimes combined. One has to do with plans for the entire family group, dealing with such matters as the length of placement, goals for the family, and the roles of parents and Home during the child's stay in the Home in relation to visiting, writing, vacations, financial support, and availability for conferences and consultation. This plan is the primary responsibility of the social work staff. The other level deals with agreed-on plans for the child while he is in the Home—what he needs, who will do what on his behalf. The two are not entirely separable, and the major direction of the second (sometimes called the "use-of-care" plan to distinguish it from the "family-agency" plan) may be outlined in the first. The more detailed second-level plan is, however, often more of an agreement between staff to carry out specifics of the family plan rather than an agreement with the family, except that as family members are brought more into the Home's decision-making process they can become participants at this level.

The social worker's responsibility for this second level of planning varies both with the Home's experience with the child and with the emphasis of the Home. If the Home is essentially a treatment center, the use-of-care plan becomes an integral part of a specific therapeutic effort, and the social worker may have a major part in determining its direction. If, however, the Home is basically a co-planning, family-oriented one, the initial stages of such a plan must be based very heavily on the social worker's knowledge of the family and the child; as time goes on, other persons, and in particular child care workers, will have their own experience of the child and his family to contribute.

Certain attributes of good planning at either level are important to its success. First, the plan should be reduced to writing. A written plan does not take the place of mutual understanding, but it does provide a summary of what has been agreed on. Verbal agreements are very easy to forget and tend to be reinterpreted as conditions change. Writing down what one has agreed to is often a help in clarifying misunderstandings. It is one thing to agree verbally, quite another to sign one's name to a written document. One wants to be very sure what one is signing. Written plans, too, crystallize thinking at a specific moment and are invaluable in identifying progress, lack of progress, or retrogression.

Second, any plan needs to specify when and under what conditions it is to be reviewed. It is absolutely essential to specify a maximum period for which any plan or agreement can be operative without a review, and this deadline must be kept, even if the informal consensus is that everything is going well. The greatest enemy of good planning is drift, which results from the failure to note little indications of change or from a series of nondecisions, postponing consideration of a situation which does not seem a major problem at the time. The decision, for instance, to separate the living arrangements of siblings at a time of conflict, or where one is dominating or taking too much responsibility for another, all too often can lead to a permanent separation and a weakening of a tie which both siblings may need later. This can easily happen if both children seem to be doing well where they are, unless there is some procedure that demands a review of the situation.

Having a deadline for review does not mean that plans cannot and should not be reviewed whenever the need arises, but it is important to be clear who can initiate any reconsideration, and how. In general, anyone who believes that the plan is not working should have this right, but some single person should have the responsibility for calling a conference when this need is brought to his attention.

Third, a plan needs to be couched in simple language that is as unambiguous as possible. For instance, some Homes have had a parent couch the family plan in his own language, since he is the person most concerned and least likely to use professional terms or pious generalities.

*Care*, or nurturing of children, is the primary responsibility of the child care worker. Again it is her primary responsibility and she is the primary caring person. She works within the Home's plan for the child, which may identify certain goals and even prescribe to some extent methods of meeting them, and she is generally required to enforce certain rules or to follow certain campuswide procedures. Increasingly, however, Homes are moving away from what might be called a "doctor-nurse" concept, in which the child care worker is a more or less mechanical implementer of other people's decisions.

Child care, or nurturing, is sometimes hard to distinguish from the child care worker's educational function, that is, what she does to prepare the child for the future through instruction, reinforcements, or sanctions. Yet in large measure child care has only indirect reference to the future. It is essentially present-oriented, having to do with the life a child lives in the here-and-now.

In part child care meets physical needs, such as food, clothing, minor medical care, rest, exercise, and the like. But all these things have emotional connotations that affect a child's well-being. Clothing may be well- or ill-chosen in terms of the child's taste, complexion, physical build, or personality. It may be consistent or not consistent with the fashion at any one time, a factor of great importance to teenagers. It may be suitable or not suitable for the activity at hand; so, of course, are hairstyles and cosmetics. Food may be physically adequate and nutritious, but it may be served unattractively, it may not take into account a child's tastes or his ethnic tradition, or it may be eaten in an atmosphere of strain or confrontation. Minor medical care—the use of Bandaids or aspirin—may be symbols of the degree of concern shown by the person entrusted with one's care. Bedtimes are a well-known battleground between adults and children, with implications of banishment, depreciation, and even punishment.

So much emphasis has been put on preparing children for adult responsibility or for the next stage in their development that rather little attention has been paid to their right to happiness now. Even a cheerful, welcoming, orderly, unthreatening home life is often described as a "therapeutic milieu," implying that it is largely a means to some future end. Childhood is a stage in growth; it is also approximately one quarter of a person's life span, in which he has as much right to be happy and successful as he does in young adulthood or middle age. A happy childhood is not only a prelude to satisfactions in adulthood. It is something to be valued for itself, and this is true even of a stay in a Children's Home that is part of a plan for the future.

A child has the right to expect a number of things from those who are caring for him, even for a comparatively short time. One of these is respect—respect for his person, respect for his difference from other children, respect for his identity, respect for his background and associates, and respect for his feelings, tastes, and opinions. For instance, he has the right not to be punished in a way that degrades him physically or psychologically; a case in point might be physical punishment at the hands of a member of the opposite sex after the age at which sex-identity becomes important or, indeed, of adolescents of any age. A child has a right not to be laughed at for his tastes, beliefs, hobbies, and preferences (including those normally associated with the other sex). He has a right to his own name, even if it causes problems or confusion with other children, or to the nickname he prefers. He has a right to be proud of his race, his ethnic group, and his culture, and to have these respected by others. He has a right to respect shown to his parents and his friends, however much their life-style may be unlike that of the child caring person. And he has a right to be listened to, to have his tastes taken into consideration—although not necessarily catered to—and a right to express his opinion without being considered impertinent, as long as his opinions are expressed in a reasonable manner. Recognition must be given to the universal fact that children have not yet acquired culturally appropriate ways of expressing their opinions on subjects on which they feel deeply.

A child also has a right to an existence which is both orderly and relaxed. He has a right to expect that meals will be on time, that there will be quiet periods for study, that whatever he does will not be constantly interrupted, that his personal possessions are respected, and that he can get enough sleep at night. At the same time he needs a life that is not unduly pressured, hurried, or regimented. He needs to be able to take things more or less at his own pace, have some time to himself, enjoy his meals. He also needs some exceptions to a routine. Although there is value in predictability, routines need varying occasionally.

Another part of child care is the supplying of affection. Children, of course, vary greatly, both individually and in relation to age and sex, as to how much, how, and by whom they want to be touched. Generally, children who have been unloved need to be touched more than do others, often in a way for which they would otherwise be too old. Thus, an eleven-year-old girl may need to sit on a housefather's knee as if she were five or six, or an older boy have an arm around his shoulder. Fear of stimulating sex behavior often holds an adult back from expressing badly needed affection, and while adults can behave in ways that are seductive, a child who craves affection and does not get it is not only denied a real need, but is likely to seek it somewhat indiscriminately at an age and manner in which it is even less appropriate. One does not learn not to need affection by being denied it.

*Education* is preparation for the future and, as we have said, sometimes looms as so important that care for care's sake gets forgotten. Education refers here to much more than the formal educational process, which is principally the role of the school, although child care staff must and do contribute to this kind of learning. Many Children's Homes, too, have found it necessary to add remedial learning or special classes for children who have expressed their rebellion in truancy, have fallen behind in school, or whose behavior is unacceptable to school authorities, because they have been moved frequently, or have been kept out of school for family reasons, or have been unable to put their energies into learning because of pressing social or emotional problems. Some twenty years ago or so most Children's Homes gave up their schools on campus in order that their children might become more a part of the community. Recently, however, Homes have found it increasingly necessary to conduct special classes on campus, not for all children (though sometimes for all if a Home is dealing only with very disturbed or even retarded children) but for those who cannot keep up with others in a community school. In this situation consideration must be given to supplying normal community contacts. A few community schools will accept children taught academically in special settings into their nonacademic or their extracurricular activities.

But education goes much farther than academic learning. It includes moral and religious teaching, socialization (even table manners), a great deal of what is normally thought of as discipline—that is, attempts to modify a child's behavior by positive and negative reinforcements—and the learning of life-skills, such as money management or preparation for parenthood. In some Homes where more or less stylized techniques are used it can come close to being the Home's form of individualized therapy.

At the same time, education by means of instruction, sanctions, and even positive reinforcement must not become so predominant a part of the child's daily life that he is constantly reacting to adult demands or trying to please someone. This may be easy to see in relation to socialization and even to religious and moral instruction—a child can hardly live in a twenty-four-hour-a-day school of manners or a Sunday school class. Too great an emphasis on table manners or on the moral implications of behavior robs a child of the chance that he needs to relax. But the same can be true of a stylized technique the use of which involves constant, rigorous application. Children today get little chance to "be themselves." There is danger in overstressing adult approval for conforming behavior, for a child can easily learn the game and become an expert manipulator while having little conviction about the values expressed in his behavior.

Educational methods should certainly stress the positive more than the negative. Unfortunately, by far the larger part of what adults convey to children in any one day is negative or corrective, rather than appreciative. For some reason, a child's acceptable behavior is often regarded as something for which he deserves little credit—"he ought to behave." Attention is centered on the times that he does not behave. There is also a feeling that punishment or correction must follow any wrongdoing; otherwise the child and others will be tempted to repeat the behavior, a theory which hardly stands up to close examination. Behind this all-too-common feeling lies the implicit assumption that the wrong is enjoyable and the good unpleasant. Yet often a child's ability to behave in an acceptable way represents a real victory on his part over fears or over ways of behaving that he has found necessary in the past to keep his head above water.

It is a commonplace that the best education is experience; this method requires adults to let a child make mistakes and profit by them. Certain safeguards need to be put around the results of making mistakes. A mistake cannot be allowed to occur, for instance, if it is likely to end in bodily injury, pregnancy, or some total psychological trauma, but a mistake may be helpful if it leads to temporary lack of money, unpopularity, the need to make amends, or the breakup of a particular boy-girl relationship.

Training in use of money and the value of work is important. In the past many Homes expected children to work on the farm or in the laundry out of gratitude or because they imagined that work would somehow become a habit if it were insisted upon. The usual result was a distaste for work. While there is certainly value in expecting children to partake in normal chores necessary to keep a cottage in good order, many Homes are now paying children for work done beyond this point, as well as encouraging them to work off campus after school and during the summer. The child, on the other hand, is asked to assume progressively more responsibility for his own support. Some Homes have developed progressive systems beginning at age twelve or thirteen in which the child learns to handle his own money more and more as he grows older. One of these systems is described in this book. The child is better prepared to leave the Home. He sees much more value in working and working well—the system allows for promotions and demotions on the job—he is usually able to save quite a bit against his leaving or for his further education, and he learns experientially, often by making mistakes in his use of his money.

One of the advantages of distinguishing education from child care is that distinction is also made between disciplinary measures necessary for orderly group living and true learning experiences. In any form of group living certain rules need to be enforced purely to maintain order, or even for public-relations purposes. These may have an indirect moral component, perhaps in asking cooperation with the general good, or insisting on obedience, but such is not their primary purpose, and in fact their so-called moral component is often nothing but a way of trying to give them a false importance. These rules are not so much educative as operational and can be highly resented by children if they are treated as moral questions. Children are aware of being manipulated. Some such distinction between operational rules and behavior which can be educational also helps in the ambivalent situation arising from the conflict between "individualization" and "fairness" in treating misbehavior. As adults we might expect differential treatment for a serious crime, or at least to have extenuating circumstances taken into account, but we would be very resentful if parking fines and speed limits were individualized. Some behavior to which adults may give moral import not easily accepted by children is better handled in the category of order rather than of morals. Smoking is a case in point.

Education, like care, falls principally in the realm of the child care worker, who should be the principal disciplinarian and educator. Others do have a part in education—the social worker, the work supervisor, the activities director, the superintendent—but a child generally needs a person or persons close to him to be the primary source of education in day-to-day living. If a number of people intervene and too often correct his behavior, or if he is responsible for it to someone "up there" who has not been closely involved in the incident for which he is corrected, the child feels he is being treated not as a person but as an object to be controlled.

In planning an educational program, whether it be in the church, or a work-responsibility system, or a plan for behavior modification, goals must be clearly defined and procedures analyzed in order to promote desirable learning. As far as is possible, too, all parts of the Children's Home community and particularly the youngsters need to be brought into the planning. A well-designed educational program can quite easily be negated if some of its procedures convey a different message than what is intended—if worship, for instance, is associated with authoritarian demands for conforming behavior or dress, or if it is seen as something imposed and therefore to be avoided. A work-responsibility program can be sabotaged by procedures that encourage continual dependence or by staff members who view increasing responsibility by youngsters for their own support as a lessening of the Home's concern for the child's welfare.

*Group-living* may be looked on as an element of both care and education. It is, however, one factor that distinguishes group care from family living and is, therefore, one of the things that Children's Homes have uniquely to give. The staff of any Home should know why it favors a particular kind of group composition, should use discretion in placing a particular child in a group, and, when a group exists or is created, must provide it with leadership and direction.

The living group is the primary one in the Home, but there may be others. Interest groups, playground groups, and groups especially created for therapeutic or decision-making purposes may also be important and can be used to complement the values of the primary group. Ideally, the living group is cohesive; attractive to its members; consistently, openly, and honestly working to develop and sustain mutually effective and socially relevant norms and values; and generally demonstrating a climate of caring and concern for its members. It is characterized by group decisions with wide participation and a sense of unity among its members. It is the opposite of a mutual "put-down" society—the fate of any group living unit where the staff exercises only monitoring, controlling, and occasionally individually comforting leadership.

The basic variable for the living group is size. The optimum number of youngsters with the likelihood of becoming a group—a single unity (as opposed, for example, to a set of sub-groups)—which can provide for a richness of interaction and interdependency is eight to ten. A group larger than ten is a risky undertaking.

The kind of living groups a Home constructs will depend a good deal on its primary purpose, as well as the expertise of its staff. The traditional peer group of one age and sex is often best suited to disturbed children, who can learn a great deal from peers undergoing the same problems and who can help each other. This is particularly true of adolescents who are most influenced by their peers. On the other hand, a Home which is primarily concerned with family problems is likely to want to use a mixed-sibling grouping, which is more like family living and helps children work out intrafamily relationships; this arrangement can also help to develop a mutual caring group norm. Caution must be exercised in separating children in a family for good. Temporary reasons, such as squabbling, or domination of one sibling by another, or an older sibling who needs to be free of the responsibility for younger ones, must not be allowed to perpetuate a separation when these reasons disappear. This is particulary true if the family is to be reunited. The children do not need to be faced with the double problem of adapting to their parents and their siblings at the same time. One Home has a policy requiring children of one family to live together, whatever their relationship, at least in the weeks before there is any plan to return to their own family home or that of a relative.

Mixed-sibling cottages do, however, demand greater flexibility from a child care worker, and if the staff is untrained, peer cottages may be more practical. The mixed-sibling cottage is more complex, in that its relationships involve not only vertical family associations but horizontal age and interest ones as well. The possibility of interfamily competition, particularly where cultural values or parental involvements are different, also needs to be kept in mind, not as a problem to be avoided but in terms of the dynamics of group living around which socialization occurs.

Group structure makes a great deal of difference. Groups vary greatly in their power structure and in their demands on a child. Some groups are rather loosely constructed, having no concentrated center of power and with a tolerance for most of its members. Others are dominated by one child or a small clique demanding subservience as the price of inclusion. Some groups are uneasy balances of power between two or more competing subgroups. A group with too little adult leadership often has a "stairstep" or a ranked organization; one that is overprotected or oversupervised often lacks subgroups and has a number of personal friendships that do not extend to others.

Groups can force children into roles, radically altering their behavior regardless of their real desires. A child may be forced into isolation and withdrawal by rejection from the group. He may play the role of scapegoat, licensed clown, or toady to the powers that be. He may himself reject the group and detach himself from its life. He may be cowed by its demands, be forced into manipulation, or organize a small subgroup more to his taste. A good children's worker in any position, but primarily the child care worker, should know not only the structure of her group and the role each child plays in it, but also its values and its relationships with other groups on the campus. Some groups are, for instance, self-contained, all-absorbing, or rivalrous with other groups, and some groups are so loose that their members make their principal associations elsewhere. Homes sometimes move from one extreme to the other as staff members react to each other or to the tone of the Home as a whole—its attitude, for instance, toward boy-girl relationships. The sociogram is a valuable tool in confirming or questioning this knowledge and might be used as a periodic check on group structure.

Another problem of group structure is homogeneity. There are arguments both for the homogeneous group and for the one with considerable variation in the degree of disturbance or level of intelligence in its members. A homogeneous group of badly disturbed children can be staffed with child care workers of unusual expertise. It can create a specific therapeutic milieu that places special demands on a particular group of children. On the other hand, some difficult children gain a great deal from association with those who are under less strain, and as long as they are in a minority, so that the prevailing tenor of the group is positive, may not need an artificially constructed milieu. The same can be said for the slow child. Some gain by association with children of higher intelligence who can stimulate them. Others may find the competition of brighter children too discouraging and may need a slower-moving life style.

The most important facet of group living for most Children's Homes is the leadership. A child care worker may attempt to control the group through authoritarian methods or may so dominate it that no real grouping occurs and no indigenous leadership is developed, or she can help the group accept responsibility for its problems, come to decisions, think through its actions, and be supportive of its members. In some situations, for example, small groups of adolescents who are at odds with society but have some desire to change, children have been motivated to form responsible caring groups, helping each of their members. Generally, these groups can bear a great deal of responsibility, even that of survival in camping situations and where the alternative to becoming a viable group is likely to be a training school or even prison. Yet, some elements of positive peer culture or guided group interaction can be used in the normal living group and the leader can become more of an enabler, a suggester, a confronter, and a synthesizer than a controller. Lack of leadership, on the other hand, can lead either to disorganization or to a child-controlled group which may develop all the characteristics of a delinquent gang, with both its virtues, such as loyalty, and its vices, largely in the areas of the use of violence and its antisocial orientation.

_Counseling_ is a function of the whole Home. It is not and cannot be restricted to the social worker, the minister, or the superintendent. Answers to questions from teenaged children in a number of Homes indicate that they see each other as the primary source of counseling when they have a problem in day-to-day living. After this, largely in relation to the adequacy of the Home's staff and their own situation, they turn either to their own parents or to the child care worker. Superintendents, social workers, ministers, and guidance counselors are sought out chiefly in their own areas of expertise or function. This pattern may vary somewhat where an institution is unequally staffed; recently, however, there has been a marked change in the kind of questions to which child care workers are expected to respond, and a far greater interest has been demonstrated by child care workers in learning counseling techniques. The setting for meaningful counseling is more likely to be a job shared together or a few minutes of private time with someone close to the situation than it is the clinical atmosphere of an office. Counseling may, of course, take place in formal situations as well as informal ones, and children do seek out people whom they believe to have either the answers or the authority to answer.

It is not in the province of this chapter to identify usable counseling techniques. These can be found in a number of publications and are taught in a wide variety of institutes and workshops.[7] They are also fruitful subjects for staff development. Some Homes prefer to indoctrinate their staff with a particular "method" such as "Transactional Analysis" or "Parent Effectiveness Training" as a basis for counseling. Although all of these methods contain important and useful principles and techniques, emphasis on a single method should not prevent the counselor from finding a way of relating to children that conveys his own style of caring and being helpful.

Counseling, as the word is used here, relates to specific problems, such as, "What should I do about my grades?" "How can I work out things with my boyfriend?" or "How can I stop myself wetting the bed?" It assumes some knowledge on the part of the child of the nature of the problem and some willingness to accept or at least consider advice. A wise counselor knows fundamentally that the child, and not the counselor, must solve the problem. He listens rather than directs, and he avoids false reassurances and taking the problems away from the child. He is also aware that to be helpful he must have some knowledge of his own hang-ups, some self-discipline in not serving his own ends in his responses, some sensitivity to feelings, and a willingness to recognize when he is either out of his depth or is encroaching on someone else's function or authority. He must be aware of how the child is using him. He needs also to know what freedom he has to counsel with children and how he is expected to report or not to report his actions.

Counseling is not therapy in the limited sense we have given this word, although it may result in some change in attitudes or behavior. It may be directed towards apparently trivial decisions—what to wear, how to write a letter—as well as to

7. See Part Three, Suggestions for Further Reading, p. 259.

apparently serious questions affecting important things such as a child's religious or sex life. The apparently trivial may, however, be the particular vehicle through which the child is asking a much more fundamental question. Asking how to dress may mean "How should I handle my sexuality?" or "What do I really think of myself?" Asking how to phrase something in a letter may really say, "How can I face the fact that I don't really know if I love my mother?" Therefore, the Home has a great responsibility for seeing that staff to whom children will turn are aware of what they are doing in this relationship.

*Therapy* here denotes specific treatment programs—physical, emotional, or social—that are undertaken on a child's behalf. In one sense, of course, everything that happens to a child in a Children's Home can be potentially therapeutic, and is sometimes spoken of as treatment. Yet use of this term suggests that something specifically dysfunctional in the child's physical, emotional, or social state requires an individualized and specific remedy. There is an implication of sickness.

If a Home is, or wants to become, a residential treatment center, its intake will be predicated upon the existence of such a dysfunction in the child. Specific and individualized therapy (not necessarily carried out, however, in a one-to-one relationship) will therefore be a necessity for every child. If children are accepted on the basis of their family situation, however, some of them will be found to be disturbed or sick, needing various forms of therapy, while others may be essentially well but confused, baffled, ambivalent, or in need of support to cope with their problems. A few may even be able to handle their situation, given reasonably favorable living conditions, good planning, and normal education. Thus specific therapy will not be needed for all children. In this it differs from planning, care, education, and counseling which are common needs of all children in care.

The most important thing about therapeutic enterprises in a family-centered Children's Home is that they be part of an individual child's plan. They must be explicit, undertaken for a clearly defined and generally understood purpose, and both limited in time and evaluated periodically. There is no room in a Children's Home for a generalized and undefined quasi-therapeutic series of interviews in which the social worker offers something called "social casework service" without either the child's or other staff members' being aware of the goals of this service.

Therapy may be offered by specialists outside the Home or by competent staff social workers, in consultation with a psychiatrist. There is some value in offering therapy by a social worker who is not the child's primary planning agent, or at least in distinguishing clearly between the two roles of the worker. The social worker's co-planning role must not be confused with any role he may play in treatment of problems; children often complain if the person responsible for co-planning asks a lot of questions irrelevant to the co-planning function. Although both services are offered by two members of the same profession there is no reason to equate them, or to insist that they be given by the same person. A therapist would need to know the child and the family's plans, but children are less often confused if they can see one person as "my family worker" and another as the person who is "helping me with a particular problem."

Therapy should not be limited to the child. A Home can, although rather few do, maintain a therapeutic service for parents who need it, perhaps in the form of marriage counseling or training in child rearing. Sessions with all members of the family, including the child, would be better still. Nor is all therapy on a one-to-one basis. Group therapy for parents and family therapy are possible and useful alternatives.

Whether behavior modification should be considered a therapy in these terms is an open question. It might more properly be thought of as an educative technique, involving the child care worker more than the therapist. However, in certain situations behavior modification may serve as a specific plan to overcome particular problems, ignoring others for the time being. If this method is used the child's full understanding and participation are essential to success.

Therapy is not limited to emotional problems. A Home's therapy may well be physical, under the direction of the physician and the nurse. This, too, needs to be part of the child and his family's plan, understood by all concerned. This seems very obvious, yet therapy which is primarily emotional or behavioral in emphasis has often been set up with little precision or planning.

*Advocacy* for children and their families is quite clearly the responsibility of the entire staff when the rights of either the family or the child are denied. But when one talks of advocacy for children one must describe it carefully. Children have certain legal and constitutional rights, and in acting to assure these one is clearly acting as a true advocate. Children also have certain moral rights which must be respected if a Home is to fulfill its function. Some of these were discussed under *Care* above, such as respect for his person, his difference from others, his identity and his opinions, freedom from degrading punishment, and an orderly existence. But if a child's individual needs are equated with his rights, in talking of "speaking for" or being his advocate, adults very often are not speaking for the child but rather for their concept of what would be good for the child. What they think good for the child may in fact be the exact opposite of what the child himself wants.

This paradox can be seen in many juvenile court proceedings. The social worker declares and imagines himself to be the advocate for the child. If the child's legal or moral rights have been violated, he may in fact be a real advocate, but frequently he is merely opposing his own concept of how children should be reared to that of the parents. The child has never commissioned him to do so, and to the child he may be not an advocate but an intervener. What he wants for the child may be desirable, but to arrogate to himself some special status of representing or speaking for the child is both unfair and presumptuous. He implies that he, and he only, is acting out of love for the child. Parents and others who may oppose his plans are seen as adversaries, when they may in fact only hold a different concept of the child's good.[8]

8. See Alan Keith-Lucas, "Speaking for the Child: A Role-Analysis and Some Cautions," in Albert E. Wilkerson, ed., *The Rights of Children: Emergent Concepts in Law and Society* (Philadelphia: Temple University Press, 1973).

It should not be forgotten that an advocate for one person is usually an adversary to another. In court this is usually the parents. Within the institution it is usually the child care worker or the administration.

A very difficult situation develops when any part of the staff—and this is usually the social worker, for reasons discussed in Chapter III—feels it has a special advocacy role for children and opposes its own ideas of a child's needs to the ideas of those entrusted with the child's daily care. Not only does this line up one part of the staff against another, but children, many of whom have learned of sheer necessity to manipulate adults and play them off against each other, take advantage of the situation. If there are honest differences about what a child needs, these should be discussed in planning sessions. If a child's legal or moral rights are being denied, then the administrator needs to know. But where moral rights are concerned it is important that the Home present a unified front, and all sides—not the child's alone—of any infringements must be considered.

Children's Homes do have a responsibility to be advocates for their children in the community and with the schools, particularly when there is evidence of discrimination against the Home's children or exploitation of them. They have the responsibility to protect children against being used by anyone, however well-meaning, for his own needs; from being patronized or shown off; from being used to assuage guilt or to satisfy someone's desire to be or to be thought benevolent; or for publicity. Christmas parties, tickets to the fair, and visits from sponsoring organizations are often exploitations of this kind.

There is, however, one kind of advocacy in which everyone in a Home ought to be concerned, and that is advocacy for laws, resources, and services to enhance the quality of family life. Families should not be subjected to the pressures of inadequate income, poor housing, unavailable medical care, lack of recreation, poor schooling, or any other of the factors that lead to the need for care of children away from home or that hinder rehabilitation. And in this the Home is in a particularly favorable situation. It can testify at first hand to the results of inadequate public assistance, punitive courts, entrapment in unrealistic credit schemes, and lack of mental health facilities or family-life education. The Home also usually has a board whose members have some status in the community and who, if the Home keeps them informed, have some power to help change things. But such an advocacy is more than advocacy for children. It is advocacy for family and community life.

# ❧❧III

# The Family and the Child Experience the Home's Services

More families than we like to think about are lost to children or cling to the outward trappings but not the essential nature of parenthood because they have not used the continuous and supportive help a Children's Home could have offered to them. Sometimes this help has not been available to them in any comprehensive and usable way. More children than we like to admit are making poor use of a Home's caring, education, group living, counseling, therapeutic, or advocacy services because their emotional and intellectual energies are consumed in trying to cope with matters which should have been dealt with when they first came into care. Some, although physically in care, have never moved in psychologically. Both parents and children may have encountered aspects of the Home in a meaningless, piecemeal way, with no coordinated sense of what is happening to them or how the Home can help them. And the Home is often vague about how it can help either child or family to use the Home in any but a muddled, drifting, or purposeless way.

In order for this not to be so, a Home needs to come to certain convictions about itself, its services, and the people it serves.

First, the Home needs to have the conviction that it exists, not to take charge of neglected, dependent, or troubled children, but to help a family find the best possible solution to its difficulties. This is a very different emphasis from that which says, "We have your child under our care, or are willing to accept him. We recognize that you have some rights to him and are important to him, and so we will be working with you, too, on his behalf. We try to help you reassume his care, if we think that is in his best interest, because a child needs his own parents." It says, rather, "This is your child. If you want our services, they are here. We may put some conditions around how we offer them, that come from our experience with how they work best, but it is up to you to decide whether you want them."

This principle may be hard to hold to when a court has removed a child from his parents and a public agency seeks to place the child in a Children's Home. In this situation, it would really seem as if the child is in the Home's charge and the parent is constrained to cooperate at best. The parent must endure having the child live somewhere other than with him; the child must endure the separation. But the basic question remains: "Are the Home's services the ones that you and he can use best, in this situation, since he may not at this time live with you? He is still your child and you are still his guardian, the person with the right to make ultimate plans for him, even if the law has intervened to say that his daily care must be undertaken by someone else."

To hold to this conviction the Home must develop a real belief in the rights of families to plan for themselves, making a distinction between those parental rights and responsibilities that are best described as custodial and those that fall to a guardian. Custodial rights have to do with caring decisions; guardianship deals with the right to plan. Unfortunately these terms are often used almost interchangeably even in legislative acts. Some courts also glibly terminate parental rights which are psychologically very active. A parent should not, however, lose guardianship rights and responsibilities on the basis of neglect or even abuse alone.[9] The pressures of child rearing in this increasingly complex

9. See U.S. Department of Health, Education, and Welfare, *Standards for Juvenile and Family Courts*, 1966, pp. 17, 94.

and stressful world are such that neglect and even outbursts of physical abuse, horrible though they may be, are often the result of intolerable social pressures. Some parents who are the victims of such pressures can, with help, be still responsible parents to their children, and may well wish to be. When a parent genuinely rejects the parental role, however, not simply finding difficulty with it or getting discouraged at times, the child must have someone else who can be the planning or deciding person in his life, and this person should become his guardian. A guardian in this sense should not be an agency, a caseworker, or even an administrator, but someone who has personal ties to the child, such as a relative or a friend. The child needs his guardian to represent him in the agency's councils, to agree with the agency on his care, and, if necessary, to protest on his behalf to or about what an agency is doing or not doing for and to him. It is a curious anomaly of our law that there is no statutory right of a child to a guardian of the person. If a child has property, a guardian of his estate is mandatory, but a propertyless child is more or less at the mercy of anyone who is feeding and clothing him, with no guarantee of the permanence of this investment.

Second, the Home needs to believe that its services are worthwhile and potentially helpful. The old-time orphanage did have this conviction, perhaps wrongly or in an exaggerated form and in relation only to the training it provided, but in the light of increased knowledge of what separation means to children and increased commitment to family life, placement is often presented as a last resort. And a last resort by definition is a final despairing hope, something to be tried when everything else has failed, and is not likely to be a valued service. Worse, even among placements, group care is often considered a last resort, a last step, when other supposedly more hopeful forms of care have proved to be unavailing. The Children's Home is still suffering from the revulsion against the barren regimentation of the orphanage and the unrealistic belief, starting in the 1920s and 1930s, that foster family care could solve all placement needs. Children were referred to Children's Homes only if foster family care had failed or could not be used by them. Recently, despite evidence that children served in group-care settings need that particular form of care and gain from it, Children's Homes are again facing an anti-institutional wave of feeling, largely because of conditions in overcrowded or purely custodial training schools and state facilities for the retarded or the mentally ill. Yet experience shows that a good Children's Home can offer a continuity that foster family care rarely provides, that its service to the whole family can be better organized and structured, as well as largely eliminating conflict between two sets of parenting figures, and that it can be particularly helpful for the child who can profit from group interaction, the child who has difficulty trusting adults, and the child in need of socialization.

Indeed, the Home's ability to help both parents and children often goes hand in hand with the perception of the worth of its service. If it sees placement of a child as the break-up of a family and placement in group care as a regretable, less personalized service for children who are too disturbed or unacceptable to live happily in a family home, its services are likely to be perfunctory at best and usually foredoomed to being a mere salvage operation. If, on the other hand, the Home sees itself as offering opportunities for a new start in family relationships, for the rebuilding of trust or fulfillment of a need for socialization, and believes in its potential helpfulness in these endeavors, then its service will probably have the necessary quality.

It has long been held that the social worker should discuss with parents all possible alternatives to placement, either referring the parents to other resources in the community or himself offering, in the name of the Home, counseling or in some cases financial aid. In intention, the principle is a good one. One must admire those workers in Norway, for instance, who will live in a child's own home for as much as two weeks in an effort to help the parents make other plans for the child than group-care placement. Yet even this long-established practice can be overdone, if the social worker is urging adoption of one plan over another and not really listening to the parents' request. The parents' plans must be considered seriously. The Home does not need to accede to them if it believes they are impractical or will do more harm than good, but in these situations it owes the parents an explanation for its reluctance rather than an attempt to sell them some other service. Some parents know that they need separation from their children for a while. Only when group care becomes the breakdown of a family, rather than a re-evaluation period, is it a measure of last resort.

When a parent does realize, however, that the family's goals could be better met through other means, the Home, having helped the family to this conclusion, owes it more than a simple mention of other available services. It needs often to help the family find another source of help, sometimes to break the ice or pave the way for the family, and to leave the door open to the family to come back if their plans do not work out. It is one thing to agree that such and such a plan would be preferable to group care, and quite another to say, "Because this other plan is preferable we cannot serve you, even if the other plan is not available." This is sometimes referred to as a "sustained referral."

The third conviction the Home needs is a real belief in the value of a structured planning process as the essential basis for all of its other services. Structure must be created, then constantly adapted and refined; there must also be a willingness to expend money and time to see that the process takes place. For instance, attendance at family conferences should have a high priority in the executive calendar, never being put aside lightly for other duties. Primary planning staff should be competent, well-supervised, and free to give time to planning. They should not be occupied with incidental duties, or allowed to indulge their need as social workers to be engaged in therapy at the expense of a good planning process. Support by the whole staff is essential in maintaining a sequential process that is recognized as a basic need for both families and children, that cannot be carried out haphazardly or in emergency situations only, and that is the right of every client system.

Definite planning structures have a number of advantages. They take the impact for the child of the overwhelming effects of placement and break it up into steps he can take one at a time. Planning structures also ensure that parent and child are engaged in concrete actions, so that they do not become either victims, however willing, of the Home's will, or detached spectators of it. Parent and child are required to look at their situation, to make plans, to do something about it. This may be painful, but if the service is to be helpful it must be based on reality.

The first step, both with parent and child, is to recognize the reasons for placement. Closely related are the expectations of parent and child from placement.

Frequently, Children's Homes accept a partial reason for placement, one that allows a parent to sidestep the truth. "We need to find more adequate housing" may be a face-saving reason, but it is fatal to the child's sense of worth and security when two years later the parents find more adequate housing and, as a result of perpetuated nonplanning, appear not to want him back. Often, too, a parent is allowed to put the whole burden of the placement on the child's behavior. Whether this is the reason given the child, the message somehow gets across, and the parent is left appearing to wash his hands of any responsibility for using the service himself.

Children of any age need to understand what is happening to them and, if possible, why. They need this knowledge in particular because one of the concomitants of placement is a deep sense of guilt. "If Daddy deserts, I am responsible. I was not lovable enough for him to stay by me." "If he dies, maybe God is punishing me for my secret sins." "If Mother goes to the mental hospital, she has been saying for six months, 'You kids are driving me crazy.'" "If I am just turned out or couldn't get along in school, it was because my behavior was bad."

There is a great temptation for adults simply to try to assuage the child's guilt through false reassurance, but false reassurance always lets one down in the end. Children know that they have in some way been involved in the family difficulty. They may need to be reassured that they were not wholly responsible and they do need to enter placement with the sense that it is one phase of a plan in which they have a part, and not that they have been thrown out, on the one hand, or taken away on the other. This last impression is easily given when the Home tries to make a success of the placement by painting its services in too glowing a light, or by asking a child whether he would like to live in the Home before the reasons for his needing to live there have been faced. The assertion that the welfare department, the court, or the Children's Home "took me away" is often the refuge of the child refusing to face the real reason why he is away from the family home.

Unwillingness to appear to criticize the child's parents to him is one reason a child may not be realistically dealt with regarding the reasons for his placement. But it is important to give the child those reasons that parents and Home have agreed on as the basis for goals and commitment rather than *our* understanding of these reasons. He should learn these not solely from the Home, but from the parents and Home together, or from the parents and then the Home, in which case, of course, they must agree. Moreover, they must be real reasons, and in one sense inevitable reasons, not excuses or justifications which can be refuted. Children need to be involved in a placement decision and, at least from adolescence on should have some power to make decisions. They need to know that placement, once decided on, will last for a certain length of time, must be reviewed at stated intervals, and cannot be wriggled out of by pleas, running away, or unacceptable behavior. If the reasons given for placement are not real, the child's participation means nothing at all.

Such an understanding of the reasons and goals of placement is particularly difficult to reach but perhaps even more necessary when a court has taken the child away from his parents for neglect or abuse, or where the referral is made to the Home as one, perhaps the final one, in a number of placements in which the parents have had little part and may indeed have been discouraged or have abandoned participation. In the first instance, the child has indeed been taken away, but not, one hopes, arbitrarily, and the purpose of the placement may be to explore the possibilities of either reversing the decision or living constructively with it. The second instance requires a real reaching out on the part of the Home to the parents with the message, "We are being asked to care for your child. We recognize him as part of your family and hope that you will plan with us so that this placement can help you all." There are parents who, because of past experiences with agencies or because they have genuinely cut the child out of their lives, will not respond to such reaching out. A surprising number will.

One social worker who planned most helpfully with parents stated once that he never liked to plan care for a child without some back-up in the family—an uncle or aunt who might not wish to accept immediate responsibility, but who was willing to be called on if the parents should decide that they could no longer play a constructive part in their children's lives. These back-up or standby resources may become very important later to the child.

Quite frankly, the purpose of many placements can best be described as exploratory. The essential question in the parent's mind is, "How much of a parent can or do I want to be?" There is no need not to face the question. It is a question which placement can often answer. If it is faced frankly it allows, too, for the possible so-called negative answer, "I don't want to be any part of a parent," which may actually be a positive move that frees the child for adoption by relatives or others. If the Home takes as its goal the reuniting of every family, as it sometimes is urged to do, it may force a parent who really does not want a child to express himself by not working with the Home, visiting only sporadically, yet insisting that he still is the child's parent. The governing will in this case is that of the Home. The parent can only express his in obstructiveness and noncooperation. For a child the goal of placement may have to be stated as "to explore whether we can go on as a family."

Children learn less from words than from actions. They see actions as symbols confirming feelings. A handshake, a kiss, a blood-letting, or a vow carry more meaning than an explanation. That is why it is important for the process to provide time in which specific events occur—the parents tell the child formally of the decision; he meets with the social worker to learn about the Home; a date is set for a preplacement visit; he meets with the superintendent, the child care worker, his parents, and the social worker to review the plan and see it signed, or signs it himself, so that he knows that his parents and the Home are working together; he is given a copy of the plan, signaling his inclusion in it; times are set for his parents' first visit and for review of the plan; and the child is given an appointment with the social worker to discuss his initial reaction to the plan. Already, we can see that the process underscores a partnership context in the family-agency relationship.

Such a procedure sets the tone for the Home's dealings with the child and with his family. The Home gives evidence that it will deal with them honestly and consistently, include them, listen to them. It is not trying to sell them on placement, or to suggest that it has taken over, or to expect immediate conformity to its demands. Such an approach makes it possible for the parents and child to accomplish the psychological tasks demanded by separation and placement.

For the child, these tasks can include struggling with the implications of separation, the feeling of things happening to him over which he has no control, the need to establish relationships with new people—the child care worker, the activities director, the administrator, his peers—and to establish new kinds of relationships with the parents and perhaps his siblings, and finally the need to make his own commitment to using the placement and playing his part in the plan. In the course of facing these tasks, the child will go through periods of despair, when he feels utterly worthless and unequal to the situation, and periods of anger, when he will blast out against everyone concerned with what has happened to him. Studies of persons who have encountered crises in their lives show the importance of allowing them to express this anger.[10] Indeed a child must do so if he is to accomplish the step of acting responsibly on his own to benefit from placement. The child who "settles in beautifully" and shows no anger is in real danger of later moving into a state of despair, with little sense of self-worth or ambition, or of becoming detached, manipulative, and unable to form meaningful relationships. This child may never fully enter the Home psychologically.

10. See in Howard J. Parad, ed., *Crisis Intervention: Selected Readings* (New York: Family Service Association, 1965), particularly the articles by Lydia Rapport.

47

It is most important in the early days of placement that the social worker be available to the child, with the child feeling free to express any and all of his feelings. The social worker's acknowledgment that things will not be easy, but that he is there to help the child, can make the child's tasks less overwhelming. If ever there is a crucial time to withhold false reassurance, bringing to a situation reality, empathy, and support, it exists in the first few days and weeks of placement.

In this whole process there must obviously be a sharing of information so that all partners in the co-planning process can make more responsible decisions. On the one hand the parent and the child need to know enough about what the Home is, and what it does, to determine whether it can really help them. This can never be a matter of selling the Home to them. The family needs to know what will be expected of both parent and child, as well as the kind of rules, disciplinary practices, restrictions on choice, and lack of certain resources in the Home, along with the things it can offer. Loyalty to the Home and approval of its program must not take precedence over reality as it will affect the family. However, this information must come at a time when the family is ready to hear it—when there is a real movement towards using the Home. It should not be offered as a come-on for the service. No family and no child can answer the question, "Do you think you would like it at X Home?" until they have decided whether separation is something they want or can live with.

The same is true of the information that the Home needs in order to decide whether it can serve the family. This decision cannot be made by the social worker alone; it must involve the entire Children's Home. Social workers were originally employed to screen out unsuitable children or those who did not need group care, and this historical situation has caused many Homes to carry out a complicated and exhaustive accumulation of facts about a child and his family which administrator, director of cottage life, and others use to make up their minds whether to admit the child. This became and still sometimes is the principal activity of the social worker in his contacts with the family, putting the child and family through a rigorous examination, including references, psychological examinations, school reports, medical records, and the like, to produce a detailed "intake study." The very language betrays its origin in the days when group care was thought of as a privilege accorded to worthy children, and suggests a fine-meshed screen through which the child may be admitted if he manages to make himself small (or in this case, admissible) enough.

Certainly the Home needs some information before it can decide whether it can serve the family. It needs to know the family's situation, how it has come to asking for group care, and what its goals are in using the service. It must have some information indicating the family's ability to carry out its responsibility. It needs to know the length of time for which placement is being asked. It needs to know what back-up plans are available, and the part, say, that an absent parent may play. It needs to know about certain concrete legal matters, such as custody, guardianship, or probation. And if it is to care for a child it needs to know, for admission purposes as well as to aid in planning with and for him, what kind of a child he is, how he copes with life, his interests, tastes, talents, and fears, and what he thinks and feels about placement. The Home needs some facts about established behavior patterns, addictions, school performance, and general intelligence. But above all it needs to know what it will be called on to do to help this family and this child. Does it have the resources, the skill, the living group, the school placement that will be of help?

The Home should therefore consider four basic questions before it agrees to a plan:

1. What are this family's situation, needs, and goals?
2. How will they use the Home's service, and for how long?
3. What kind of a child are we being asked to care for?
4. What will we need to do if this family is to be helped?

Again there is a matter of time in the the search of answers to these questions. Some answers will emerge from the family's and the Home's exploration of the family's needs and goals. Some may have to be asked for specifically, at relevant times in the planning process.

The social worker may need some evidence to support his answers. He may, for instance, think it wise to ask for a psychological test, not because it is an intake requirement but because there are unexplained contradictions in the picture he is getting. Since the Home is to care for the child, he probably will want an up-to-date medical report. But he does not need a lot of unrelated facts simply because they are part of a required study, or a lot of secondhand impressions. If the social worker is worth his salt and has been truly working with the family, not just asking questions about them, he should be able to give the Home enough information on which to base its decision as to whether it can and will help.

Once family and Home have agreed in principle that a period of care in the Home for the child will be helpful, a plan needs to be worked out which will deal with the role of each of the interested persons in the placement. The Home will agree to do certain things and perhaps not to do others. The parent may agree to visit, to provide vacations, to pay part of the cost of care. The child, according to his age, may make certain commitments. The goals of placement will be made clear, as will the times for the plan to be reviewed, and the conditions (such as remarriage of a parent, or his leaving the state) which will require a new plan to be made. Some of the planning may be tentative at this time, with emphasis on the need to re-evaluate the plan in three months on the basis of actual experience. It should not be forgotten that the reality of placement may produce unexpected reactions in both parent and child. Nevertheless, the plan must be specific enough to give the child a sense of the mutuality of the enterprise; some clarity as to the purpose; and answers to such questions as, "Who is in charge of me now? Am I being abandoned or do I still belong to my family? When will I see my mother? How long is it planned for me to stay here? What part am I expected to play? What is it leading to?" Such specifics make it possible for a child to avoid being overwhelmed by the apparent totality of his physical move.

Incidentally, at this point, it might be wise to state a strenuous objection to the practice of forbidding contact with the child's own home for a month or more at the beginning of placement so that the child can "settle in." This practice dates from a time when parents were regarded as disturbing influences on a child's desired adjustment to a new and "better" regime, about which the fewer questions raised the better. The parents were presumed to be a force in favor of the child's former, less moral or less orderly living, against which the child needed to have time to build up resistance. Yet in these first few weeks the child needs more than at any other time to know that he has not been abandoned, that his parents are still there, that co-planning is followed by co-working. A plan should call for close communication in the earliest stage of placement. A telephone call on the night of placement is often a real source of assurance.

If the child has been in on the construction of the plan he has at least some sense that his parents and the Home are working together. But the Home to him up to this time has been represented by the social worker. When he comes to the Home, it takes on quite a different aspect. The person closest to him is then the child care worker. Above him and beyond his group living situation are such persons as the director of campus life and administrator. These are the people who affect his daily life. He needs to know that they are in on his family plan and intend to help carry it out. He needs to know that they know about him, his fears, his tastes, even the things he finds it hard to do, and try to understand him.

Part of this transfer can take place in a preplacement visit. But more useful still are the family conferences which are held in the process of making the plan and culminate in a formal meeting to review it and share it with all concerned. Here the child begins to see that in talking to the social worker he was in a real sense talking to the Home, that the Home is a team, and that the person closest to him, the child care worker, is an important part of the team and is as prepared as any other member to try to understand and help him.

She must convey to him that she is very much part of the

staff—not merely someone to whom he is delegated, who does not know much about him, who can be manipulated against others in the staff, or with whom he can fall into the same kind of self-defeating but still desired relationship that he had with his parents.

The free interchange of information within the staff does raise the problem of confidentiality. Distinction should be made between knowledge of the plan and the child's needs as opposed to dwelling on the "gory details" of the past. Most information was withheld from child care workers in the past not because of any unwillingness on the part of parent or child to have people helping him know these things, but from the administration's or social work staff's fear that unprofessional staff would use information prejudicially. Parent and child, in most cases, shared information with the child care worker anyway.

The family conference is the time at which the child sees with his own eyes his parents and the Home sign an agreement to which he may add his own signature.

The day of placement is a day of destiny for the child, for which, one may hope, he has been prepared through a preplacement visit and by actual preparation for the details of the day—who will be bringing him to the Home, what he may take with him, whom he will meet, when he will be saying goodbye to his parents, what is planned in the cottage that evening. The Home should also have prepared for his coming by providing places for his things, making arrangements with the school, and allowing time for questions and answers.

But too much emphasis can be put on the day of placement. The initial shock has been weathered; the child is finally within the Home. There is a very real danger, with the parent now invisible, that the Home will take full charge of the child, go to work to straighten him out or undo the mistakes of the parents, and forget that the child is attempting two very difficult tasks at the same time—getting used to being away from his parents and learning to take on people who do parenting things to him.

Homes must be careful in their desire to see the child adjust. Indeed, the child who adjusts too quickly is flying a danger flag. Placement is something one needs to be somewhat disturbed about. Continued discussion of the plan and its goals and regular reviews of the use-of-care plan (the more specific plan for the child while he is in the Home) and its relation to the family-agency plan are needed to carry the child through this experience. The Home needs to be aware of how the child is handling placement, particularly if this appears to be either by docility or by hostility and aggression. The Home needs to consider, also, the child's relationship to the group and to the particular child care workers responsible for him and to his siblings. All too often the first arrangements, made on the basis of what is at best partial knowledge and sometimes just expedience, become the continuing arrangements by default. Unless the child protests quite vigorously, plans tend to be continued unthinkingly.

Yet if the child needs help in the first weeks of placement, the parent needs it even more. He is struggling with his guilt, his apprehension, and his sense of relief. The child at least has the visible presence of the Home to support him and people to talk to; the parent is often alone. A national study shows that if a child is in care for three months the chances are that a parent, left to what the authors call a self-healing process, will let the situation develop into a long-term placement.[11] Even more, perhaps, than the child, the parent needs to be engaged in some process. The explicit goal of discovering how much and what kind of a parent he wants to be can offer some structure to help him; so can preparation for the first visit, the first weekend at home, and evaluation of these events. It would not be too much to say that as the parent is helped to handle the earlier months of placement, so may he handle all of it. It might also be hazarded that most parents lost to the child and to the agency are lost in those neglected first few weeks after placement.

Both parent and child are subsequently involved in a regular process of review of the plan at agreed-on intervals, in many cases around visiting and vacations. Both are also sometimes involved in crises of various sorts, such as runaways, accidents,

11. Henry S. Mass and Richard E. Engler, Jr., *Children in Need of Parents* (New York: Columbia University Press, 1959).

or illness. Many a parent has re-established his parental role in the wake of a child's illness. More and more Homes are experimenting too with bringing the parent in as part of the treatment team in terms of a child's behavior or unhappiness.

The nature of a review, either of the family-agency or the use-of-care plan, needs to be spelled out. Reviews should not be simply diagnoses of the present situation or accounts of what has happened. They should be, on the other hand, evaluations of developing trends in terms of the family's long-term goals. Parents and agency should ask themselves if this situation is developing in such a way that the long-term goal is still possible or likely. If abandonment is developing, this should be recognized now, while the child is still young enough for adoption. They should consider what progress has been made and in which direction plans should move at this time. The five possibilities— return home, assumption of responsibility by relatives, continued placement with strong parental support (a plan which should not be condemned as it sometimes can offer the most constructive plan for a family, comparable to a boarding school arrangement), some other type of placement, or adoption—should be discussed and the parents' movement toward any of them recognized. Reviews should promote greater clarity about the degree of parenthood the parents can or wish to exercise. This is a time for challenge, rather than for discounting apparent weaknesses in the plan.

More is called for here than an understanding of the child's and the family's needs. There must be a plan for which parent, child, and staff can be held accountable at the next review, and it should be a plan of action rather than a way of looking at the situation.

At one particular time the child may need to have another piece of structured planning to rely upon. This is when, in the course of placement, he becomes an adolescent. The rationale for a specific adolescent reassessment is that no matter how carefully Home and child have worked together, adolescence alters, or should alter, the Home's relationship with a child. An adolescent relives or tries to resolve many of his problems, particularly those of relationship and identity, that were unresolved earlier but have been "on the back burner" during the so-called latency years. This situation calls for a new contract, not so much between parent and Home, with the child playing his part, as between the child and his parents and the Home. The adolescent is no longer someone who takes his signals largely from adults. He needs not rules but some limits within which to experiment. He has the power to make placement almost impossible and even to reject his parents' plans for him.

Generally it has been found that cultures that recognize this new status as some kind of puberty rite have been more successful in living with their adolescents than those that do not. In the Children's Home some different policies may be called for which recognize greater responsibility—perhaps the beginning of a work-earnings-responsibility plan or a new arrangement with the child care worker in relation to having to ask permission for what the child wants to do. One of the difficulties adolescents have in living in Children's Homes with children of different ages is that all ages tend to be treated alike. Adolescence is a time when a youngster often needs to explore all possible alternatives to the one he is experiencing and to know that he is being told the truth about them before he can make use of his plan. A child, particularly one whose plan calls for him to stay at the Home until graduation with perhaps rather minimal support (and this does happen), may need to test out the supposed promise five years ago of an aunt that she would take him "if the worst came to the worst." He may want to build on his relationship with an interested friend to see if a foster family relationship is possible; these self-selected foster family Homes are sometimes successful, particularly if the envisaged relationship is not so much a family one but a home base from which one goes to boarding school or college. He may want to retest the relationship with a parent who has until now been out of the picture.

The Home's responsibility here is not to follow the youngster's often somewhat illusionary wishes; it is rather to allow him to face these illusions and test their reality, not in words but by letting the child confront the persons he chooses to seek out, while keeping him within the reality of the family context and having in mind the child's legal status and responsibility. If the ghosts of the past are to be laid to rest they must be seen for what they are, not pooh-poohed or ruled out of court by adult fiat or moral judgment. Working with an adolescent at this stage calls for an almost blazing honesty and willingness to listen. It is not done without involving the parents, but they too may need to face the child's growing independence and desire to plan for himself. Like parents of adolescents, living at home, they may need to weigh their own desires and the possible effects of insisting on them arbitrarily.

Some Homes set up a contract directly with a youngster who is moving towards independence both of his family and the Home. This may be part of a work-earnings-responsibility plan, indicating a new relationship with a young person who has largely taken on his own planning. It may involve plans to live off campus, in a group home or hostel, or perhaps a more independent status on campus, with a child care worker who can serve more as a counselor when needed than as the person responsible for the youngster's care or education.

The last step in planning with parents and children is for the ending of placement and for continued service, if this is needed. Placement may be ended in a planned way because the service has served its purpose or is no longer needed: the family may be ready to reassemble once again, or other plans, for independence, adoption, or home-base foster care, may have been made. Sometimes these options have been tested out in shorter periods of time, during the summer, perhaps. The need and desire for further service has been explored and a plan made. The Home's willingness to take the child back into care has been clarified.

Or a placement may end because it is not serving the parents' or the child's needs. The child may need some service that the Home cannot provide. The parents may not be using the service. Despite what he and the Home agreed on, he may be actually abandoning the child to the Home while insisting on his right to be the child's nominal parent. Here the Home, knowing what happens to children in such a situation, may have to refuse to be used in such a way, insisting that the parent either take on full responsibility for the child or abjure it. To offer service to someone does not mean to do his bidding if the result is harm; it helps no one to allow him both to have his cake and eat it. Homes sometimes give in to such situations out of their protective feelings for the child. They cannot bear the thought of the child returning to such a disinterested parent. The child is at least safe in the Home, they feel, and in order not to risk "losing" the child the Home tolerates the very situation which leads to the child's being "lost."

Some placements end, too, because they become intolerable to parent or child. The parent's guilt may cause him to snatch the child back in an unplanned way; the child may run away, marry, or act in such a way that the Home feels it cannot keep him. This last situation ties in with the most tragic reason of all for terminating a placement—dismissal for what are generally called disciplinary reasons.

Situations do arise in which a child's behavior is uncontrollable and may be a threat to the welfare of other children. Other plans may need to be made for him. But these plans should be made by the family, with the help of the Home, which is saying that its particular caring service can no longer be part of the plan. Making a different plan for a child should not be thought of as a disciplinary measure. That kind of thinking is a vestige of the time when an orphan's being in a Home was a privilege accorded only to the more promising children. The child, by his nonconforming behavior, forfeited his opportunity. To dismiss a child for bad behavior in the Children's Home of today is both to burden a child with a second rejection and to put a premium on bad behavior for the child who "wants out." This is particularly so when dismissal is linked to specific acts such as drinking, sexual intercourse, vandalism, or theft. The Home may be unable to help a child who does these things, but there is no need to make of this inability a disciplinary matter. The argument that if one does not dismiss a child for such acts others are encouraged to do them places an archaic and unrealistic reliance on deterrence through example. Dismissing the child summarily, returning him unprepared to the family where his difficulties developed, is to wash one's hands of the situation, doing more harm than good. And to fear that his continued presence on the campus while other plans are being made will contaminate other children shows little understanding of the sophistication of today's youth.

There may be situations involving violence or a refusal to stay on campus, perhaps from guilt feelings, in which a temporary place is needed for a child to stay while plans can be made. Some Homes have used a "standby" foster home, where a child can stay for a short time as a guest with a family not involved with his problem, to gain perspective on the problem and allow time for planning. But hurried plans to return home because the child has been dismissed violate the whole concept of planning. Indeed, sometimes the greatest help a Home can be to a child and to his parents is in the moment of his leaving. Continued assurance of the Home's concern may provide the base on which a family can learn to trust itself. Studies show that the gains made by a child in care are continued if there has been meaningful interaction between the Home and the parents during placement and that good planning at discharge and support to the child and family during this process are the central factors in the family adjustment after the child returns home.[12] If the child's leaving is poorly planned, everything gained in placement may be lost.

Opinions differ about the extent to which the Home offers an aftercare service. It is necessary in this stage to balance the support given by continuing contact with the family against undesirable continuing dependency on the Home. When children graduated from Homes in a parentless condition it was natural that this dependency should continue, and it sometimes did so to an exaggerated extent. On the other hand, a helping process does not suddenly end at one of its crisis points, and many children and families will need help in making adjustments to their new

12. See Melvin E. Allerhand, Ruth E. Weber, and Marie Haug, *Adaptation and Adaptability: The Bellefaire Follow-Up Study* (New York: Child Welfare League of America, 1966); and Delores A. Taylor and Stuart W. Alpent, *Continuity and Support Following Residential Treatment* (New York: Child Welfare League of America, 1973).

situations. Some may not. In some situations a well-planned return to the family home may signal a new-found independence; both family and child may resent any attempt on the part of the Home to continue contact. But if the relationships during care have been constructive and helpful there is every advantage in offering continued help. It is interesting that some youngsters remaining in care have seen the Home's continued interest in their companions who have left as evidence of the Home's concern.

Probably the best approach is to engage in a gradual process of disengagement while leaving the door open for the family to ask for further service if they need it. Sometimes a return home, even if planned, is to a degree in the nature of an experiment. This may be recognized in the form of a deliberate trial visit, or, if the plan appears to be good to all concerned, it may be assumed that the child will stay but that the Home stands ready to help in any way that it can. At the same time, if services are needed, such as counseling, these should be found in the local community.

The kind of involvement that will be undertaken between the family and the Home should be planned before the child returns to his family. Where it cannot be planned—if the family, for instance, wants to leave this on a contingency basis—a visit by the worker to the family within three months after the child's return, as an expression of interest, is a good minimal piece of structure. Families may find it difficult to ask for further help if there is any implication that they have failed once more.

Some Homes offer as part of their service opportunities for higher education for children who have been under their care. Designed in the first place for the child who graduated to independence, such plans might not be confined to these but offered to any youngster who has used the Home's service and for whom it would be helpful, irrespective of whether he remained in the Home until high school graduation. Indeed, it might be good policy not to offer such help until the child has been out of the Home for at least a year. Youngsters who have grown up in a Home need a period of emancipation from institutional living, a time to find their own way, and are much more likely both to make mature decisions about their future, and less likely to reject or to accept the offer as signifying continuing dependency, if they can have this time away from their feelings about the Home. Perhaps such scholarships could be offered at any time after a year and before four years after the child has left the Home.

Structure itself needs to be built on a concept of norms. In the total experience of a family with the Home we have outlined a number of sequential steps. For most situations these should be givens, not useful things "we will do if we have the time" or goals to be attained "if we can." But situations will arise in which a step becomes inappropriate or impossible—a parent disappears, a child needs immediate care in the middle of the planning process, a child care worker is called away on the day of a family conference—and the orderly process is interrupted. When this occurs the important thing is not to hope for the best despite the lacuna, but to recognize the departure from the norm and devise ways of accomplishing the same ends in some other way. A norm should prevail unless there are very good reasons to diverge from it.

The steps, then, in the process, can be recapitulated as follows:

1. Inquiry. Elimination of obviously inappropriate inquiries. Ensuring that a request for service come from the family; if the inquiry comes from a third party, specifying to custodians other than the family that the family must be involved.

2. Exploration with the family of their goals and of the services offered by the Home. Exploration of alternatives and, if necessary, sustained referral to other sources of help.

3. If placement is agreed on as a possible means to goals, clarification of reasons for this, shared by parent and social worker with child.

4. Mutual obtaining of information about the situation and about the services of the Home.

5. Discussion of situation with staff who will be concerned with child and decision to offer placement by the Home.

6. Working out with family the family-agency plan, with clarification of responsibilities of all concerned.

7. Preplacement visit by child to the Home and preparation for day of placement.

8. Preplanning by staff for child's coming, including discussion with group and preliminary use-of-care plan.

9. Family conference on the day of placement. Signing of family-agency plan in presence of the child. Copies to all concerned.

10. Setting of date of first visitation. Reassurance by telephone if possible that child is well, parent still available.

11. Intensive help to child in handling separation feelings in first few weeks of placement.

12. Structured involvement of parent in early weeks of placement, with use of visits.

13. Regular review of both family-agency and use-of-care plans; involvement of parent in the first, essential; in the second, desirable.

14. Reviews if situation changes or in crises.

15. Adolescent reassessment if child reaches this age in care.

16. In some cases, a "junior-senior" or "approaching independence" contract.

17. Planning for leaving the Home and structured aftercare or follow-up services.

If this kind of process can take place, there is every chance that a group-care placement will be of real service to family and to child.

# XXIV

# Structuring and Staffing
# the Home

Most of us are familiar with the classic table of organization that appears in the manual of most Homes. This starts with the constituency, the board, or the superintendent, according to its scope, and indicates whom each supervises, or directs. A typical chart of this kind may read in part:

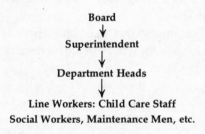

In this chart power flows downwards or is delegated, as do the scope and importance of decision making. In some small Homes, morever, which have no department heads, all decisions are the superintendent's or the board's, except as they are specifically delegated to line workers.

This kind of understanding of the relationships between

staff is undoubtedly valid for any organization whose eventual product is an artifact created by that organization. If the product is, for example, a car, the product is envisioned and designed, and its cost projected, at a high level of administration; lower echelons are less and less aware of the total product; and the lowest of all may do nothing more than put thousands of identical rivets into identical holes in a small part of the product.

When an organization's product is not a thing but a service, however, this chart does not truly represent what actually does or should happen. It is representative only for certain general kinds of decisions, such as budget, form of organization, overall policies, and perhaps ultimate decisions about children, such as admission or discharge, and even then a wise administrator finds that he must rely to a very great extent on input from those closer to the child and his family than he.

An organization whose basic purpose is to render service is very different from an industrial concern. The service actually reaches people, not at the hands of the administrator, but in their contact with the line worker. Thus the line worker makes, not a few very restricted decisions, but a great many, perhaps not of very great moment one by one, but cumulatively constituting the product—that is, the service. Moreover, most of the actions or decisions made by line staff cannot be prescribed. They are often extremely complex, involving attitude, verbal and nonverbal signals, understandings, and relationships that cannot be supervised in detail, although they can be given general direction by teaching, support, and review, or developed to be constructive rather than harmful. Yet, some Homes act on the illusion that such actions can be prescribed, clinging to the hierarchical concept suggested by the table of organization. These Homes are likely to see themselves as essentially producing a thing—a child product who believes and behaves in a prescribed way—rather than offering a service.

Four kinds of staff can be identified as needed to meet the needs of families and the children who are part of them:

1. Primary planning personnel.

2. Primary caring personnel, who are also responsible for a number of educative functions.

3. Specialists, further classified as those who perform primary diagnostic and therapeutic functions, such as physicians, dentists, psychologists, and other psychotherapists, and those whose functions are primarily educative, such as teachers, ministers, and recreational directors.

4. Maintenance personnel, including both those who take physical care of buildings and grounds or provide essential services such as food and those who maintain financial security or facilitate communications, record keeping, etc.—business managers, public relations officers, and secretaries. The duties of these will, of course, vary with the size and functions of the Home or of the agency of which it is a part. Except for their contacts with children and families, which will be discussed later, these people are part of a business organization which may be administered on a more or less hierarchical model, and therefore their relationships in their business capacities will not be dealt with here.

*Primary planning personnel* are generally known as social workers. It may seem curious to mention them first, as they are the latest comers to the child care field. There is, however, some danger in thinking of these people as representatives of a profession rather than as staff members responsive to particular needs.

Social workers were first used by Children's Homes in the 1920s primarily to screen admissions. Homes were becoming aware that not all children prospered in group care, and, conversely, that some children were too disturbed to be cared for in a particular Home. A few Homes saw the value of counseling with applicant families which would in some cases result in alternative and perhaps more favorable plans for a particular child—say Mother's Aid or placement with relatives or in foster family care—but the social worker's skills valued by the Home were largely investigative and evaluative. Social workers were also used to plan for children who could not stay in the Home.

While the child was in care, however, the social worker's

position was somewhat anomalous. He was not part of the on-going process of the Home. On the other hand, he was often the only person on the staff with professional education and identity. Through his professional education he had something of the status of an expert, and therefore he began to be called on when child care staff were unable to handle a situation. He was expected to be able to "treat" the child or to suggest better ways of handling him, a role that he usually undertook willingly as his profession became primarily psychoanalytical in its orientation.

His was, however, a dangerous situation. A child care worker whose child was referred to social service was forced to admit that she had in some sense failed. An expert had to be called in. The social worker, on the other hand, tended to interact with the child care worker only when the latter was frustrated and in fact had often acted unwisely or with what appeared to the social worker as lack of understanding. At the same time the social worker's "instant therapy" was frequently unsuccessful, since he was in a singularly powerless situation, seeing the child infrequently, in contrast to the child care worker, who lived with him. Advice to the houseparent was often ineffective as well. The profession's value system was largely libertarian; the child care worker saw her primary duty as one of control. She resisted advice that she felt would weaken her authority or carried it out grudgingly, mechanically, and unsuccessfully.

The problem was further compounded when the social worker, reacting against the prevalent ethos of control and working from a position without disciplinary responsibility, let himself be used by the child as a listener and an advocate against authority. When one adds to this the facts that social workers were often nearer in age to the child than they were to the child care worker, and that their theoretical knowledge or skill in one-to-one therapeutic encounters rarely included experience in living with a group of hard-to-handle children, the tensions that arose between social worker and child care staff are not difficult to understand.

There were several directions in which Homes could go from there. In some, social workers claimed a right to be the principal determiners of the Home's policy and child care practices. They either attempted or in some cases were permitted to supervise the child care staff. This arrangement had some validity in a Home primarily concerned with treatment of the child's disturbance; the social worker, often as the representative of the psychiatrist or psychologist, assumed, as it were, the role of the doctor; the child care worker assumed that of the nurse. This pattern, which does have some logic to it, is still maintained in some treatment centers, modified perhaps by allowing greater input from the child care worker into team decisions, but even in these centers it is being called into question. It definitely does not fit the "living-experience" or family-centered Home. When the caring emphasis is on the quality of living, education for life, and group activity, the child care worker is often more experienced and even more of an expert than a caseworker.

In some Homes, the social worker remains in this anomalous position, claiming a right that is not accorded to him either by the administration or by the child care staff. When a Home begins seriously to consider what needs to be done in the way of planning with parents and children, rather than how it uses its social work staff, a different pattern emerges. Planning becomes both an integral part of the Home's service and in many respects the key service of the Home, with the social worker as both the initiator and the coordinator of the family plan. It is not, however, his plan alone, but that of the entire Home, in partnership with the child and his family.

In this plan, child care is a part, but it is not the planner's duty to prescribe or supervise child care. His duty is rather to recognize child care as a primary resource, to know its quality so that the care that the Home provides is indeed what the plan calls for. The planner may contribute his ideas for this care, but only as a member of the planning team and not out of any special expertise or position with the child. He can ask as a planning person whether care can be adapted to do certain things which would make the plan more workable, but he must do this as a coequal colleague with a special responsibility and interest, not as a director of how each child shall be treated.

The social worker will still need to see children, some more frequently than others, but with the definite purpose of discussing and testing how the plan is working and not out of some generalized responsibility for all that happens to a child. He may still need to see the child whose behavior is puzzling or at time of crisis, not because the child care worker has failed but because the child's behavior or the crisis may be signals that the plan needs to be revised, or because it may be impossible for the child to accept care unless some part of the plan is modified or clarified. Moreover, these reasons for seeing the child must be easily explicable to other members of the staff.

It should be remarked here that "primary planning person" and "social worker" are not synonymous terms. The education given to social workers teaches them, by and large, to do a sensitive and realistic planning job, although many social workers need help in learning the specifics and even the philosophy of planning. But "social worker" is a wide term, and a graduate social worker may be an expert in group work, in staff training (adult education), or in individual therapy, enabling him to be employed in any of several different slots in the Home's operation. When one person is given two different roles, however, they must be distinguished. To discuss the co-planning role does not mean that a social worker would not see a child for therapeutic reasons, perhaps at regular intervals, but when he does do so it is because the child's plan includes this therapy. He does not carry out therapy as an independent activity on his part. Some Homes help to clarify this situation by divorcing the two functions completely, so that one's therapist or counselor is not necessarily the same as one's family worker. This has on the whole helped children to make better use of both.

The question of whether a graduate social worker—one with a Master of Social Work degree—is necessary to the planning job is a difficult one. Planning demands as much sensitivity, skill, and, to some extent, knowledge of family and child development as does therapy; yet it presently enjoys a somewhat lower status and perhaps is less recognized as a special field of technical knowledge. The supervisor or sole worker in a planning program should, if possible, have a graduate degree in social work rather than in some more treatment-oriented discipline such as psychology, but in actual practice many planners have only a bachelor's degree and must depend on their supervisor's help in refining their skill.

The *primary caring staff* are the people who have been progressively known as "matrons," "houseparents," and "child care workers." In the training, payment, and status accorded these workers the United States has lagged far behind many European countries. Originally, in the orphanage, the matron was often an object of charity herself; she was usually a widow, a single person, or, if the Home's theology permitted this, separated or divorced. A study in the 1950s demonstrated that her average age at entering on her duties was from fifty to fifty-five, and the average age of persons on the job was over sixty.[13] The matron often had little or no experience with children, even her own; preference was frequently given to women who had few ties outside the institution. The surprising thing was that, possibly by a mixture of good fortune and natural selection through the rigors of the job, this era produced a handful of individuals who were really skilled and devoted child care workers. A very few of these were able to adapt to changing conditions and are still in practice.

The task assigned to these workers was primarily managerial and monitorial. Little else was possible with the number of children they had to care for. Housekeeping skills were highly valued—an early advertisement for matrons required the ability to make soap from lye and emphasized that this was "no job for a lady." Her contact with children involved keeping order, seeing that children were fed, washed, clothed, put to bed, and awakened on time. Minor infractions of order were corrected by summary penalties. More serious ones were referred to the superintendent or even to a special disciplinarian. Because of the matron's vulnerability, disobedience and disrespect were con-

13. Study conducted among its members in 1958 by the Group Child Care Project (now Group Child Care Consultant Services) of the University of North Carolina. According to its recently published *Profile of Member Agencies* (1975), the mean age of houseparents on the job was 45.3 years.

sidered major problems and resulted almost automatically in corporal punishment, often in the cottage itself, the disciplinarian having been called in to support the matron's authority. The genius of the few very successful matrons was that they transcended the managerial and monitorial role to become nurturers, counselors, and group leaders despite the system in which they worked.

Beginning in the late 1930s and continuing through the 1940s and 1950s, more progressive Homes began to recognize, in theory at least, the crucial importance of the workers now called houseparents, although one Home at least refused them this title on the very logical basis that they should not and could not replace the child's own parents. This Home called them counselors. Fewer children in a cottage made both terms somewhat more realistic. Married couples, too, were sought for the caring job. There was considerable interest in staff training and something of a proliferation of workshops and institutes. Yet at a time that Great Britain, for instance, was providing a year's professional education to prepare workers for the field and classifying those so trained as residential social workers, training for the child care position was rudimentary and the pool from which child care workers were drawn had not altered significantly. Even today, two major objectives have not been reached. There is only a hint of anything like a career ladder for child care workers, or even for levels of competence in the field, and training is still seen as beneficial but not as a prerequisite to practice.

Yet there have been some advances. Training, although still somewhat minimal, is more widely available, particularly of late through community or technical colleges, although some of this training is more suited to the day-care operator than to the child care worker in a Children's Home. Younger people are entering the field but tend to leave it rather quickly for their families' sakes. There is a move in Congress to establish a minimum salary for child care workers.

The job, in many instances, is seen as primarily that of parenting or nurturing the child's development, and much training is directed towards the control of behavior problems of various kinds. Nurturing has been added to managing, but the roles of counselor, team member in planning, and group leader are given little attention.

One of the signs of a change from this position is the institution in some areas of the shift system, whereby three or more child care workers work eight-hour shifts with the same group of children.

There are arguments both for and against this system. Some welcome it as indicating the end of the illusion that the child care worker is in any way a parent and that the cottage is her and the children's family home. They see it as establishing her as a professional, preventing the possessiveness of the worker who speaks of "my children," and mitigating the nervous strain and the labor of being on duty twenty-four hours a day. Yet others consider the need of the group for a consistent leadership, and, for younger children at least, a single person or a couple to whom one looks for general guidance. Those with this point of view tend to double-team the cottage at times of stress but leave one person or couple in charge. It is important to remember that, while the managerial and nurturing roles need to be added to, they still remain part of a child care worker's job.

The lack of required training, status, and pay for the child care worker is remarkable in view of the breadth of her responsibility. She is not only the primary caring and educative person, outside the confines of formal education, she is also the primary group leader and the second most active (behind the child's peers) counselor for children. She is an evaluator of a child's progress and as such takes an active part in planning for him. She may be involved in therapeutic plans for him. She is his advocate. Moreover, unlike some staff members, she cannot partialize these roles or even play one role at a time. She functions in the midst of a swirl of constantly shifting activity. Her best counseling may take place while she helps a child iron a dress. An incident at the dining table may necessitate her intervention in the group process. She needs poise, flexibility, and the ability to make and hold to decisions as well as knowledge and skills as a group leader and counselor.

Of the *specialists* on the staff rather less needs to be said. Each is expert in a particular phase of the child's experience; none is an expert in every aspect. Although in a residential treatment center a psychiatrist may prescribe a good deal of what happens to a child, his prescription needs moderating in view of the multiple realities of group living, and in the family-centered Home there are even more variables to take into account. It is a good rule to remember that the proper place for an expert is on tap, and not on top.

Specialists may be members of the staff, or they may be contractors with the Home. Their special relationships with other staff are discussed later.

*Maintenance* or *auxiliary* staff members can be of great value to children. Sometimes the first person a child can learn to trust is a yardman or a cook—someone who has little or no direct responsibility for the child's behavior, whose contacts can be casual and yet appreciative. Children whose self-image is very low sometimes find that they can identify with workers in a humble position. In the days of the all-white Children's Home it was often the black handyman to whom the more uncertain children turned.

These positions of "undemanding relationship" must be carefully analyzed. Some persons in this group also act as work-supervisors and as such are serving as educators. They need to be part of the child's team and to participate in plans for him. But perhaps they can be spared details of the child's daily behavior. A child deserves to have someone who does not know that he wet the bed this morning, someone who can give appreciation for the child just because he is.

We have now arrived at the first step in constructing our inverted table of organization.

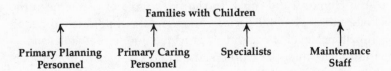

**Families with Children**

| Primary Planning Personnel | Primary Caring Personnel | Specialists | Maintenance Staff |

Later classification will depend very largely on the size of the Home and the need of the superintendent to control operations. If the Home is small, the superintendent will probably be the one to give support both to the primary planning and the primary caring personnel (for reasons of clarity this model will consider only supervision and coordination of the primary planning and caring personnel). Thus we have:

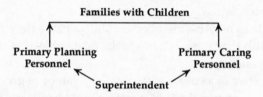

If the Home is somewhat bigger, or the superintendent is much occupied with raising funds or public relations, or if the superintendent is not a professional person and has little experience in supportive supervision, the model developed in the 1960s and used quite widely looked like this:

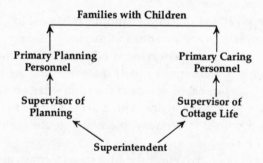

This model can be regarded as a stage in the development of the Home. It did much to clarify the role of planning in the Home and to place the social worker and the child care worker on a functional level of equality. It provided, too, professional supervision for both social workers and child care workers from persons who had specialized in these fields.

# Structuring and Staffing the Home

Yet it had its disadvantages. Frequently the director of campus life found himself supervising from ten to twenty child care workers as well as a number of maintenance personnel. The existence of two separate divisions also caused interface problems. One social worker or one child care worker might find himself working with ten or more persons in the other division. Moreover, the decision-making team on any matter of planning tended to be the triad—director of social service, director of child care, superintendent—at a level somewhat removed from the scene of the action.

At this point some Homes, after quite extensive systems analyses, turned to what is known as the unit system. In this system the child population is organized into a number of units, consisting of perhaps from three to five cottages, or twenty-four to forty children. Each unit is under the direction of a unit director or coordinator who has both child care workers and social workers under his supervision. Such a plan does, however, require some centralized planning activity that works with family and child before the child is assigned to a unit—what is still called "intake" in many Homes but is actually much more than a funnel through which children are fed into the units. It is concerned with services to families both before and in some cases after the child's coming into care, and with families who may never in fact make use of group care. Perhaps such an activity might be called the department of off-campus planning. We now have the following picture:

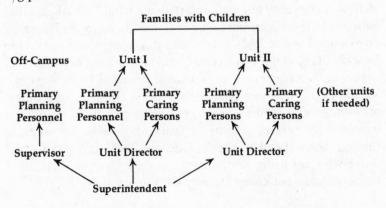

Here again, depending on the size of the Home and the responsibilities of the superintendent for external operations such as fund-raising and public relations, a professional person may be needed to give direction and support to the unit directors, especially if they are not themselves social workers. Such a person might be called director of professional services.

In the family-centered Home, it is essential that units be created to include whole family groups, whether the children live together in the same cottage or not. A unit, in fact, provides the means whereby siblings who for a period would be happier not living together can yet remain in close contact. Differentiation by age or sex defeats the whole purpose of the system. It requires a social worker to work with only one part of a family. Creating geographical units to serve areas of the state where the family lives might be desirable but may be impractical, in that it reduces the flexibility of a unit to accept children and can be disturbed by the mobility of some families. Geographical identity on a large campus is desirable, but not perhaps absolutely essential, as long as a sufficient number of unit activities are planned. Ideally, too, a unit should contain a variety of alternative living experiences.

Some homes have considered the possibility of functional units—one unit, for instance, for slower children, one for the more disturbed. There are arguments both for and against such grouping. A slower pace and less competition would and does help some slow children, but it is attained at the cost of lack of stimulation. It does permit some specialization among child care staff. A more sensible function difference would actually be that between long-term families who will need to be in the Home for an extended period and those whose stay is uncertain or likely to be short. If the Home has an emergency, temporary, or designedly preliminary placement program these do need to be separate. Mixing children whose relationship to the Home is very different—those who need to accept group living as the mode of their existence for several months or years, those who are working through the immediate shock of leaving the family home, and those who are using the Home as a very temporary shelter—makes any kind of group life very hard to maintain.

The middle "management"—the word is hardly appropriate—in the Home, whether this be directors of cottage or campus life or unit directors or coordinators, must be professional people. Whether they must be social workers is debatable. Many other disciplines are training people for human resource development, and some successful people in these positions have come from education or pastoral work. Too, some social workers are still so wedded to a casework approach that they find it difficult to operate in what is essentially a group-leadership and consultative position. What is important, other than knowledge and group-leadership skills, is a concept of supervision that is enabling, educative, and supportive rather than directive. It should be emphasized that the arrows in our charts do not indicate orders handed down, but rather show support given. The supervisor or director needs always to remember that he is there in order to help the line worker do his job better. That is why some believe that the supervisor of child care workers or unit director should not be empowered to punish children for anything that they do on campus. Too often, in the past, "support" for a child care worker meant administering physical punishment at the child care worker's behest.

Supportive, educative supervision has been described numerous times in professional literature. Perhaps three elements of it need especial emphasis here:

1. The supervisor must always recognize that his job is to supervise the worker and not the child. He is the generalist, the child care worker, the specialist. He knows what is generally good practice, what has worked in most cases. He can challenge the worker to think things through, present alternative theories of causation or methods of operation, even play the devil's advocate, but he cannot possibly know as much as the child care worker about how the child behaves or how he interacts with other children, his effect on the group or the group's effect on him.

2. The basic material with which the supervisor works is the feelings of the child care worker. A suggested action is still the child care worker's to put into practice. How she feels about her

job or about the particular child, her sense of being appreciated, supported, and understood are the factors which will influence her ability to do this. Her personal hang-ups are also important. The supervisor is not so much her boss as he is advocate and representative. He has the right to hold the child care worker to standards and to require independent action and decision. He needs to help define the job and to relate it to others on the campus, but he should not do the job for the child care worker.

3. Supervision should not be restricted to crisis situations. It should be a continuous process with regular times set aside for evaluation of the total situation as well as for problem-solving. This means in turn that the supervisor, child care workers, unit director, and still more the director of campus life must have the time to give to the supervisory job. Many Homes expect one person to supervise twenty or more houseparents and to perform at the same time a large number of managerial duties, perhaps as liaison with schools, director of activities, or assistant superintendent. It is one of the great advantages of a unit system that the span of control is reduced to more manageable proportions.

In supervising social workers these principles are generally understood. Child care supervisors are generally less able to insist on the basic necessities of their job, and are frequently called on to perform the impossible.

The extent to which the director of campus life or unit director should have direct relationship with children is difficult to prescribe. He is, and can be, a court of appeal if the child feels himself to be unfairly treated. On occasion, but optimally very rarely, he may have to intervene between child care worker and child. He may become involved in situations affecting the unit or the campus as a whole, or situations between cottages, and he may want to counsel children on matters of campus or unit interest. But he should take care not to become the principal counselor and disciplinarian.

In this respect it is important for Homes to specify who gives permission and who can restrict for what on the campus. It is very confusing for both child and staff if the director of campus life gives permissions that are normally the child care worker's, especially in the form, "it's all right with me if it is all right with your houseparent," which puts the child care worker in the position of being, perhaps for very good reason, the denier of something the director has in essence approved. There may be permissions and decisions which need both child care worker's and director's approval, but the child care worker, as nearest to the child, must then make clear that she will consult the director and give a decision based on their agreement.

The role of the superintendent and to some extent that of the unit director, working through his staff, is partly one of leadership and partly one of support. It is also one of keeping things in balance, especially between the equally essential concerns of caring and planning. It may be good planning, for instance, for a child to visit his parents, even if the experience is painful and results in some disturbance. But the child care workers rather than the social worker bear the brunt of this disturbance, which may also affect other children in the group. Homes frequently come to grief because one arm—either the planning, or maybe the therapeutic, or perhaps the caring arm—has become predominant, relegating the other to insignificance. For this reason it is very important in the two-division model for a director of campus life or supervisor of houseparents to have equal but not necessarily identical professional qualification and status with the director of planning or social work. In addition, the superintendent, if he is not a professional must understand and respect good planning operations.

In the early days of group child care the superintendent played the role of father to all "his" children, and many even adopted "Father," "Daddy," or "Pop" as official nicknames of which they were very proud and insisted on being called by. Later, in a revulsion against this presumption, superintendents and executives, particularly those who were not professionals, were relegated largely to managerial and development tasks. Both social workers and child care staff claimed their right to be the most important figures in a child's life on campus. Some superintendents virtually abandoned any involvement in the lives of children, ceased to know them even by name, and took no part in decisions about them.

Yet children do need someone who symbolizes the agency to them, and so do their parents. Someone must be able to answer the question: "What can (or will) this agency do for me?" to say nothing of, "What are the limits of tolerance?" A superintendent need not assume the role of Big Daddy to symbolize these things to parents or to children. He does need to be part of the family conference at the child's admission and should in fact call this conference. He should be involved whenever question is raised about a child's inacceptability to the Home. He may not wish to question the decision of his professional staff but he alone can take responsibility for the final action. The superintendent also represents in any conference the administrative and public-relations aspects of any decision, not necessarily to overrule considerations of good planning and good child care but to represent his adminstrative concerns.

For optimal results, a superintendent should be visible to children, not in an authoritative way but in an approachable way, as a symbol of the Home's total interest and concern.

We have spoken here of the superintendent, but some agencies, especially those with multiple functions or several campuses, are headed by an executive director and may have a resident director, director of professional services, or some other designated head for the Home. A decision may be called for as to who represents the Home's totality to parents and children.

The board is the final undergirder and supporter of the program. Its primary responsibilities are to select an adminstrator, to support him as long as he performs responsibly, and, on his advice, to adopt overall policies for the Home and accept responsibility for them, interpreting them to the constituency. For this last reason it is very important that the board understand what the Home is doing, and that it take part in the planning of any major changes of direction. A board dominated by an executive whom it "trusts implicitly" and never questions is a broken reed in a crisis or when the executive resigns. Failure of such a board to understand what has happened may undo the work of years, particularly if it acts to select an unqualified succeeding executive. At the same time, a board, while retaining its right to question and even overrule on occasion, must trust its executive, support him, and follow his lead in general. It is particularly important, then, for the board to be kept consistently appraised of the failures and difficulties of the program as well as of its successes. It must not interfere in the administrative process, nor deal directly with staff or children except on invitation. It must act always corporately—a board member should have no authority as an individual.

Behind the board stands the constituency, and our final model may look something like this, in a unit system:

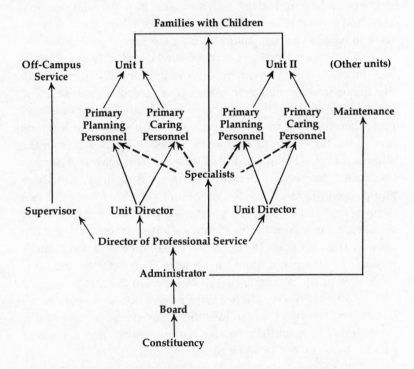

The position of the specialists is important. They are shown here as consultants to the primary planning and caring personnel. They also serve children and their families directly. This brings up the question of the Home's centralization or decentralization. The services of the old-line orphanage were almost entirely centralized. Even such obvious child care functions as food, laundry, and clothes buying were centralized. The children ate in a common dining hall, sent their clothes to a common laundry, and received clothes from a common stockroom. In addition, such services as recreation, liaison with the public schools, religious instruction, and even discipline were centrally provided. So were a multitude of permissions relating to dating, going off campus, and having friends visit from the community. The Home, too, operated under a multiplicity of campuswide rules that constrained the child care worker in areas such as dress, bedtimes, study periods, intercottage activities, and boy-girl relationships. The child care worker had little discretion as to how these services were to be used for the children under her care.

Of late, many Homes have developed a more cottage-based model, with many more services and decisions centered in the living unit. Some have gone so far as to decentralize the budget, allowing each cottage to plan for itself within agency-prescribed limits. This is in general a healthy move, but it can be carried too far, to the point that each cottage is isolated from the others and operates in a world of its own. This may also happen in a group home or a detached cottage off campus, but these groups are integrated into the community in a way that units of a campus cannot be. Children often need groups other than those of the living unit; one of the advantages of a campus is that it can provide such groups. Therefore, some balance between centralization and decentralization seems wise. The trend at present is more toward the cottage-based model than to the institutional.

The unit system offers a compromise between overcentralization and too much decentralization, but even one unit can be institutional or essentially cottage based. Again, there must be a balance between the two principles.

But the mark of a really productive service agency is the degree to which it learns to operate as a team for the benefit of families and children, whatever the distinction of function or the relative power of its component parts may be. The basic principle of a team is that in significant decisions there is input from all those with knowledge of the situation or affected by it, and these same persons participate in the outcome. Everyone does not necessarily agree with the decision, nor is the ultimate decision one person's responsibility. The concept of dialogue is important; i.e., it is not a team decision if one person collates the written reports of others.

The basic internal team in the Children's Home is the one that plans with families and children. The operation of plans may be the ultimate management responsiblity of one person, the unit director, for example, but such plans as are formulated are contributed to by the child care worker, the social worker, the parent and others as needed, such as the teacher or work supervisor, who come into contact with the child. The child himself may be a part to all of the plan, or some of it. These planning people meet on a functional and not a hierarchical basis—all of their inputs are important to a decision. It follows too that anyone in this group is entitled to the same information about the family or child's situation as any other. There can be no withholding of confidential information significant to the child or the family's development from members of the team if such information is needed for a wise decision.

Another type of knowledge necessary to good teamwork is the sharing of constraints. Executives are often wary of sharing negative constraints as they exist in the realms of available money, community or board acceptance, or legal requirements, both with staff and with children. To admit that these constraints exist appears to diminish the executive's authority, whereas in fact the executive will seem much more human to others if he acknowledges these constraints. Acknowledgment of them does, however, raise the possibility that some of them can be modified, or even that they will ultimately appear less as real restraints than as imagined ones, sometimes arising from the executive's fears of what might be the reaction of the board or the constituency. Fears, for instance, of public or constituency reaction to racial integration have been far greater than the actuality; so have fears of racial difficulties on the campus.

Teamwork is also important in solving campus problems or in establishing internal policies and procedures. Such things as standards of performance, dating policies, working programs, visitation policies, and recreational programs, including the use of facilities such as a gym or a swimming pool, are best arrived at, at least initially, by vertical committees or task forces.

The essence of a vertical committee is that it includes at least three elements—administration, persons who must carry out the policy, and consumers, or persons who are affected by it. Sometimes a fourth element—noninvolved persons who can view the program objectively, either from a common-sense or an expert base—is useful for balance. Thus a committee trying to arrive at standards of performance for child care workers might include an administrator, perhaps the director of campus life or unit director, one or more child care workers, an expert on writing standards, and, as consumers of the service, both a social worker and one or more youngsters. The consumers, particularly the youngsters, are more likely to see the impracticality of some part of a program as it intermeshes with other programs or pressures on those affected by the program.

The inclusion of youngsters in decision making is an important element in any administrative plan. This is dealt with in more detail in one of the articles on particular subjects that form the second part of this book. Here perhaps it needs only to be said that any program or rule into which young people have had input, and been listened to, either in the cottage or on the campus as a whole, is assured of much greater acceptance than if it is established without such participation, no matter what its merits are. And what is true of youngsters is often true of adults as well.

# ❦❦V

# The Home
# in Its Societal Context

No agency exists in a vacuum or is wholly autonomous. It forms part of a number of systems and has close relationships with others. A church-sponsored Home, for instance, is a member of several systems:

1. The system of its sponsoring church, which may own its facilities, appoints its board, contributes the major part of its funds—although this is increasingly not the case—and, in general, provides its theological and dogmatic beliefs and underpinning as well as the reason for the agency's existence.

2. The community system, which provides it with services, such as schools, health services, and recreational activities, and whose goodwill at least is essential to its well-being.

3. The social service system, and within this the child or family welfare system in particular, which provides it with referrals, accepts referrrals in return, may educate or train its workers (through schools of social work or through institutes and courses), and certifies its professional staff as well as being the source of professional standards, ideas, and methodology.

4. The governmental system, of which the Home may not be a part but by which it is constantly being impinged on. The Home exists in relation to certain laws, such as those on child

neglect or adoption, guardianship, or school attendance. It must observe ordinances on health, fire protection, and zoning. In most states it is required to be both chartered and licensed on a continuing basis. It may be affected by state or national personnel policies in such areas as pensions, minimum wages, and occupational hazards. If it receives any money or services from the government it must observe state or national policies on nondiscrimination. These relationships, in the instance of a particular Home, are shown graphically on page 85.

Other systems may be mentioned to which it is accountable, the economic system, for one, and, indeed, the family system of each of its children, for the whole nature of systems involves both constraints on the member of the system (the Home) and the contribution of this member to the system of which it is a part.

Thus a church-sponsored Home owes to its sponsoring church system the carrying out in a practical way of the church's mission and beliefs. It may have some responsibility to serve families in the church, although this has long since ceased to be an exclusive responsibility. In the past it was sometimes expected to evangelize for a denomination or sect. Now this is generally understood in a more general sense, i.e., that if people are treated or helped in a Christian and therefore a loving way, they will be more able to understand and accept a gospel of love. Homes, too, of a particular denomination may be presumed to owe some implementation of beliefs on which the denomination places particular stress, such as abstinence from alcohol among Baptists or pacifism among Quakers. The Home also has the responsibility of providing a service worthy of the sponsoring church.

One possible and not wholly unworthy role for either a church-sponsored or a community agency is to provide a superior service to a particular group, or to provide a service in which certain cultural or religious values are stressed. Before a Home undertakes such a responsibility it should make sure, however, that its service is indeed superior on the whole, and not merely superior in one aspect (say, the quality of religious instruction) and inferior in other, possibly more far-reaching, ways. It also

# Systems Affecting Epworth Children's Home

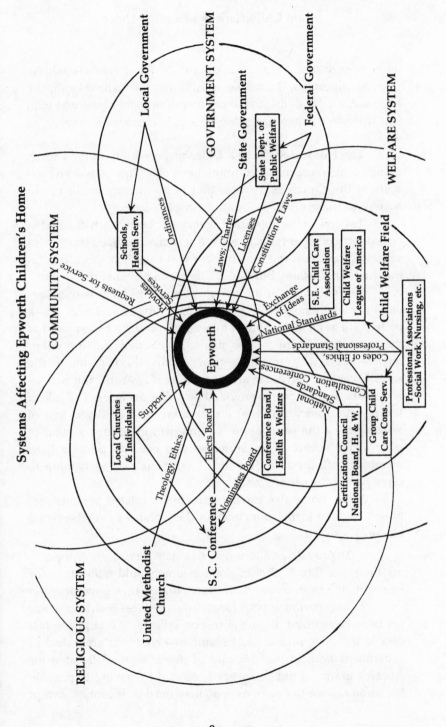

85

must be sure that what it has to offer is not offered elsewhere. The contention that the workers in a church-sponsored Home are necessarily more dedicated, more moral, or more concerned with spiritual values than are those in a public program may be an illusion.

The Home does have a wider responsibility to the church system that transcends denominational ties. This is its responsibility to the church as a whole and to the private sector of our society, as these undertake social service tasks.

The role of the voluntary agency has been much debated in our society. While originally private agencies provided the bulk of service to families, and government was usually a subsidizer (in the thinking of some, but not of others) and frequently a coordinator and invigilator of the private service, offering its own service only where no private agency was willing or able to do so—a pattern still seen in the almost total assumption by government of the institutional care for the mentally retarded and the delinquent—public programs have grown so that this is no longer the case. Except in particular areas, such as New York, the nation-wide bulk of child care is provided by public agencies. The role of the private agency could, at a minimum, be considered that of keeping alive the principle of voluntarism in society, a concept particularly attractive to churches who need to provide their members with an outlet for their charity, as well as helping to carry part of the service load.

More thoughtful private and church-related persons see, however, three further functions of the private or church-related Home. These are:

1. To provide an alternative to a state service, thus preserving the possibility of choice. Some people would rather turn for help to their community or their church than to their government.

2. To experiment with functions or services which have not yet been recognized as public responsibilities. While in the last decade the government has become involved in a great deal of experimentation, in part because of public money allocated for research grants, a public agency is limited by having to provide the same service to everyone who may need it. It cannot, except

86

purely for purposes of research, select a group to be served or undertake a very expensive service for a few. Moreover, the availability of public research funds is unpredictable. It is certain that government will need to spend its funds on larger matters of social engineering, such as the control of delinquency or illegitimacy, or epidemic social problems, such as drug addiction, or child abuse. Service for less obvious personal problems may again fall to the private agency.

3. As a critic of the public endeavor. This may be a particularly important function of the church agency. Public social work in this country is by necessity humanist, or to be more accurate, humanist-positivist-utopian, in its philosophy, although this humanism has Judaeo-Christian roots. With much of this philosophy a church agency may agree, but there are places at which a Christian may feel he must take issue with trends developing in the realm of secular social science. The church agency must at least offer an alternative. For example, social science may become, from the Christian point of view, too totally concerned with theories of behavior control or theories that tend to glorify the contemporary secular culture, or, in an effort to relieve pain in any and all circumstances, may be denying the possibility of growth in responsibility through the acceptance of suffering; the Christian here may think the social sciences are showing a tendency to "play God" or to create cultural idols.

These are, of course, debatable matters and to many might seem unimportant. It is not suggested here that a Christian is necessarily right in calling a halt at these points. Yet implications of such ideas are far-reaching for the manner in which people are treated, and in all these instances the Christian has a specific viewpoint derived from his basic beliefs which may make such ideas quite unacceptable to him. It should, of course, be equally clear that the humanist may criticize a church agency that is, for instance, judgmental, unmerciful, self-satisfied, or so convinced of its rightness that it can tolerate no dissent.

Some of the obligations of a Home to its constituency may, in fact, conflict with its role as a member of some other system. This is likely to happen most frequently when the demands of its constituency are detailed, when they are based on misconceptions (such as the belief that the Home is caring for orphans), or where the Home is treated as a subordinate agency of the constituency rather than a contributing part of a system. Unreasonable demands sometimes made of a Home are that it should produce a certain kind of behavior in its children, that it should become a "perpetual Sunday school," emphasizing religious doctrine at every turn, that it should be constantly available for inspection by church groups and always in apple-pie order, that it should accept without question the well-meaning but patronizing charity of church groups, and that it should operate on a totally inadequate budget, particularly in regard to staff, often on the mistaken theory that if an undertaking is "Christian" it should not need adequate manpower or skill. But these are the darker aspects of its membership in a church system, ones that it must act to correct through interpretation of its work. Membership in a church system may be one of a Home's greatest strengths, providing it with direction, inspiration, and dedicated involvement. This is likely to be so when the Christian nature of the Home is clearly manifested in the way the Home and its staff act towards families and their children, rather than in the induced moral behavior of its children or their professed piety. In the past, many Homes maintained what they thought of as a Christian operation by purging themselves of the very clients who needed them most—the so-called sinners—and keeping their hypocrites and their pharisaicals.

The Home owes to its community, first and foremost, that it be part of some overall plan, perhaps loosely conceived but nevertheless at least implicit, for all families and children in the community. Whatever its motives, it is doing little good if it is duplicating a service that is already being given, or if it is offering a service for which there is little need, in which case it will either be unused or will be tempted to accept children which it is ill-equipped to serve.

This raises the whole question of specialization versus generalized service. Some Homes, out of a feeling of responsibility for all children brought to their attention or belonging to their constituency, or because they are unwilling to think in terms of a whole community's needs, accept children into care, often with inadequate planning, with little consideration for the real needs of the child or the family. Such Homes respond to the family's distress and the child's need for shelter, or to the urging of a court or a welfare department, and while their motives may be laudable, they can do a family and a child a real disservice.

Three principles might be set out here:

1. If a Home is to respond to a wide variety of requests, it must be prepared to develop a variety of services for children who, for instance, need short-time or long-time care, foster-family or group care, more or less structure in daily living, schooling at various levels, normal living, or a treatment situation.

To have a single service which is expected to serve all children is to try, like Procrustes, to fit the sleeper to the bed and not the bed to the sleeper. It is a sad commentary that even today a child whose parents turn to the church for placement has perhaps four chances out of five of being cared for in a group, while one entrusted to the state because of neglect or dependency will almost inevitably be tried in one or more foster-family homes. This is not so much a matter of differing beliefs in the values of the two kinds of care—most social workers at least recognize that some children need one kind of care and some another—as it is that each group has only one type of care readily available to it. Few Homes have the resources to provide this variety or can deploy their resources with ingenuity sufficient for a wide variety of needs to be met without producing a watered-down service. Sometimes, too, the effort to meet too wide a range of needs means poor service for all. Thus, certain Homes may be wise to specialize in short-term care, or in service to the alienated adolescent, to slow-moving children, or to victims of family breakdown.

2. There is real value in knowing one service well and carrying it out with expertise. One Home is doing a beautiful job with teenaged girls and their families who cannot get along with each other; it has a structured one-year program directed to working through this problem, yet it is constantly being pressured by the community to accept long-term placements of slow-

moving girls who need remedial schooling, for whom there is no resource in the community. So far the Home in question has held its ground, while acknowledging the community need, but being unwilling to crowd out the very successful and needed service it is giving. At the same time, the Home is exploring the possibility of establishing sometime in the future a facility for the slow-moving child. This will mean that for a time some girls in this group will go unserved, but serving these girls at this moment would be a poor use of a staff trained to provide a specialized service. Should the need of the slow-moving child increase, however, and that of the alienated teenager decline, the Home may well think of retooling.

3. There is a kind of Gresham's Law of service. Poor service to any group tends to inhibit the development of a really adequate service. Because a part of the need is met, perhaps by the mere provision of shelter, the real needs of a group appear less urgent and the community assumes that the problem has been solved. Sometimes it actually works to the detriment of a group of clients to offer them a partial or a less than professional service.

Obviously some kind of balance needs to be struck between specialization in order to provide a superior service—something a private agency needs to offer—and meeting the most pressing need in the community. Agencies can become too precious in their intake policies, too careful not even to try to serve a child who does not fit into the group it believes it can best serve. Unfortunately, however, the children most usually excluded are those who require a service that the Home is not willing to offer—that is, the most difficult children. Specialization in the easy is not a particularly honorable course.

Even when a Home is unable to offer a specialized service, however, and is caring for children who, although not easy to care for, are within its capabilities to serve, there is a further dimension of community planning to which church Homes in particular have paid little attention. Historically, each denomination has developed its own service with little regard for what other denominations have developed. It is not unusual to find, within a hundred-mile radius, three or four large Homes serving essentially the same population, and with comparable facilities and skill. Each may, in addition, have developed group and foster-family homes, often in the same territories. They may differ slightly in philosophy, in facilities, in the characteristics of children and families with which they are most successful—the tempo of life on some campuses or the degree of structuring may, for instance, be particularly helpful to slow-moving children on one campus and to highly competitive ones in another—and they are often a sufficient distance apart that visitation would be much easier for a particular family in one than in the others. Yet only the last factor of all these distinctions, and that one somewhat infrequently, determines which family works with which Home. Although Homes no longer serve their own denominations exclusively and a large proportion of the families using them are only minimally involved with any church, it appears to be largely a matter of chance, of someone's knowing of such and such a Home, that determines to whom a family will turn. And once a process starts with a Home the family is likely to continue with it.

In a few communities there are the beginnings of intake agreements, and in those communities where, for financial reasons, most families become engaged first with the public welfare service, more discrimination is used in steering families to where they can get the best help for a child. Here an outside agency— the publice service—is the distributing agent. The use of the Homes arises from external judgments and not from the Home's self-knowledge or experience. For the most part, any ecumenical planning with families in this country is very much in its infancy.

Some communities are at least dreaming of a community-wide family bureau, probably under public auspices, to which families who are not necessarily aware of what facilities exist in the community or may not be aware of what a Home could do to help them may turn for advice. Such a center could make referrals to Homes, but in such a system something more than information-giving is required. There needs to be some system of sustained referral and some accountability on the part of Homes to such a source, even where no payment for care is involved. At a minimum this might be a report on the discussion with the family about their use or nonuse of the Home's services and a report when services are terminated. If the planning with the family discloses needs that the Home cannot meet, there should be referral back to the bureau or to a more appropriate agency. Every effort should be made to see that families and children do not fall between available services and that they are not left in some vague limbo of a public responsibility. Such a bureau should be authorized to call together all possible resources in the community to meet the needs of a family.[14]

Quite another responsibility a Home may have to its community is taking a position of leadership in community affairs as a whole. The Home is often in an excellent position to observe what happens to children in our society, under existing welfare, educational, or health laws or provisions. It can document the need for resources such as kindergartens, special education, mental-health centers, shelter or emergency services, and, above all, adequate income maintenance. It sees the result of lack of resources or facilities that are poorly staffed or misdirected. And it usually has a board whose members can be sensitized to the problem and who have considerable social and political power.

Again, a Home is part of its immediate community. One Home, for instance, in a large city was instrumental in organizing a series of "safe houses" for children who might be accosted or assaulted on their way to and from school in a high-risk neighborhood. Another led a community in a clean-up campaign. Homes, too, can provide communities with recreational facilities, meeting places for community activities, and centers for such activities as parent effectiveness training or marriage enrichment.

The Home's responsibility in the child welfare field is also a large one. Beyond fulfilling its role in the community's child care system, it can contribute to professional knowledge through research and through sharing with others, in conferences and on paper, its successes and its failures. It can experiment, not only

14. See the pamphlet issued by the Citizens Committee for Children of New York, "A Dream Deferred" (1971), and its elaboration in Alan Keith-Lucas's "Co-planning and Advocacy in Child Welfare Services" in Felice Perlmutter, ed., *A Design for Social Work Practice* (New York: Columbia University Press, 1974).

for itself, but for the field as a whole. Most new concepts in the field and much of the theory developed around them have been the direct result of something done in a Home, perhaps in an emergency, that proved useful and could be adapted to other situations. The use of the family conference, the use-of-care plan, back-up planning for children, and adolescent reassessment are all practices now accepted as useful and essential for most families or children that were originally devised to help with a single situation. Such programs as the work-earning-responsibility plan described later in this book were developed in response to a Home's dissatisfaction with its work program.

Research in Children's Homes has hardly begun to scratch the surface of the many problems Homes could help solve. Questions such as the characteristics of families that offer some hope for reestablishment, the factors that lead to unexpected teenage rebellion, the criteria for when a family of children can or should live together are ones that need to be answered more authoritatively than they have been at present. Experimental indicators do exist in all of these areas, but these have been based on too small a sample or too wide a set of variables.

Private child care agencies also have a responsibility to help in the education of social work students and students in other helping professions by providing field instruction. Many social workers, for instance, have little idea of how to operate in an institutional setting; many more need this knowledge and experience if good planning with families is to become a reality.

The Home's responsibility to the public sector raises the whole question of accountability in a more complex way. The Home is accountable to its constituency. It is accountable to the families which it serves. In a number of court cases recently, where a child's behavior or mental health has been involved, Homes have been required to show that they are doing something positive about the child's condition rather than simply providing an alternative to the parents' supposedly inadequate care. But a Home is also accountable to the public welfare system of its state or community when it accepts board payments for children—what is generally known as purchase of care. This practice, almost universal in the Northeast, is becoming much more general in other parts of the nation. Some denominations with strong convictions about the separation of church and state have held out against it, but even there there appears to be some weakening of the principle in the face of the rapidly escalating cost of good service.

For clarification, it might be good to review the normal sources of income of a church-related or private Home. These can be classified in ten categories:

1. Endowments, either through gifts or legacies, which provide a Home with a regular income or with capital funds. These are the Home's own business although it should be pointed out that they can act as much as a constraint on the Home's program as can government grants, especially where money is given for specific purposes which do not fit the Home's program or exclude certain kinds of service. Homes have felt themselves constrained sometimes to build cottages or other buildings they should not build on their campuses because money was available or for fear of offending a wealthy donor. A legacy may prescribe service to white children only or exclude children with both parents living or, in one well-known instance, illegitimate children. In the search for this most assured form of financing the Home needs to be very careful that money does not control program.

2. Gifts for specific purposes, for which the same caution needs to be issued.

3. Collections, or appeals to friends of the Home for regular expenses. These, if given in cash, can usually be used for the Home's purposes, but can become an embarrassment if the traditions of the community favor gifts in kind, such as used clothing or entertainment that carries a patronizing feeling or, as sometimes happens, overstress material gifts at Christmas.

4. Regular budgeted support from the church's benevolent budget or from a community fund. Many church Homes are finding that this source of funds represents a smaller part of their budget than formerly and gives rise to the question of the reality of the church's sponsorship of the program. In some denomina-

tions, the tendency has been to identify this part of the budget as programmatic—that is, to rely on endowments, payment for care, and voluntary giving for the basic custodial program, the bricks and mortar, food and clothing, and to regard this contribution as the factor that raises the level of service to one worthy of the church and its mission.

5. Payments for service by the families served. This is a small but increasing part of the budget. Care should be taken, however, that parents and relatives take responsibility for general support and not for functions that are properly those of the Home, such as allowances and clothing. Part of using a Home's service is recognizing that there are aspects of a child's life the Home must provide equitably for all children under its care. To allow a parent to exercise these custodial, rather than guardian-ship, responsibilities can conceal the reality of the service.

Support from the family should include, in the Home's thinking, Social Security and veterans' benefits for a child, as well as court-ordered support payments, since these are not payments by government on behalf of a child but rather family income to which the child has a right independently of his care in the Home. It would be as illogical to consider these government payments as to make a distinction between a family's earnings from a private employer and those earned as a policeman, gar-bage collector, or member of the armed forces. If the United States ever moves to a family allowance for children, as have Britain, France, and Canada, Children's Homes need have no hesitation in accepting this as legitimate family contribution to the cost of child care.

6. Payment for care by the state or county. This is a very different matter. It acknowledges the state as the custodian of the child and therefore the primary planner for him. The Home is then in danger of becoming little more than a facility which the state uses as part of its planning process. Much therefore depends on the degree of delegation the state is willing to grant and still maintain its own accountability for the money spent. If the state, for instance, controls the child's visits to his parents, or must approve the child's care in a group or foster-family home, the

private agency's freedom to plan is severely circumscribed. The parent, too, finds himself forced to plan, not with the people who are actually able to help him by engaging him in his child's care, but with an agency whose relationship with him is primarily based on its legal right to take charge of his child. His own contribution to this care, both moral and material, is denied by the fact that the Home is receiving a board rate from the state. If, on the other hand, the board rate is simply an expression of the state's interest in every dependent child and is treated as a family allowance for children who need care away from home, then the Home may be free to plan constructively with the family. The state would need only the assurance that the child was still in need of care and that this was being given in an acceptable way that recognized the rights of the family and the perceived need of the child. The distinction is an important one. In the first instance the state controls the placement, making decisions in the particular case. In the second it approves the Home to serve families and children and provides it with the financial means to do so.

In being willing to approve a Home as qualified to provide service with payment for so doing, without having to control the individual planning in each case, the state has the right to require a certain accountability from the Home. This is not simply a matter of a license or the meeting of standards. It should include some form of reporting to justify continued payment. One suggestion is a requirement that there be, at least quarterly, a planning conference involving the parents which is reported to the state, as well as a reporting of termination of service and the reasons for it. If church-related or private agencies are to accept payment for care from governmental sources, this seems a reasonable requirement.

The question of short-term use of a private facility by a public department which is planning with a family and will continue to do so but needs temporarily what a Home can provide is another matter. One Home has developed a policy which limits such placements to six months. If care will be needed for longer, the Home must be free to plan with the parents directly.

Another possible danger in accepting payment for care is

the premium it may put on acceptance of children who may be entitled to such funding, and even the temptation to take, for instance, court custody of children in order to ensure payment, when this is not what a family needs. Payment for care may be essential to the existence of some agencies but it can become the kind of constraint that can twist a Home's purposes.

7. Individual sponsorship of children. This is a somewhat difficult area, particularly when it involves clothing and allowances at the sponsor's discretion. Some children may gain greatly from the support of an outside family. For many, however, it engenders a divided loyalty or a false obligation. Certainly it should not be relied on as a regular way of providing needed things. It too often serves the interests of the sponsor rather than those of the child and should never be used indiscriminately or apart from planning for the family.

8. Grants, either from government or from foundations, for particular projects or services, such as the training grants that were formerly available under the Elementary and Secondary Education Act, or grants for special studies, special projects, or research. Since these are projects which the agency itself initiates, there is little constriction on the autonomy of the Home. The major problems with this kind of grant are that the Home may become dependent on grants to do what it should be doing itself, and that the existence of grants in a particular area may tempt the Home to emphasize programs for which grants are known to be available.

9. Direct grants from governmental sources. These do obligate the Home to some extent to do what the grantor requires and are therefore somewhat suspect if the Home wishes, as it should, to retain control over its most sensitive decision—the particular families and children it is prepared to serve. Only a Home can determine accurately at any one time whether care for a specific child would meet the objectives of its plan with the family. In the past, some Homes have feared being compelled to accept particular children so that they hesitated to sign the Civil Rights Compliance, even though they had declared their intention of serving families and children of all races.

10. Incidental income from a number of miscellaneous sources, such as for example farm products or the output of some vocational training programs.

It is not easy for an agency to keep in balance both the sources of money with which it operates and its various obligations to the systems of which it is a part. Yet if the agency is to be strong and vigorous, offering a real service, it needs to be clear about the constraints under which it allows itself to operate. It cannot opt out of the community or welfare systems or ignore its relationship with government, however attractive such autonomy may appear, without greatly restricting its potential for service. Yet it also needs to retain its freedom to render the kind of service it both wants and is equipped to give.

# PART TWO
## Essays on Specific Topics

# Introduction

Part Two is organized into seven areas, following the outline of the seven helping methods as found in Chapter II of Part One. This part presents selected materials of recent vintage, appropriate to the area under which they appear and, in the authors' opinion, the types of material that will be particularly useful to practitioners.

A wide range of styles and types of selections is included in Part Two. The reader should know in advance that no effort has been made toward uniformity in style, nor does the content logically flow as would a single essay.

These materials are linked together by their focus on practice. Some have been written by practitioners, some were developed by practitioners in workshops, and others were presented by students of the practice scene. Each selection is meant to demonstrate one or more aspects of the area under which it is included, or to share an experience, either of an individual or an agency, that is related to the area. The articles that are somewhat theoretical have been selected on the basis of the authors' experience of materials that practitioners find usable.

The content of Part Two will further define the concepts inherent in the seven helping methods of the family-centered children's home. Many of the articles should prove useful in the training of personnel for group child care.

# Contributors to Part Two

ROBERT L. COATES was formerly a consultant for Group Child Care Consultant Services, University of North Carolina. He is now in private practice in Lakeland, Florida.

THOMAS E. CURTIS is professor and former chairman, Department of Psychiatry, University of North Carolina.

RAYMOND FANT is director of Group Living, Bellefaire, Cleveland, Ohio.

MARJORIE L. FARADAY is a consultant on the staff of the Group Child Care Consultant Services, University of North Carolina.

DRUSCILLA HARTE, at the time of writing, was a child care worker at Episcopal Child Care Services, Charlotte, North Carolina.

JACK KIRKLAND is director of Black Studies, Washington University, St. Louis, Missouri, and a former board member of Group Child Care Consultant Services.

JUANITA PERRY, at the time of writing, was a child care worker at Episcopal Child Care Services, Charlotte, North Carolina.

JOHN Y. POWELL is director of the Thompson Children's Home, Episcopal Child Care Services, Charlotte, North Carolina, and a board member of Group Child Care Consultant Services.

DOUGLAS POWERS is professor in the Department of Human Development and Learning, the University of North Carolina at Charlotte, and psychiatric consultant to Episcopal Child Care Services.

MELVIN E. WALKER is director of Campus Life, Kennedy Home for Children, Kinston, North Carolina.

EUGENE WATSON is associate professor, School of Education, University of North Carolina at Chapel Hill, and a former board member of Group Child Care Consultant Services.

# 🌿🌿A

# In the Area of Planning

1🌿 Helping Parents Become More Responsible

*From a workshop held at the Chapel Hill
Workshops, 1969*

CLIFFORD W. SANFORD, *Consultant*
LUCY ANDERSON, ALLAN JARRATT, PATTI VAN WAGNER,
FRANK T. WILLIS, *Writing Committee*

Although the staffs of child care institutions would readily agree that parents of the children in our care should be more responsible, there seems to be an undercurrent of resistance in fulfilling our obligation to help parents assume this responsibility. While social workers speak about the concepts of the dignity and worth of each individual, self-determination, a nonjudgmental attitude toward clients, and beginning where the client is, these concepts are not always apparent in our daily work with families.

Historically many social problems have been dealt with by removing people from society and the milieu in which the problem occurred. Thus many Children's Homes, through expressed policy or by attitude, have discouraged active involvement of the family of a child in residential care. In its parental function, institutional philosophy has at times denied the reality and pervasive influence of the natural family. In its protective emphasis, the institution, working with the child apart from his family, has really undermined his identity and the development of his dignity as an individual.

By the act of holding families to their continuing responsibility, we can enhance their dignity as self-directing individuals. When we take the responsibility for making decisions we remove the opportunity for the recognition of self-value. Taking over, doing for, "knowing better than," are the pitfalls we dig in the path of the parent.

Actually, the agency does not have the power to decide whether or not the parent should be involved. He is involved by the very fact that he exists. He is involved in the mind and life of the child. Therefore, we must ask, are we being ethical when we do not encourage the right of the parent to participate responsibly? It is at the point of his active participation that we begin to help the parent understand his responsibility.

By assuming responsibility the parent gains self-respect and the process of responsible participation becomes an affirming experience. Consequently, the child begins to see his parents actively accepting their responsibility and this in turn increases his self-esteem since he is so closely identified with them. The agency is the helper, the social worker is its agent.

The entire child care agency is involved in the process of enabling families to function more successfully. Whereas the attitude of helping the child as a part of his family ideally permeates the institution as a whole, the social worker is the specific person to interpret the institution to the client and help him understand the limitations and conditions on which help is offered.

The common characteristic of most client families is the experience of failure. Most often, this takes the form of deteriorating relationships. A turning point is needed on which to rebuild. This is the kind of clue we take into account when we determine how we are to perform. Of course, services are provided not only to meet the families' immediate pressing needs, but to provide opportunities for continuing growth. Agencies have the capacity to reverse the pattern of failure and irresponsibility through their faith in each person's capacity for growth and change, and by supportively offering bits and pieces of reality (such as conditions on which help is offered) with which the parents must struggle and cope.

Many times parents or other family members make inquiries regarding the placement of children in a group setting because this is the only way they know to approach the problem. They know that they have a problem. Probably they know this by the evidence of it, rather than by identifying the nature of the problem. They feel that the solution would be to have the child in what they consider to be a more secure situation. During this initial stage we present the framework through which help is offered and we build the means by which parents are enabled to take advantage of available alternatives. Thus, the helping process is communicated in such a way that the family can grasp hope for a revival of relationships. This experience can represent a new beginning for the family in making responsible decisions.

Though we encounter a few parents who have lived in Children's Homes, most parents have no real concept of what goes on there. Initially, then, the social worker should discuss with the parents the purpose of the Home, how children are treated, and what it can offer their child. Policies governing the care of the child need to be explained thoroughly to the parents, so they may consider these in the light of what they think their child needs. They should be encouraged to ask any questions they wish in order to make sure they understand.

The attitude of the worker during this first meeting is all-important. He should at all times express the attitude of the concerned helper. Though he may know his field, he is no expert on this family, nor is he their decision maker.

After the services are explained, the worker must enable the family to decide whether they desire these services for their child. Do they think this is really what he needs? The worker needs to know the problems that have been occurring so as to help explore all alternatives and resources. However, the parents must be aware that they, at this point, are the ones to decide whether to use this particular agency. If the parents decide that they do wish to use the agency, the worker must prepare them for receiving the services.

Many parents never fully understand what is happening to themselves or to their child. They often do not understand who has custody of their child, nor do they understand what rights they and their children have. It is the task and indeed the obligation of the social worker to explain to them what has happened, what is now happening, and what possibly can happen.

Parents need to know what services they are asking for; they must decide if it is what they really want; they must be prepared for the time when these services will begin. Only the social worker to whom they have gone at this time has the opportunity to enable them to plan adequately for their child.

When the worker and the parents feel that the services are understood, the basic admission policies must also be thoroughly discussed. The parents must again be assured that the basic decision is theirs. If they decide to make application, the agency then tries to determine the needs of the family and to decide whether the services offered will fulfill those needs.

Admittedly, few parents are functioning responsibly at the beginning of the helping process. They must be given much support in the initial stages as well as genuine understanding of their present situation.

Even when referrals are not initiated by the family, but through other community agencies who may hold custody of the child, we need to involve the parents directly in placement plans with the referring agency and the residential facility. The right to decide whether to use service is then out of the parents' hands, but the decision to enter into the use of service will be one of the major determinants of its usefulness. There is no justification for sidestepping our responsibility for a thorough planning job regardless of the source or urgency of the referral. Through this initial phase of the helping process we are attempting to help all persons involved to fulfill role expectations. And a thorough exploration of all areas prevents problems later in care.

In cases where parents are totally out of the picture, such as through death or refusal to participate, the agency which has custody must agree to become involved with the helping process.

In any case, early and frequent conferences with parents are a must. These must be at least as intense as the intake. Maas and Engler in their study, *Children in Need of Parents*,[15] indicate that most children in foster care (institution or family) for approximately six months without active work with the families remained in care for eighteen months. If after eighteen months the children are still in care without active work with the families, they are practically assured of growing up as foster children. In other words, long-term placement is inevitable when families are not involved actively.

Another condition to consider is that the parent must talk with the child about his placement. The parent must tell him that he, the parent, has decided to place him in the Children's Home. The child needs to see, hear, and feel, from his parent, what is happening to him. Reality and truth must be dealt with. We cannot uphold a deceptive situation. The social worker plays an important supportive role in helping the parent understand how to tell his child that he must leave the family home.

At the time of admission, the agency and the family should enter into a written agreement specifying responsibilities. This agreement symbolizes the partnership that has been established. Although it carries no legal authority, it formalizes the commitments, and somewhat binds what has been decided upon by the parents, child, and the agency. The agreement is a piece of reality around which the partnership begins to grow. It should include at least the following elements:

1. A clear statement of the reason for placement.
2. Agreed-upon responsibilities of the parent.
3. Agreed-upon responsibilities of the child.
4. Agreed-upon responsibilities of the agency.
5. A clarification of procedures for keeping communications open, through conferences and visits.

Since we cannot take the parent's place, we must bring him in when possible. There are many children now in care for

15. Henry S. Maas and Richard E. Engler, Jr., *Children in Need of Parents* (New York: Columbia University Press, 1959).

whom this kind of planning has not taken place. Where this is true, the worker must recreate the prelude, attempting to capture the essential elements of a new beginning.

In many cases we need to spend more effort and money in attempts to trace lost parents. Each child will have a different reaction to the idea of finding his lost parent. Again the worker must assume an important supportive role in reestablishing a family relationship. When relationships have been reestablished, we then need also to enter into a partnership with this family and begin planning more meaningful care.

Initially, the agreement should be a temporary one. The partners should have a conference and reevaluate the agreement within, at the most, three months. At this point, we focus not upon the irresponsibilities of the parents, but rather on the strengths and limitations of the agreement. Although the type of agreement and the frequency of review is determined to some extent by the projected length of care, the one trap we do not permit the parent or ourselves to fall into is that nebulous state, "indefinite."

In summary, helping parents become more responsible is an action on our part, the nature of which depends upon:

1. Our attitude about ourselves as helpers and about those needing help.

2. Knowledge of the resources of our agency, of social work principles, but also of much more and certainly of the nature of the child-parent relationship.

3. The extent to which we offer a helping process which, from the initial encounter, stays with the parent where he is, respects his right and capacity for growth and change, clarifies the conditions on which our agency's help is offered, and supportively holds him to functioning responsibly regarding those facts necessary to begin coping with help, to the end that he realizes he now faces an opportunity for a new beginning.

## 2❧ The Parent as a Member of the Decision-Making Team

*From a panel discussion presented at the Chapel
Hill Workshops, 1971*

*Moderator:* CLIFFORD W. SANFORD
*Social Worker:* KITTY BASS
*Parent:* CYNTHIA MOORE
*Child Care Worker:* CAROLYN TRENT

MODERATOR: This is a situation in which the staff of a Home and the mother of a child worked together on a child's problem. Ms. Bass, would you begin by telling us something of the situation as the Home saw it?

SOCIAL WORKER: Ms. Moore had asked us to make a plan for her two children back in 1967. Both she and her husband were in mutual agreement that our agency could be of help to them. Since then we have been involved together in looking at how we can make the plan effective. What we wanted to share with you today was a very crucial turning point in this family, as we worked together around the problem of the behavior of their eleven-year-old girl, Terry, in a group care situation. Perhaps by discussing how we went about working together to solve the problem we can see better how we were able to bring the family closer together, and became involved in seeing something happen that we all felt was really exciting.

The problem really became acute when Terry was reported by the school for inappropriate behavior with boys both in the classroom and after school. Terry was a child who looked as though she were eighteen. Her skirts were certainly short and she wore high-heeled shoes and a lot of makeup, and sometimes she would wear padded bras. We were not greatly concerned about that, but she was hard to live with. She had a violent temper at times and she was a very negative little girl. She would play us all against each other. She had a problem with her boy-friend, too. She would sneak out to see him and was going steady, and at eleven we were concerned that that was rather young.

This is not the only side of Terry. The other side of Terry is a very intelligent and attractive little girl, a very nice person who does well in school, is very creative and artistic, and has a lot of strong points to work with.

We realized when this problem was particularly brought back to us by the school that as an agency we had somehow been working separately with the child. The social worker had seen her, the houseparents saw her at the cottage, and she saw her mother every weekend and on vacations, and went for visits. But somehow we just could not change Terry's behavior. We had tried for a year or two, and we now felt a real need to get together and look at what we were doing.

MODERATOR: Ms. Trent, would you speak about the problem and how a decision was made that working separately was not effective? From your perspective as a group parent, how did you three begin the process of coming together?

CHILD CARE WORKER: Well, we knew that we had to get together, because Terry would go and tell her social worker that I said one thing, and I would tell Terry that she could not wear all this makeup, and she would say that her mother said she could; and she told her mother that I said she could. We knew that in order to work with her we had to get together.

MODERATOR: Where did the motivation to get together come from? What was the spark?

CHILD CARE WORKER: She did have many problems that I knew I could not deal with alone. I called the social worker, who called Terry's mother, and we decided to get together.

SOCIAL WORKER: I think the school's intervention was one thing that was a turning point. It helped us both decide that we had better get with it. At that particular time, there were involved a relief child care worker and a cottage supervisor as well as Ms. Trent and myself. We said, "Look, we've got a problem. We have to do something." So one Monday morning we just sat down and started talking. That's how it really started. We had all gone our ways separately and needed to get together. Then Terry's mother and I had been meeting on Monday nights, but we had not been dealing with any behavior problems. We had just been looking at general plans for the family.

MODERATOR: Ms. Moore, on some given Monday night, then, Ms. Bass said something about your need to get together as a team. Perhaps you can't remember the exact moment, but do you remember some of your reactions to this idea of involving more people than just the two of you, and your reaction to the idea of working on a specific behavior problem?

PARENT: I think that in order to answer that, I have to go back to the beginning of my relationship with the Home.

When my children were first placed at the Home, I felt completely cut off as a mother and a parent, and as a person involved in their lives. At that time, there weren't any conferences with social workers or anyone in the agency. I merely went to the Home on Sunday afternoons to pick up my children for a couple of hours, visited with them, and took them back. I had no way of knowing if they had a problem at the Home or in school, if they were sick or well; I knew nothing about them other than what I heard from them on Sunday afternoon. This constantly made me feel useless, that I was an utter failure as a mother and had nothing to contribute to my children or their lives since I wasn't able to give them many material things. Not being involved in their lives and not knowing what was happening with them was making me very anxious. I don't know whether it was the change in the policy of the Home or a change in personnel that made a difference. I began to have conferences with the children's social worker. At that time I used these conferences for purely personal, selfish reasons. There were no actual problems to deal with, it was merely to have a link with my children. I didn't feel like a mother, and I felt that I couldn't be a mother. I felt that rather than looking upon me as a true mother they felt I was a fairy godmother type of person who only came to visit on a Sunday afternoon. So I went to conferences wanting to be on the inside rather than on the outside looking in.

At the same time, I was skeptical. I really didn't see the advantage of just going in and sitting there talking. I felt it was pretty pointless because, after all, my children weren't with me and I knew that, and I thought sitting there talking with somebody about it wasn't going to be worth two cents. But I was wrong, very, very wrong. I started having conferences and I found that in talking with the agency or Ms. Bass, I gained confidence in myself, felt I had something to contribute to my children and their lives, and believed I could contribute as well or maybe better than a mother who had her children at home to care for. I gained confidence from working with these people that gave me strength.

Then after we had been having conferences for a time, we came to realize Terry had problems, and we started to focus more on specifics than on general discussion of plans for the family. At that point we were willing to knuckle down and start working as a team. I feel that we've come a long way from the beginning when the children first went to the Home. I know I feel a lot better. My children and I are a lot closer now. I couldn't help my children with their problems before, because in the first place I didn't know what their problems were and in the second place I didn't know my children. You can't know a person intimately when you see him only two or three hours a week, and know nothing else about him other than what you can observe in that short period of time. So I was really helpless. I found that I could not relieve their problems without help from their housemother, who lived with them daily and knew them better than I did. I could learn to know my children better through her. And I could not help my children with their problems without going through their social worker, discussing the problems and sharing them with her. Or perhaps she would share a problem that came up, and then the housemother would follow through with it.

SOCIAL WORKER: You were asking about what happened that time in October when we all decided to work together, after Terry was reported by the school. I called you and you came that night. And all of us sat down together and looked at the situation.

We decided together how to go about helping Terry—her behavior and what her problems were. We tried to be more specific about her problems. We decided, after we had pooled our knowledge, that Terry was really crying out for us to give her some experience that would provide an inner control for herself. We felt that if we could give her some support and yet at the same time some assurance, we could help her feel more secure. We did this specifically by limiting her and explaining her problem to her. She would have fifteen minutes to get to school and we expected her back fifteen minutes after school was out, and for a while she would need to check with the housemother about going to parties and going places through the day. Ms. Trent, do you remember some of the other specifics that we came up with that first meeting?

CHILD CARE WORKER: She had to be in at 6:30 and she was limited as to where she could go. She couldn't go all over the campus. She could only go into the back yard.

SOCIAL WORKER: Then some of the specific things we did were this. We decided that we would meet that night, and then we would meet again in two weeks after she started restriction, and then we would meet in two more weeks at the end of the restrictions, to evaluate her progress with her.

We had planned to meet with Terry every two weeks, which we did for the first month that she was restricted. Then we had planned to meet again in November; we just got involved with Thanksgiving and all the Christmas parties and the holidays and we didn't meet at that time. But Terry got off restrictions and she came home for three weeks for the Christmas holidays.

CHILD CARE WORKER: When Terry came back, she had been restricted for a month and then all of a sudden she was completely free again. We didn't sit down with her to talk to her, and she had the free run of the whole campus and could do whatever she pleased, and so she let us know about it.

While she was on restriction we saw a real change in her behavior, but at a later point—after Christmas—things reversed themselves. We had questioned ourselves as a group whether this had been a valid change in Terry or whether she was acting for our benefit to try to manipulate and get out of these restrictions. At this point, we knew something had happened but didn't know exactly what it was or why it had happened.

MODERATOR: Ms. Trent, you were living in the cottage with Terry regularly during all this time. This was Terry's first occasion to sit down with you, her mother, and the social worker to focus on her behavior. Until that time you had dealt individually with Terry about her behavior, and the social worker had also spoken to Terry about it. Following this beginning experience of Terry's somehow seeing all three of you working in unity, did you begin to notice any shift in Terry's feeling about adults around her telling her what to do, or any feeling about being at the Home and finding a way of making constructive use of being there? Did you notice any kind of change in her?

CHILD CARE WORKER: Terry was very hostile at first when the social worker would talk to her and I would talk to her, and so at one of the meetings we decided that Ms. Moore would tell her, as her mother, what her restrictions would be—and that's the way it would be. Her mother told her at the meeting that we all agreed, and since she was her mother she was telling Terry she would not be allowed to do this or that—then I noticed a change in Terry.

SOCIAL WORKER: We think that was the real turning point in Terry, after Christmas when she kept letting us know by her behavior that she recognized our togetherness, and it started with her being out and coming in late—you know—a series of things. Then she was restricted for a week and she was perfect for a week.

I think the final incident when she really asked for help was when she and her boyfriend were making out in the field in back of the house and the other kids were calling her names.

That night, Terry felt terribly guilty over what she had done and Ms. Trent found her with a knife in her hand. We realized that we really had to help Terry, and so the next day we really got together to see how we had failed to meet Terry's needs. We decided that we had first given Terry a lot of attention and then none, and had not followed up our last meeting with her. This is when we started another turning together with Terry. I think that this is when her mother told Terry just how things were going to be, and we were able to follow up by weekly conferences, team conferences, and conferences with her mother. At that point we put Terry on definite restrictions, feeling that this would give her the security of being able to get angry and then settle down and know that we were still there. And this we felt was more a turning point than the other.

CHILD CARE WORKER: But we didn't just restrict her at this time. We gave her other things to do. She's involved in ballet now, she does a lot of baking and cooking at home and at the cottage, and she is involved in many different things to give her other outlets.

MODERATOR: Did these ideas come out in your conferences?

CHILD CARE WORKER: Yes, they did. Somewhere someone sparked the idea that maybe we should take some positive approach to this.

MODERATOR: How did this seem to you, Ms. Moore, this kind of planning together around some positive things—happy, healing things in the cottage or at home?

PARENT: I think the first thing we did a little differently where Terry is concerned was the conference approach. After Christmas we realized that we had not followed through, and that we really had to do something. We abandoned the approach where we had said, "Now, Terry, how do you feel about this?" and we took the approach of, "Now, Terry, here we are, we are all together again. We all feel that *this* is the way it is going to be." We found that Terry responds to this approach. Part of Terry's problem had been that she could not handle situations and responsibilities. We realized that we had erred in giving Terry the responsibility of choice. We told her, "This is the way it's going to be and on the other hand there are going to be more things for you to do. If there is something that you are interested in, we'll try to arrange it for you, so that your restrictions will not be a prison, but there will be activities for what you want to do."

We also arranged a time for Terry to spend with her social

worker each week. Terry had always resented these meetings, and didn't want to come and lots of times wouldn't show up. We told her that this was one more responsibility that she would have. She wouldn't have to go to the office and sit down coldly and be expected to start talking. Activities were arranged—a trip to the pet shop to look at the animals, or something like that—and thereby a more inviting atmosphere was provided. Terry began to open up and talk more about her feelings and some of her problems.

SOCIAL WORKER: This meant a real change for me. It was pretty exciting after we got started, but I was kind of scared at first. I tried to negotiate some kind of contract with Terry about her coming up to talk with me; she hated it. So after thirty minutes of saying, "I hate you, I can't stand this office; why do I have to come up here?" we decided that she would have no choice about keeping the time with me, but she did have a great deal of choice about how she used that time. I also provided her with resource people who could help her learn to do things she was interested in or see things that she was interested in seeing. So I think there was a real difference here in our approach to Terry.

PARENT: Speaking of being frightened, I don't think anybody was more frightened of Terry than I was. Quite frankly, I was scared to death of her. You can't imagine an adult's being scared to death of an eleven-year-old child, but I was. Terry really came on quite strong. But thinking back on it, I believed that if I put my foot down to let Terry know that was the way it was going to be, I was going to alienate her, and I would have a war on my hands. And you had to be pretty tough to come out on top. After we began to work together and Terry knew that we were working together and that we were all standing firm—we were like a brick wall in front of her—she knew that this was the way it was going to be. I knew that I couldn't say "Yes," when the rest of them were going to stand there and say "No." I felt that together we were a little bit tougher than Terry was, too, so I'm not afraid of Terry any more.

I can look at Terry now and say, "No," and she can start throwing her tantrums and her fits, but I can say, "Well, just go ahead; it's not going to do you any good." She usually straightens up. We've got some more problems still. She's not perfect. We've got a lot to learn yet, but the things that we have learned and the progress that Terry has made are so encouraging. It is good to know that Terry is becoming the real person that she is. She is learning who she is and she is able to handle growing up.

MODERATOR: Ms. Trent, Terry's mother has spoken of finding real strength in this experience for her role as a mother to Terry. What has this experience meant to you as a group parent?

CHILD CARE WORKER: Well, I couldn't have made it without the support of Ms. Moore and Ms. Bass, because I was a little afraid of Terry too, and she can make life really hectic in the cottage. When you try to restrict anything, she starts fights with all the children, and it's very difficult to live with her at times, but knowing that I had Ms. Moore's support and Ms. Bass's gave me a lot of strength, too.

MODERATOR: Here is a youngster with a problem—a set of problems—and all three of you obviously somehow reached the point where you like each other and feel good about being with each other. We've said some nice things about a change we've seen take place in Terry that everybody feels good about, but if we were to go back and put our finger on one or two or three specific things that the agency did to make all of this possible, what would it be? What has happened, since this all started in the fall, that somehow provided a framework for the kind of work that has taken place among you three?

SOCIAL WORKER: The thing that I keep thinking about is that we had time to do it. We had time to talk together and plan. We had adequate supervision and a chance to look at these problems and plan what we were going to do.

MODERATOR: What do you think were some of the objectives that you and the agency had in mind, when you began these conferences with Ms. Moore?

SOCIAL WORKER: I think that at that point we were more interested in planning for the children—more or less looking towards making a goal for a family, looking at where they were going, and the direction they were headed. But when we learned to be more specific we were able to work more effectively.

MODERATOR: Are you suggesting your agency has learned that by focusing on specifics and making time for conferences, some of the generalities begin to find their place in the total picture? Has some of this taken place?

SOCIAL WORKER: As long as we kept to generalities, it wasn't very productive. I think that when we look at something in particular we are able to bring about progress.

PARENT: The first thing we did was to recognize that there was a very desperate urgent need for us to act. At this point, we didn't know what we were working with. We were just as lost as Terry was. We were beating our heads against a wall. We were pulling against each other. So we had first to recognize the need. Then we had to decide what was best to do, when we should start, how we should begin. The first step was to get together and talk about it. The more we got together, the more we looked at it, the more we learned about Terry's situation. We began to get very deeply into the problem. We found things that we would have never realized were there before. We really analyzed both the problem and ourselves; in order to make this thing work, we had to examine ourselves quite critically. We had to acknowledge just exactly what our moods were, and how effective we actually were.

CHILD CARE WORKER: I think that includes the difficulty of the first few times we functioned together as a team. I wasn't sure of myself, of my role as a team member. The only way to find this was by working together and feeling comfortable enough to say, "Golly, I don't know how to go about this."

MODERATOR: Did your agency give you any choice about this? Could you have avoided the process?

SOCIAL WORKER: I guess we could have if we really hadn't tried, or wanted to bring about a change.

# In the Area of Planning

MODERATOR: Then this was not a matter of policy or structured method of operation. These conferences that you were having were not mandated by your agency as policy procedure. The agency did not expect you, as the social worker . . .

SOCIAL WORKER: Oh, the agency expected me to get involved with the family and to work through these problems, but I think *how* we went about doing it was something that all of us were able to work through together.

MODERATOR: Let me open up the floor for questions from the audience.

QUESTIONER: Did Terry have any person to serve as her advocate during this period when she was facing a three-against-one kind of situation?

CHILD CARE WORKER: She didn't need one. It took all three of us to keep up with her, didn't it?

QUESTIONER: Well, did Terry in fact see it as three against one?

SOCIAL WORKER: I think that at first she saw us as all against her, and then later on, as we broke down her defenses, she felt that maybe we were all with her.

QUESTIONER: Was there a psychological evaluation of Terry?

SOCIAL WORKER: Yes. We were concerned that we were doing the right thing. We were insecure and uptight, and asked for an evaluation by our psychiatrist; he told us we had done well.

MODERATOR: I want to emphasize that this agency has first-class supervision and consultation.

QUESTIONER: Obviously, at one time Terry had been able, in her situation, to manipulate different individuals, and perhaps therefore did not know whether or not she could trust adults. Now that there is a united front, have you discovered any shift in the way in which Terry reaches out and trusts the three of you?

SOCIAL WORKER: There has been a change in my relationship with

Terry. I don't know who changed more, Terry or myself, but our relationship is quite different now. I feel that a great deal of it had to do with my structuring our time together in a different way.

CHILD CARE WORKER: I think so too, but I think it helps her a great deal to know that I respect her mother, and that I respect her ideas, and that we all work together. I think that makes up for a lot in her relationships with adults.

PARENT: I find that I no longer dread being around Terry. I look forward to it. She's pleasant to be around, she's more open, she's warmer. She has gone so far as to confide personal things and this is a big step for her. She has found that she can tell me something that she's done or something that she feels, and I'm not going to condemn her or punish her, and I think she's beginning to learn that we understand, or at least we're willing to try to.

### 3 ❧ Assisting the Dependent Child before and Following Discharge

*From a paper given at the Ninth Annual Workshop for Personnel of Homes for Children, Austin, Texas, 1967*

MARJORIE L. FARADAY

From the first moment a child enters the institution, we must begin to plan for the day we will help him leave us to find a fuller, more satisfying life as a member of a family group or as a young adult assuming responsibility for himself in the community. When we talk about what we can do to help the child around discharge, we really are talking about everything we do to help the child during the entire time he is with us.

Leaving the institution should be a planned and orderly process, and the focus of our concern, of course, is the child. Who is he and what is he like? We're working with a child who has been forced by circumstances—internal or external, but usually a combination of both—to take a kind of side trip on his journey from infancy to adulthood. His detour may be long or short, straight or circuitous. We know that the road has been bumpy and that he will not get back on the main highway of life at the same point he left it.

Therefore, those of us who have had responsibility for his care during this period have had two main jobs to do. We have had to be specialists, providing the help the child needs to handle this crisis and come through it as strong and as secure and as soon as possible. At the same time a child's just plain growing and developing also must continue through the troubled times in his life. So we have had to perform parental functions and help him meet the usual needs of his body and soul and emotions so that he will be ready to pick up his life at whatever point he reenters the community. We have not dared let ourselves get so focused on his troubles or so isolated from the world outside the institution that we lose sight of our deeper purpose. We are only some of the many adults in the child's life who have a part in helping him along the way to become a mature, responsible, self-confident citizen in a free society.

This child did not come to us unencumbered, or having parked by the roadside all the luggage of his past experience, relationships, joys, sorrows, angers, fears, achievements, confusions, and failures. He brought them all with him. Periodically during his time with us, he has needed our help while he unpacked them, shook them out, mended some, discarded some, added some new ones, and refolded and repacked the whole lot of them. Sometimes the place has seemed so hopelessly cluttered with all of the feelings he brought with him from his past that we have wondered if he has room in his life for anything we have to give him.

We did not know him before he came to us, yet we have not questioned his right to make enormous demands on us physically, spiritually, and emotionally, nor has he, and we have not expected him to give us anything in return. When he leaves us, he will take a big part of us with him, but we want him to go with his soul and personality as intact as possible. We know the results of our labors may not be visible for a long time, and we have no assurance that we will ever hear from or about him after he leaves us, so we may never know what we have accomplished. One of the hardest parts of all for us has been that frequently, and in soul-shattering ways, he has made it abundantly clear that he did not want to come to us; he does not like being here; this is not his home and we are not his family; that, given the choice, he would rather be *there* with *them*; and he does not feel the least bit of gratitude or appreciation to us, however graciously and efficiently we have functioned as hosts, teachers, cooks, nurses, laundresses, and all the other people his living and growing require.

Now the child is at a crossroads, getting ready to go on to the next part of his journey, and he will be going without us. The impending change, like any change in life patterns, has two very important ingredients: it is both an ending and a beginning. The child will not just be going *from* the institution; he also will be going *to* something else, and each of the many possible "going to's" has different implications. Whether he goes to an atmosphere of love and stability or to one of rejection and chaos will make a difference in what kind of emotional girding of the loins will help him most. While we are helping him bid his farewells here, we must help him prepare for what is waiting for him there.

The reason for which the child is leaving the institution needs to be reckoned with, too. He may be leaving because he is ready to go or in spite of the fact that he is not. His leaving may represent the resolution of whatever problems made it necessary for him to come or it may be because we cannot help him. He may have "grown out of" the institution and is leaving us to take up life on his own or almost on his own. He may have to leave only because he has reached the institution's age limit, even though he still needs and could benefit from more time with us. Whether his leaving signals a kind of success or represents another failure in a young life already surfeited with confusion and unhappiness will have a big influence on the kind of help he needs and gets from us. This, then, is the child who needs and has a right to our help. How can we give it to him?

# In the Area of Planning

We have already taken the first big step. We have gathered together everything we know about the child, his situation, his relationship with us, and his feelings about all of these things. This is the foundation on which we can plan how we will help his discharge from the institution to be as positive an experience as possible.

Planning involves many things, such as timing, which is more than just assessing the child's readiness to move and setting a date. It means trying to plan the discharge to avoid unnecessary breaks in the child's routine. A move during the school term, for example, may increase the tensions and the number of adjustments the child has to make all at once.

Planning means looking carefully at all the factors. Discharges at Christmas time, for example, can have both advantages and disadvantages. There is a school recess, and the reunion with family may be a positive potential. This should be weighed against any meaning it may have to the child to spend the holidays with the people with whom he has been living, being involved in the institution's holiday activities. Moreover, the holiday season puts extra pressures on staff, and the resulting fatigue and time limitations may affect our ability to give the child as much help as he needs.

The decision will differ, according to the individual child and his situation, but we should consider the full meaning to the child of any occasions and events which may be important to him. Has he been practicing for a role in a school play or looking forward to his cottage group's camping trip? Depriving a child unnecessarily of pleasures he has been anticipating can increase his unhappy feelings about the move and about the total institutional experience. Careful planning will allow time for staff feeling to be examined and reconciled. It will take a lot of emotional gymnastics to sort out our eagerness to have the child succeed and our reluctance to admit that he can get along without us. We must neither underestimate nor overemphasize either his strengths or his limitations. Once the decision to terminate the placement has been made, however, individual staff feelings and opinions must merge into a unified force to help the child. Differences of opinion among adults about the child's readiness to leave and about his potentials for success are damaging to the child and will reinforce all his anxiety, fear, and confusion.

Realistic planning takes into account the time needed for all the things it takes to wind up placement: required physical examinations, getting the child's clothes in shape, arranging for transfer of school records, etc. Cramming a medical appointment into the last hectic days can throw everyone into a panic. Arriving at a new home with inadequate or outgrown or unrepaired clothing can be humiliating. The joys of an all-new wardrobe, assembled at the last minute, may not compensate for the comfort and self-identity familiar clothing can bring. Advance attention to these things will leave staff freer to devote time, energy, and emotion to helping the child handle his feelings about the move.

Usually the child will know about and be involved in the general plan for his leaving before he knows exactly when it will take place. He has a limited capacity to "keep his cool" when such an important change is imminent; he can handle knowing that it will be happening "sometime soon" better than he can handle comfortably knowing the exact time scheduled for the move.

We all know what can happen to the best-laid plans of mice and men! Discharge may be precipitous rather than planned, and we will not always be able to delay it. The child may have to leave before he is ready, and staff will have to do everything they can—and then just a little bit more—to make the move as positive as possible in spite of their feelings about being party to something they believe cannot be good for the child.

The child may learn about the move before we want him to, and we will have to help him handle a longer period of anxiety, uncertainty, and mixed feelings of all kinds. Factors beyond our control may catapult a carefully planned discharge into twenty-four hours of chaos, and we have to throw the plan out the window and cope. We will want to plan as carefully as possible but we are used to sudden changes when we work with children. When urgency demands action and precludes planning, we will take a deep breath and fly by the seat of the pants. As long as we focus our efforts on the child's feelings, he and we probably will come through it reasonably intact.

We know that the child is having, and we know the antidotes for, unhappy feelings. Knowing what to expect, for example, takes away some of the fear of the unknown. We can help a child, therefore, by telling him about the general plans which are being made, and we can discuss with him as much of the process as he needs to have explained.

He may regain some sense of order and continuity to life if we review with him the reasons he came and what has happened since he has been here. It is good to help him identify changes which have occurred in him and in his life situation.

We can talk with him about how these changes will affect what he can expect after he leaves. If there have not been any significant changes, we must help him avoid building false hopes. We can tell him what we know about where he is going, making sure it is realistic and not wishful thinking designed to please him or us.

A good part of the child's life revolves around school. It may help him handle some of his insecurity, therefore, if we give him some information about the school he will be attending, how far it is from where he will be living, whether he will be walking or take a bus, what kind of children he will meet, whether the teachers will know he has been here with us, how he can expect to measure up to the general academic level, what kinds of activities the school offers to meet his particular interests, and dozens of other details that are terribly important to the child and can give him handles to grab hold of. He can use some of the same kind of information about other important areas in his life such as the church he will be attending, scouts, or other activities. Any information we can give him about any area of his future may be helpful.

The child needs to know where he stands with staff. Can we find the fine balance in our own feelings that will help him see that we are not sending him away, but that we do want him to go and that we want him to have new opportunities and experiences? We do not need to be afraid of letting him know that we will miss him. Being missed is an important part of being loved and needed and these are essential parts of living.

His natural desire to leave, combined with his equally natural need to cling to the familiar, is causing him enough pain. We cannot give him the additional burden of feeling disloyal to us or the institution because he wants to leave. We know that an institution is not the answer to everything for him, and that he needs and has a right to want more than it and we can give him. He knows this, too, so let us acknowledge with him and help him understand that mixed feelings about staying or going are natural and right and that we have them too.

We can boost his sagging self-confidence about his ability to make it in the next place by reminding him gently that he had the same doubts about coming here and he has made it here. We can boost his self-esteem by pointing out some of his successes and strengths. He needs so very much to know he is not all bad!

If planning includes a predischarge visit—and usually it will—the child may have an overwhelming surge of anxiety and panic when that time comes. Having a staff member who is important to him take him to his home may make the trip less frightening. It can also put a floor of reality under the discussions about the setting into which he is going, as the staff will really know about it, and he will know that we know. When the visit ends, having the parents bring the child back to the institution may help ward off any fear that the institution is taking him away from his family again.

The trip in either direction can be more than a necessary mechanism in a predischarge visit. It may provide just the right chance for the child to have just the right person available to talk with, alone and uninterrupted. We need to learn to watch for situations that afford these dividends.

Some children, of course, will not be going to their own families. When this is true, foster parents, staff from the other institution, or other adults who will be caring for the child after he leaves can take a similar role in predischarge planning and visits. It can be a real source of reassurance and security to the child when caring adults who represent both the ending and the beginning of this important step join forces actively in planning for and helping him.

Any interchange between staff and parents at the time of discharge may help symbolize the return to the parents of the responsibility which they have surrendered temporarily to the institution. Most important of all, any time staff and parents are involved together we have a chance to reaffirm for the child something he desperately needs to know: we are aware that he has parents who are important to him and who will be treated with dignity and respect.

# ❧❧❧B

# In the Area of Care

## 4❧ The Content of Care

*Developed from a discussion at Epworth Children's Home,
Columbia, South Carolina, for submission to a
committee of its governing board, 1974*

Group child care in a Home such as Epworth provides for all
children:

1. A plan, modifiable at need, shared with him, and regularly reviewed by all interested parties, made with his parents
and/or guardians, governing the goals, conditions, and extent of
his stay in the Home.

2. Opportunity to work out his relationship with his parents through correspondence, visits, etc., and help in understanding and coping with these.

3. An individualized plan for his use of care, shared by all
significant staff, and reviewed at regular intervals, or when the
need to change it becomes apparent, establishing specific goals
and assigning responsibility for their implementation.

4. Reasonably comfortable and attractive housing, including some degree of privacy, a place for his own possessions, and
opportunities for relaxation.

5. Acceptable facilities for sleeping and personal hygiene.

6. Adequate personal clothing suitable for school, play, church, etc., and chosen with consideration of individual preference, coloration, body build, etc., and within the limits of current styles.

7. Nutritious and attractively served food in needed quantities, served in unhurried circumstances.

8. Attention to both long-term and temporary health needs and appropriate remedial action.

9. An orderly living style with some predictability, but some degree of flexibility where needed.

10. One person, or a couple, to whom he is responsible for his day-to-day behavior and from whom he receives affection, acceptance of his worth as a person, and concern for his well-being.

11. Participation in decisions that affect him consonant with his age and opportunity to express his opinions, preferences, and complaints within the limits of acceptable behavior.

12. Respect for his person, his identity, his background, his friends, and his personal behavior.

13. Peer relationships in a group that does not oppress him or reject him for reasons over which he has no control.

14. A living group small enough that his individuality is not submerged or ignored.

15. Regular attendance at public schools.

16. Provision for study in the Home and normal adult assistance with school tasks, including provision of needed materials.

17. Religious nurture suitable to his age, both in the Home and in the context of the church.

18. Regular participation in worship both in the Home and the church.

19. Discipline of a predominantly positive nature designed to help him learn acceptable behavior and to make moral decisions.

20. Experiences within safe limits to make mistakes and to learn from them.

21. Experience within safe limits with children of the opposite sex.

22. Experiences suitable to his age in working and in handling money.

23. Instruction in social graces, personal hygiene, and everyday life skills.

24. Experience in cooperation with others and in the assumption of common tasks.

25. Advocacy of his rights within the Home and in the community.

26. Periods of unscheduled time in which the child is free to play or to pursue acceptable interests.

27. Planned vacations with parents, relatives, or other interested persons.

28. The right of access to the director of child care and to the superintendent, if he believes that his rights have been violated.

In addition, group care at Epworth offers special opportunities for children on an individual basis. These again can be divided into those which are planned with the child or encouraged as part of his use-of-care plan, in which there is some commitment to follow through once begun, and those which the child can make use of at will. Those that are planned for some children, with varying degrees of participation on the part of the child are:

1. Special education and/or tutoring.

2. Specific arrangements for diagnosis and for courses of therapy conducted either by Home personnel or by specialists on contract or in other agencies.

3. Structured off-campus work and earning opportunities.

4. Planned participation in group activities provided by the Home, specifically at this time Boy Scouts, choir, and team basketball.

5. Specialized disciplinary or education plans agreed to either as conditions for placement or to overcome specific problems, e.g., behavior-modification plans in relation to certain behavior, or restrictions from certain activities, where these have been agreed to as part of the use-of-care plan.

6. Planned instruction and experiences that develop a child's talents, such as instruction in art or music.

Activities that are purely voluntary on the part of the child are not the sole responsibility of the child to work out on his own. The Home has some responsibility within its resources to facilitate any of the following that the child wishes to participate in and can do so without danger to the child or others and without disruption of ongoing programs.

1. Participation in planned recreational activities on a voluntary and occasional basis.
2. Pursuit of a hobby.
3. Participation in Methodist Youth Fellowship.
4. Participation in extracurricular activities of the child's school.
5. Visits to and from acceptable friends in the community.
6. Opportunity to relate to staff members outside the cottage at his own pace.
7. Counseling from appropriate staff members.

*A Note on Priorities.* Absolute priorities cannot be established for any specific period of time, as some activities are fixed in time and can only be carried out at that moment, while others are more flexible. Activities in Group 2 may also, for the individual child, take precedence over activities in Group 1 at any one time.

Activities that should not in general be set aside for any other purpose include visits with parents, school attendance, church and church school, medical care of an emergency nature, and specific therapy. In a second group are those which have priority over others but not over the ones listed above. These include study periods, disciplinary restrictions, planned activities to which the child has made a commitment, and work assignments.

## 5 ❧ The Right to Fail

*From the Chapel Hill Workshop Reports, 1968*

CLIFFORD W. SANFORD

The other evening just before dusk we (my neighbor and I) happened to be on the terrace when the young fledglings (from the brown wren's nest) appeared from beneath the leaves of the geraniums—summa cum laude graduates lined up at the edge of the old weathered gray, near-collapsed flower box.

One by one they braved the precipice. One by one they flopped awkwardly to the plum tree—all but one little fellow who toppled ignominiously into the mint bed below.

We sat waiting nervously, helplessly, to see what happened to him. His mother came back and hopped beside him a moment, taking off to the nearby rock wall with a short spurt of speed. He tried his wings again and got as far as the rung of a stool by the table. She came close and then sailed off again. He tried for the wall and bumped into it. She called to him from the top and he tried again—and made it.

The relief I felt was astonishingly intense and I started to laugh and applaud, but my neighbor watched with solemn face. The little bird family's struggle, near-failure, and triumph were too poignantly like the struggles, failures, and triumphs of the human race.

Most of us, like the wrens, muddle along with varying degrees of persistence and courage, doing what we can for our families, hoping that we're building strong wings for soaring.

Sometimes our fledglings fall, too, but as my neighbor said, "Who among us, great or small, dares stand up against the ultimate and terrible nature we do not know and dare not defy?"[16]

Almost every group of child care workers engaged in inservice training or a workshop experience has at some point been compelled to enumerate those qualities which are basic to personal daily involvement in borrowed children's lives. Three of those qualities, ones valued by child care workers themselves, which are always listed are patience, understanding, and respect. "These words comprise a wholehearted conviction that even the most difficult child is to be met not only with a sense of duty or

16. Celestine Sibley, "Little Brown Parents Struggle, Their Fledgling Nearly Fails," *Atlanta Journal-Constitution*, 23 June 1968.

even pity (God forbid) but with a deep respect for the capacities and possibilities that lie dormant in him."[17]

We have seen this conviction at work. We've seen it working in the Children's Home superintendent who counseled a bright high school junior planning for college. We have seen it evident in the housemother who encouraged youngsters to function as a group, setting some of their goals, sharing in the continual planning regarding their day-to-day life together, or bring one of their own group members face-to-face with behavior that was challenging the group's cohesion. We have seen it in the housemother of a ward of the severely retarded as she exerted tremendous emotional energy to "listen" to the "talking" eyes of a mute, paralyzed retardate.

On the other hand, we have witnessed the opposite in the superintendent who hastily dismissed a youngster (twelve years in the Home's care) who slipped out one night to meet her boyfriend, or in the case of a child who tests the housemother with vile language—challenging authority, or in the housemother who suddenly and painfully learns that it was her "model" child who had been influencing others in the cottage to shoplift in the stores downtown.

The wholehearted conviction about the value of patience, understanding, and respect "is not always easy to attain when one is confronted with a solemn, suspicious boy or a brash, immodest girl, or with repeated disobedience in spite of kind admonishment. It is only human to become impatient and angry, and sometimes even to feel betrayed,[18] or to feel that one has failed.

If we can shift the focus from a consideration of *our* feelings about *our* failures to those of the children in our care (not a simple shift because frequently we cannot differentiate the two) we will discover a matter of serious common concern.

In a recent essay, William K. Zinsser laments America's use of the word "dropout" as a synonym for failure. He calls it

17. Gisela Konopka, "What Houseparents Should Know," *Children* 3, no. 2 (1956).
18. Ibid.

America's newest dirty word. We should hear some of what he has to say:

What I resent is that we only apply it [the term "dropout"] to people under twenty-one. Yet an adult who spends his days and nights watching mindless TV programs is more of a dropout than any eighteen-year-old who quits college with its frequently mindless courses to become, say, a VISTA volunteer, living and working with the poor. For the young, dropping out can often be a way of dropping in.

To hold this opinion, however, is little short of treason in America today. A boy or girl who leaves college is labeled a failure and the right to fail is one of the few freedoms that this country does not allow its citizens. The American dream is a dream of "getting ahead," painted in gold wherever we look. Our advertisements and TV commercials are a hymn to material success, our magazine articles a toast to people who made it to the top. Smoke the right cigarette or drive the right car—so the ads say—and the girls will be swooning into your deodorized arms or caressing your expensive lapels. Happiness goes to the man who has the sweet smell of achievement. He is our national idol, and everybody else is our national fink.

I want to put in a word for the fink, especially the teenage fink, because if we give him time to get through his finkdom—if we release him from the pressure of attaining certain goals by a certain age, he has a good chance of becoming a national idol of a different sort, a Jefferson or a Thoreau, a Frank Lloyd Wright or an Adlai Stevenson, a man with a mind of his own. We need mavericks and dissenters and dreamers far more than we need junior vice-presidents, but we paralyze them early by insisting that every step be a step up to the next rung of the ladder. Yet, in the fluid years of youth, the only way for boys and girls to find their proper road is often to take a hundred side trips, poking out in different directions, faltering, drawing back, and starting again.

"But what if we fail?" they ask, whispering the dreadful word across the "generation gap" to their parents, who are back home at the Establishment, nursing their "middle-class values" and cultivating their "goal-oriented society." The parents whisper back: "Don't." . . .

What they should say is "Don't be afraid to fail!" Failure isn't fatal. Countless people have had a bout with it and come out stronger as a result. Many have even come out famous. History is strewn with eminent dropouts, "loners" who followed their own trail, not worrying about its odd twists and turns because they had faith that their own sense of direction could be trusted. To read their biographies is always exhilarating, not only because they beat the system, but because their system was better than the one they beat.

Luckily, such rebels still turn up often enough to prove that individualism, though badly threatened, is not extinct.[19]

Children come to our institutions because of family difficulties, homes broken by death, illness, or strife—few by death, some by illness, and most by strife. They also come because they themselves are full of emotional problems, are physically handicapped, or have committed an act unacceptable to society. As far as our culture (and the child himself) is concerned, he is spawned of failure. The tragedy is that he has not had experiences which teach one to handle failure with some success. He has learned that to avoid failure one simply does not try.

The common subculture feature of our residents is not necessarily that of poverty. The phenomenon more common to all of our children is that of failure. It is interesting to note the concern about this matter in other disciplines. Considerable research has been done in the field of education in recent years on the subject of chronic underachievers. It is a bit upsetting to review the findings of that research in the light of traditional impressions of institutional care. It seems that a common conclusion has been that "Home environments of underachievers have been described as containing more stress on conformity and 'goodness.'"[20]

With a core philosophy which has grown out of our society's first efforts to deal in an organized way with the "social dropout," and a residual form of service designed in a past era to meet the needs of that period, we are still too often plagued with practices that work against the child's unlearning the old within the context of all that the old meant to him or learning new patterns within a new environment which allows for a hundred side trips, poking out in different directions, faltering, drawing back, and starting again.

The extent to which the institution finds it possible to align itself with the total family, to grasp the need for forming a partnership, will mirror the extent to which the child is enabled to do his unlearning in the context of the reality of his family situation. The extent to which the

19. William K. Zinsser, "The Right to Fail," *Look*, September 1967.
20. Stephanie Z. Dudek and E. P. Lester, "The Good Child Facade in Chronic Underachievers," *American Journal of Orthopsychiatry* 38, no. 1 (1968).

institution builds an in-depth, personalized caring upon the impersonal characteristics for which the institution is so well known will reflect the extent to which it can help the child discover that failure isn't bad in itself, or success automatically good. We are moving away from the idea that complete control of the child's environment almost automatically will force him into normalcy, as his previous, destructive, environment forced him into emotional disturbance.[21]

Routine and order, meaningful to the security of growing and developing youngsters, if allowed to become ends in themselves, are not going to allow for the messy process of the youngster's circuitous movement toward independence.

In the face of the generalized constrictive image of the institution, I am personally convinced that no other form of foster care possesses the potential for individualizing a child's experience as does group care. Furthermore, we have not scratched the surface of what is involved in helping children in and through groups.

It is profoundly significant that little attention was given to the needs, the demands, the skills of the houseparent or child care worker prior to the 1940s and that, since that time she has been designated the key staff member, "the hub of the wheel." The cottage or unit [she] supervises has become the focal point of institutional life. The child-houseparent relationship is seen as a major avenue for growth and change in the child. The houseparent is the adult on whom the child is most likely to lean and with whom he becomes most vulnerable. This advancement of the houseparent to the role of "professional" is the most dramatic change that has taken place in recent years.[22]

David Wineman quite wisely reminds us, however, that even the most "professional" houseparent has difficulties holding onto her philosophies and techniques when the setting itself is designed to promote conformity, recognizes only "goodness" as evidence of appropriate childhood behavior and occasionally says of the youngster caught up in the struggle with failure, "He must need some other kind of care."[23]

21. Bernard Scher, "What Does it Take to Work With the Disturbed Child in the Group Living Situation?" Reprint of address, 1956.
22. Hansel H. Hollingsworth, "The Child Caring Institution on the Move," *Annals of the American Academy of Political and Social Science* (1964).
23. David Wineman, "Control—Discipline and Punishment," *Serving Children Through Institutional Care* (Proceedings of Fifth Annual Child Care Seminar, University of Wisconsin, May 1964).

# In the Area of Care

Polsky and Claster show that the child care worker's energy is applied to two primary areas of function:

1. The custodial function, that is, maintaining the system, fostering compliance with the routine, and monitoring the children's behavior.

2. The nurturing function, that is, enabling the group to experience some degree of self-direction, promoting cohesion in the life of the group, and helping the group find some of its own goals and move through a process of trying them out.

They suggest that all of these functions are necessary, but that group life becomes more meaningful as a means of fostering growth and development when we begin to place more emphasis on nurturing and guiding the group as a group.[24]

There will continue to be varying pressures that play upon the houseparent's understanding of what is expected of her. During the next few years the field of institutional care is certain to continue to search for a firmer concept of what the role is and how to give appropriate training and supervision for it. In the meantime, the houseparent is going to hold to certain principles to give a sense of stability and sureness to what she does with the children in her care. And she is going to continue to be faced with children who need her in relation to their completely normal human right to use failure as one of the major means of learning life's lessons and finding oneself in one's own life situation. She is going to be continually faced with the fact that no two youngsters will grow and develop at the same pace or with the same intensity.

Houseparents all over the country are coming up with a common set of guides gleaned from their own experiences. These guides are their own protection against impulsive responses to a child's upsetting behavior. They are at the heart of being professional, in that they assist them in remaining aware of the child's needs in deference to their own. They help them to find ways to work constructively within a setting which might be constricting in its general nature.

24. Howard W. Polsky and Daniel S. Claster, *The Dynamics of Residential Treatment* (Chapel Hill: University of North Carolina Press, 1968).

If the child is assured the right to succeed on his own terms and fail as often as may be necessary along the way, it will be because of the houseparent's daily efforts, amid all the problems of troubled youngsters, to help each move toward his own potential at his own pace.

## 6 ❧ What Young People Say

*From the Chapel Hill Workshop Reports, 1968, where it appears as "Talking with Teenagers"*
ALAN KEITH-LUCAS

In the past year it has fallen to my lot to talk to and with a number of groups of teenagers in Children's Homes, sometimes as part of a study, and on three occasions at least because the executive or someone else has been concerned about what seemed to be happening on campus. There had been some sort of blow-up. And this has set me thinking about the teenager today, and in particular the teenager in the Children's Home. We have all heard, of course, of the generation gap. We all know today that teenagers do not have much use for us older people. We talk a good deal about teenage hostility and gripes. And although, in one sense, these meetings I have held could be thought of as gripe sessions, and although some of the youngsters showed some hostility to some adults, hostility was not the predominant mood. I would have said that the mood was nearer to frustration or despair.

This brings me to another observation. One of the saddest things about teenagers in institutional care is the number of them that we lose. Depending on the Home, we lose them in different ways. Some persuade parents who are not really able to care for them to take them back. Some run away. Some tell us frankly that they want to leave, and do. Some girls rush into marriage as a means of getting out. Some know exactly what it will take for us to tell them that they must leave. They become disciplinary problems. Others stay on with us, but do so sullenly and with little attempt to learn from us or to adopt our values. As one child said to me, "I want to stay in this Home for what it can do for me but I sure do despise the people who run it."

You may think this is an overdrawn picture. You will remember the teenager who covered himself with glory and was pleasant and cheerful to live with, and I know that this sometimes happens. Yet far too many are lost. Far too many fall by the wayside and either leave in an unplanned and hasty way, or live out their time pretty uncomfortably. And some who do remain are the clever manipulative children who have learned to play the game but not to grow up and think for themselves.

Or you may point out too the number of teenagers who "freak out" of their own house, become hostile or delinquent, or rarely if ever speak to their parents, and you may think you are doing a pretty good job—which is probably true, comparatively—but remember something, if you will. You cannot afford to make mistakes that parents do. The child at home may get off the track, but he has a home to come back to when his wild oats are sown. The child lost to the Children's Home has nowhere. If he leaves he becomes a dropout and that may be the end of his hopes. Also, the saddest part about it is that the child we lose in this way is not always the one who came to us, say, at the age of thirteen, already upset and adolescent, but often is the one who has grown up with us, and who was perhaps a pretty good kid in his earlier years. Indeed, there is some evidence that the more conforming a child is at ten or eleven, the more chance he has of growing up to be a difficult adolescent.

I am not suggesting that the difficulty many Homes are having with their older children is the houseparents' or the Homes' fault. I am suggesting, however, that it is a serious problem, and one that we can learn something about. And one of the ways we can learn about it is by listening to what teenagers are saying. So I am going to share with you what some of these children have said.

First listen to a boy: "Look at me. I'm eighteen. You wouldn't believe it, would you? I behave like a thirteen-year-old. That's how old this Home is."

There is a great deal of truth in this. Children's Homes have rules and routines that are primarily designed for the younger child. The staff makes decisions for children. It tells them what to do. It arranges recreation largely on a younger level. It even punishes youngsters on a childish level. Corporal punishment, for instance, persists longer in Children's Homes than it does in families outside—even those who believe in it. In one Home I know of the most paddled age group is girls thirteen and fourteen—girls who are supposed to be learning to treat their bodies with respect. In another, incredibly, it is fifteen- and sixteen-year-old boys. This was perhaps bearable for the older child as long as he thought of himself as a child and as long as the culture outside the Home thought of him as a child. But the teenager today knows a great deal more than teenagers did thirty years ago. He feels himself to be nearly grown up. He goes to school with boys and girls of his own age who are pretty independent and used to making their own decisions, spending their time much as they want to, arranging their own social life. As another child said, "It never seems to occur to people that teenagers make their own social plans," and another, and there's real pathos here, "Maybe when I'm twenty I can stop after school and get a coke."

Now I do not doubt for a moment that the Children's Home has to have routines and rules. But I do have many doubts about whether the seventeen- and eighteen-year-old can live with them twenty-four hours a day. Rules are the last thing that a teenager needs, especially rules that apply to him and the six-year-old alike. He needs limits. He needs to be stopped from doing things that are basically dangerous or harmful, and many teenagers seek such limits. But there is all the difference in the world between meeting his request with a "No, it's against the rules," and with a thoughtful, "Well, now, is there any good reason why you shouldn't?" Rules are easier, of course, but rules are for children, not soon-to-be adults. They are helpful in helping a young child learn what the world wants of him, but they are simply deadly for the child whose habits are now established and who now needs to learn to live in a world where one does not do everything by rules.

# In the Area of Care

According to anthropologists, those societies are most successful in handling the problems of their young people that recognize the teenager is no longer simply a child and give him some status as an adult. This is certainly true of the Jews, whose teenagers are the least delinquent of all groups in America today —and the Jews have, for boys at least, a ceremony, the Bar Mitzvah, in which great emphasis is laid on a child's coming to the age when he is reponsible for his own decisions. In former times, when church life was much more of one's whole existence, the child became a man or a woman at baptism or confirmation. When children used to leave school in the eighth grade, they graduated from childhood to adulthood at that point. But nowadays, with a prolonged period of education, we make no such distinction. A child becomes adolescent, and we neither mark the fact nor treat him any differently, except that we find that he now rebels against things which last month or year he accepted without rancor. If we cannot manage to help him move from rules to limits we can perhaps help him know that we know that he is adolescent; we can perhaps give him more control in some areas of his life, such as his clothes or his allowance, or the time he gets back from school or goes to bed, or how he decorates his room, or whether he joins in a group activity or finds recreation for himself, that will help him know that we want him to grow up.

Along with the feeling that one is treated as a child goes a very real fear of the future. Listen again: "I'm scared. When I leave here, I won't know how to act." Why not? Have we not taught you? No, we have not. We have given you rules, it is true. But mostly these rules have forbidden you the only thing from which you really could learn—the experience of doing something within more or less safe limits. We have not taught you to handle your feelings for the opposite sex. We have tried to prevent your having such feelings, as if we could somehow prevent you from having them ever, in the outside world, when we will not be there to help you. We have not taught you to handle money. We have bought things for you, or made you save your money. You have no experience in spending money, wisely or unwisely. We have not prepared you in any way for the multitude of decisions that you will have to make as a man or woman. We have continued to treat you as a child. Is it a wonder that many boys rush into military service when they leave a Children's Home, so that they will continue to have decisions made for them, or that girls marry young, to have someone decide for them?

Listen again to a boy: "The moment I come back on campus, even from school, I tense up. I'm on my guard. I feel that I'm being watched." And another, "Isn't a home a place to relax?" Most of us, maybe because teenagers are somewhat unpredictable creatures, are at heart deeply suspicious of them. If they hold hands, we imagine that they want to go to bed together. If they stay too long on their way home from school, they want to hang around street corners and become part of a gang. Perhaps we have heard too much of the waywardness of modern youth. Perhaps we tend, too, to be mildly jealous, because they enjoy life so much. But very few Homes really trust their teenagers. I visited one this summer which did. It was a satisfying experience to walk freely off campus with nothing more than a casual statement, "We're going for a walk. We'll be back in an hour or so." Of course, to be fair, this was in Texas, where if the young people had been intending to run away, there was nowhere to run to but miles of sagebrush and rattlesnakes, but when I put it up to the youngsters they said, "Oh, yes, of course we're trusted, at least until we do something wrong." Again, as one boy tried to explore his feeling of tensing up, he said, "It's constantly being talked at. My shirt isn't buttoned. My room's untidy. And she doesn't like my table manners, or maybe it's my tone of voice." Another added, and listen to him, "We can't act like teenagers here." "How do teenagers act?" I asked. "Oh, you know. We're young and we're noisy, it is a part of being our age." These children are growing up in a world that has a distinctive teenage culture. It is noisy and rambunctious. Just go sometime to a teenage dance or a party. But why is it noisy? Not because these are undisciplined children, but chiefly because it is a safety valve. The teenager is caught between childhood and adulthood. He is possessed of vast energy for which there is little use. He craves excitement. If we don't want him to use this energy and to find this excitement in antisocial ways, then we have to let him let off steam in more

# In the Area of Care

harmless ways. Teenagers everywhere need places where they can be themselves and be as noisy as they like—out of the cottage, perhaps in a teenage center with minimum supervision—the sort of supervision that will quell a riot or break up a too-fervid twosome, but will not interfere with what is normal teenage behavior, however crude or zany it may seem to us adults. Children who do not find this excitement do one of two things. They either create it for themselves in a semidelinquent way—the latest theories of delinquency suggest that it is largely a reaction to frustration in the environment that does not allow a child to fulfill his needs legitimately but does provide illegitimate means—or they relapse into hopelessness and apathy. I shall never forget the boy who described to me his dream in school of what he would do when classes were over. He woke up, he said, with this question ringing in his ears, "What'll I do after school?" And the answer, in tones of the deepest despair: "Go back to the Something Home." Go back to the same old routine.

I will admit there were other problems here, the failure of the Home, for instance, to help him come to terms with the years of enforced dependence that suddenly stretch ahead of the adolescent, the pressure of a program combining a much greater expectation in school than previous generations ever knew, and a lot of manual work at the institution—about which I might say a word. I'm not against children's working, but for many of our children we have not recognized that the modern school program, plus the work we demand, leaves him no free time at all. Listen to a girl: "I never get peace to think things through." Again and again I find that one of the teenager's greatest frustrations is that there is no time to think and nowhere, if there were time, to do it. In this, and perhaps in some other matters, such as dress, or normal relationships between boys and girls, perhaps we are behind the times. Perhaps we have not realized how much things have changed in the past twenty or thirty years. As a girl told me this summer, "The world marches on. But the dear old Something Home does things as it always did."

But perhaps the most constant frustration that these children express is summed up in the statement, "If we say what we think, we are being sassy." We seem, in institutions, to be almost

**143**

pathologically afraid of any hostility to adults. "Any signs of insubordination," I am quoting here an agency manual, "should be reported at once, to the superintendent," and, from a punishment record, "Making a face at a housemother behind her back, six licks"—and this is a sixteen-year-old boy. All too often, too, we imagine hostility when it is not there, when a teenager is merely saying what he thinks, or expressing his opinion. We expect him to obey implicitly, on every occasion, without argument or question. Now, of course, we have to have obedience, and arguments are ungracious and sometimes ugly. But a certain amount of hostility, an ability to challenge, to ask for reasons, to give one's opinion, are both natural and necessary parts of the growing-up process, the way in which a child breaks away from his absolute dependence on adults and becomes an adult himself. I am much more afraid of the adolescent who says, "Yes, ma'am," on every occasion. He is the truly retarded child. And much of this seeming hostility is not hostility at all. Twice lately I have been told that I could not get anything out of a particular child, that he, or she, was too hostile. Yet in both cases when this happened, this was the child in the group who struggled most faithfully to try to express to me exactly how he or she felt, who was the fairest to adults. And each one ended the interview by accepting a great deal of responsibility for his own feelings, with one girl's even asking for psychiatric help. I came to the conclusion that these children were not really hostile. No one had asked them the right question before. And the question that needed asking was not, "Why are you so angry?" or "When will you learn to obey?" or "Why can't you be pleasant?" but simply, "Can you stand it?—can you stand living here, at your age, and how can we help you do it?"

To be an adolescent is hard enough. To be an adolescent in many Children's Homes is almost impossible. When the Home treats you as a child, forbids you the culture that is yours, expects of you the subservience of a child half your years, is suspicious of you—listen again: "Every time I talk privately to someone my own age someone thinks I'm plotting something"—it makes for further defeat. I have a horrible hunch that many of those we lose are the ones who really have the most to offer.

# ❦❦C

# In the Area of Education

7 ❦  A Working-Earning-Responsibility Plan
and Its Implementation

*Compiled from two reports by Melvin E. Walker at the Chapel
Hill Workshops, 1970 and 1971, and a letter from
Mr. Walker to the authors, 1974*

The Kennedy Home Work-Earning-Responsibility Plan grew from
the need to rethink previous policies about children's work. The
Home had for some time been modifying former practices under
which children were expected to work during the summer and
after school and on Saturdays. Seniors were now required to live
and work off campus during the summer months and manage
their own living and financial arrangements. Other teenagers
were assigned jobs on the campus during the summer and received pay for work beyond a minimum number of hours. Children earning more than $35.00 a month were expected to care for
their own clothing. Weaknesses in this program included little
incentive to do a good job, the large amount of unpaid work
required before paid work was reached, an absence of any graduated process whereby children undertook progressive responsibility, no provision for responsibility during the school year, and

the arbitrary assigning of responsibility for clothing at a certain income level without year-round planning. Also, the general attitude to work on the part of most students was somewhat grudging. Some teenagers associated their allowance with the unpaid work they performed and felt themselves badly underpaid.

To wrestle with these problems, a consultant from Group Child Care Consultant Services was invited to spend a day on the campus to discuss with the staff our present program and how it could be improved. We decided to develop our program to include those things we felt were lacking. The first meetings were with the administrative staff. Houseparents and auxiliary staff who were to be involved in the program were invited to serve as consultants. As the basic plan was formalized, committees of houseparents and children were given time to study and discuss the program. Then the final plan was formalized and printed. This plan was then discussed with all staff members and then with all children who would be involved in the program. At these meetings, the date was set for the program to begin.

The first principle we adopted was that everyone should be expected to participate in cottage chores. Cottage chores were defined as anything that was for the common good, as determined by the child care worker. Anything beyond this was classified as work.

We then decided to group children into five age-grade groups, as follows: ages six to nine, ages ten to twelve, ages thirteen to fourteen, fifteen-year-olds not seniors or juniors, and seniors and juniors.

We decided on the expectations we would hold for each age group to assure a growing attitude toward work and personal maturity. This was done first with the juniors and seniors and then progressively with each younger group.

We worked with the work supervisors to determine the number of necessary jobs we would have available on campus. We did not list any job that we did not feel was necessary work that should be done. Each job was listed with a job description and the supervisor for each job. These jobs were put into a list and a group of older teenagers ranked each job—one, two, or three—according to its desirability. They were told that the most desirable job would receive the least pay. There were twelve full-time jobs (thirty hours or more each week) and thirty-three half-time jobs (fifteen hours or more each week) designated for the summer.

It was also necessary to consider the budget in determining just what we could afford to spend in this type of program. Part of the consideration would be the savings to the agency in allowances, clothing, dry cleaning, etc. We also considered cancelling a janitorial service at the church to make both work opportunity and funds here available to our young people. The hourly rates of pay were established on the basis of this information, and used figures ranging from $.30 to $.50.

A year later we were able to report $6,600 paid to students who worked on campus, and savings in allowances, school supplies, clothing, dry cleaning, janitorial service, and farm, dairy, and garden jobs that would otherwise have to be performed by paid staff of $6,900. This does not, however, take into consideration staff time spent in coordinating and managing the program.

Our social service department was also consulted as to what cooperation from relatives and friends would be needed to make the program workable. It was felt the child would be less inclined to become involved in the overall program if he could get money from home just for the asking. A letter was drafted and sent out to each family member and visiting sponsor explaining the program and its purposes. Their cooperation was requested in not giving the children money and clothing except on special occasions.

Our final program can be expressed schematically as follows:

**Schematic Representation of
Kennedy Home Work-Responsibility Plan**

| Age or Grade | Work Available | Allowance | Clothing | School Supplies & Fees, Lunches |
|---|---|---|---|---|
| 6-9 yrs. | Emergency only | Yes | Supplied | Supplied |
| 10-12 yrs. | Some opportuni-ties in summer | Yes | Supplied | Supplied |
| 13-14 yrs. | Part-time (15 hours) in summer | No | Allowance of $125 p.a. | Fees and lunches only paid |
| 15, not seniors or juniors | On-campus throughout year. 30 hrs. week in summer | No | Allowance of $75 p.a. | Lunches only paid |
| Seniors and juniors | Off-campus throughout year. Special arrangements for athletes or those unable to find job | No | No allowance | Student responsible except for class ring, grad. invitations |

In addition, we established policies on hiring, promotions, and dismissals, savings, and on what is known as the Junior-Senior Contract.

The program was initiated at the beginning of the summer. A day was set for the hiring. The jobs were listed with pay and supervisor. Each child had an opportunity before hiring day to study the jobs available. On the day set, the group of fifteen-year-olds and up met at the office. The oldest child not a junior or senior had the first choice of the jobs. The hiring continued with the next oldest down to the youngest in the group. No difference was made between boys and girls, although some jobs listed physical requirements for the job, i.e., able to lift one hundred pounds. After this group, the thirteen- and fourteen-year-olds were hired in the same way.

It was also made clear that children could receive a pay raise during the summer if their work was of high quality. Those who failed to perform could also be dismissed from a more desirable or higher-paying job and be assigned to a less desirable one. This provision, which we see as very important, has been the hardest to administer. In fact, the only significant change made in the program since its inception was adopted after four years' experience, when it was observed that some supervisors were more prone to increase salaries than others and also seemed prone to promote everyone under their supervision, rather than to recognize individual effort. The Home now requires an individual conference after three weeks between the young person, the supervisor, and the program coordinator. This conference points out success and failure of the worker's effort, and either considers him for a salary increase or indicates what change is needed to be considered for one.

Conversely, there was some indication that youngsters were being fired on impulse in the heat of some disagreement. To avoid this, the Home now requires that when a disagreement arises a formal conference is held with the supervisor, the child, the houseparent, and the work coordinator. At this conference the young person is warned of the change needed in order to keep his job and that unless change is made he will be discharged from this job on the next offense. This seems to be a safety valve for both child and supervisor and firings have been rare.

Each child was asked to place 10 percent of all money earned into a savings account to remain there until he leaves Kennedy Home. During the summer months, some money is withheld from pay to be given back during the school months (ages fifteen and up—$6.00 weekly; thirteen and fourteen—$3.00 weekly). No child working on campus is allowed to have as pocket money more than $3.00 of his weekly pay. The remainder of his pay goes into his savings. This savings can only be spent with permission from the houseparent. A local bank works with the Home in keeping these accounts. The child's being able to see his bank book with the amount he has saved has been an inspiration and caused an increased interest in savings.

Juniors and seniors were asked to work with the social service department to obtain jobs for the summer. The seniors also were asked to find living quarters off campus. After these plans were formulated, the junior or senior signed a contract with his houseparent and caseworker present in an individual conference. Other concerned individuals were present for this signing such as director of cottage and campus life, director of social services, pastor, and superintendent.

Some planning needed to be done for children who are too disturbed for a regular work program. Six youngsters out of approximately fifty-five teenagers were assigned in the second summer to special projects under the direct supervision of the coordinator. These special projects have no particular production goal and the primary emphasis is on the young person himself. The work has been mostly painting outbuildings, roofs, fences, etc. Since no other staff member is involved in these particular projects, the young person himself is totally responsible for the end product, good or bad. He is able to see clearly what he and he alone is accomplishing. If the finished job is not satisfactory, he simply does it over again since getting the job completed within a specific time limit is not a factor. The coordinator-supervisor starts the youngster on the job, gives instructions, and leaves. During the day he returns frequently to give guidance and redirection. Some of the youngsters involved in these particular projects probably could not have made the adjustment here otherwise. Even though production was not a goal, it has been high, and the face-lifting from all the new paint is quite apparent to all who visit our campus.

One other project undertaken was the dismantling and demolition of an old residence on our campus. Three of our more aggressive boys chose this job and have really had an outlet for some of their strong feelings. At the same time, they have learned the difference between "dismantle" and "destroy" and are able to see value in salvage of something no longer useful otherwise.

Athletes presented another problem. The Home decided to compensate youngsters for wages lost because of conflict between sports and working hours and to pay half of the cost of athletic equipment.

Our goals in establishing the program were fourfold:

1. To help develop good work habits.
2. To help develop healthy attitudes toward work.
3. To gain skill in handling money.
4. To take responsibility in buying and caring for clothes and other personal items.

We feel that these goals have certainly been met and surpassed. Those youngsters who were in the program for juniors have been able to do it responsibly. They know what it means to be on the job at the required time, to take direction from a supervisor whom they may or may not personally care for, to plan ahead with their supervisor for coming events which may take them from work, or to accept the fact that the event may be as important to the employer as it is to them. They have learned what it means to budget needs and to know the pleasure of having money at times to buy what one wants within the limits of what one can afford. Clothing and its care have taken on new importance.

Those who are in their second year of on-campus work can claim equal strides and should be even more ready to face the requirements and rewards of off-campus work.

It has been rewarding to our staff to see a number of young people who felt very little self-worth and who maybe had never done any physical work in their lives begin to take pride in a job well done. The attitude changed from concern about what could be gotten from the agency and others in the way of material goods, to an attitude of earning and even asking for extra work for some particular article of clothing desired or some event to attend. We have seen younger children waiting in anticipation for the time when they are old enough to be a part of the regular program and during the meantime constantly asking for "spot jobs" to earn extra money and to have something to do.

No value can be placed on the relief from boredom and the air of busyness now apparent on our campus. We continue, of course, to hear some gripes about the work, but they are half-hearted and rarely is there heard what seems to be common now to young people in communities everywhere—"There's nothing to do around here."

## 8 ✕ Sex Education in the Children's Institution

*From an address to the Chapel Hill*
*Workshops, 1969*

ROBERT L. COATES

An acquaintance of mine once remarked, "There is an unwritten conspiracy among adults to keep children stupid about what goes on in the bathroom, what goes on in the bedroom, and what goes on in the family budget." Unfortunately this is all too true in many families and in the majority of Children's Homes.

In college a close friend of mine, nineteen at the time, was shocked to learn that babies are not born through the navel. A twenty-two-year-old married woman I knew confided to her friend that she did not understand how it happened that she was pregnant. What a pity that these two persons reached this age in their life very ignorant of some fundamental information in sex education. I wish I could make myself believe that they were both rare exceptions, but many young people and children are no more informed. Perhaps your children have more information. I hope so, but it is safe to assume there are gaps in knowledge which might be described as sophisticated ignorance of a sort.

Sex education is an important part of our overall task of preparing children for the future. When we are stressing manners, responsibilities, satisfying curiosity or the concept of God's love, we are contributing substantially to a framework of attitudes and information which can assist us in helping children assimilate the story of growth and reproduction. If we approach sex education as separate and unrelated to other needs and expressions in life, we are saying to children that this topic does not really belong in our everyday adjustment. Questions and feelings which children have about sex are very much present every day, and if we believe otherwise, it is an indication of how unwilling we are to face reality about it. If we do not talk with children about sex, who will?

We face a twofold responsibility—presenting and listening to *facts* about sex, and discussing *feelings* about sex. Often our attitudes (feelings) give us more problems than factual information about sex. Stories and jokes about sex are common, in some degree, at all age levels. These reflect our curiosities as well as our anxieties. If we can first admit that discussing all aspects of sexual growth and development makes us uneasy, we can begin to learn by and thus be more helpful to children. Perhaps we are reminded of our own childhood when the subject was considered dirty or unladylike. Perhaps we fear a child will ask us for information we do not have or will inquire about our own sexual experiences of the past or present.

Children are literally bombarded with attitudes about sex through a multitude of ways: television programs, advertising, news reports, movies, magazine and book displays, styles of dress, stories, songs, language, in addition to the quite obvious stimulus provided by their own bodily functions and growth. Thus stimulated, the child has feelings and questions stirred up. If we do not offer our help, where can he turn? In defense of truth and the whole story, we are forced to present a more complete and honest exposure to the facts and to the context of these facts.

There is nothing wrong or bad about the child's questions. The idea of "wrong" or "bad" is too often introduced by the adult's response. Let us vow to end the era where healthy questions are rebuked by unhealthy attitudes and begin an era where feelings of the child are given welcome expression. Sex education is one of the few areas (drugs may be another) where good, simple, honest questions are answered by a volcano of systematized lies, distortions, and plain avoidance. The latter is usually done by postponing an answer until later, much later. The reason some children keep asking the same questions is that their nose tells them that the truth has not yet been found. Children are acutely sensitive to how we feel and withdraw or suppress questions when they sense the adult is uncomfortable. The adult's rush to quell his own anxiety has been at the expense of the child's failing to obtain information then or later.

Can we not just permit but actively encourage his coming to us for a discussion of sex information? We must care enough to work hard at overcoming our discomfort to be of help to the child. We are in a strategic position to help place sex information in a broad context of life's goals and rewards. We are close by and available to teach when the child is ready and eager to learn.

It is not easy to change one's attitudes, but it can be done. We will not make the effort until we are convinced it is actually in the best interest of the child.

The basic principles in being helpful are present in sex education. We must listen, with our heads and hearts, to what a child may really be asking. We must recognize the question is important to *this* child *at this time*. We must attempt to keep our own feelings out of the way. A standing joke in the Army Medical Corps tells of the corpsman who injects himself with morphine upon discovering a severely wounded soldier. We obviously are of no help when our own feelings are so great that we cannot give our attention to the child.

If one feels that masturbation is repulsive and horrible, how can one possibly really be helpful to a child who might want to discuss his own worries about it? Any persistent nonconstructive behavior in a child should be viewed as a symptom that the child is seeking to cope with something. Frequent and repeated masturbation over many months is actually a disguised cry for help. Too frequently it has been the event triggering adults who are troubled about their own feelings, to lash out with fury and stop the behavior at all costs.

Our own anxieties may lead us to "shoot the works" and tell the child all we know. We make the mistake in assuming that one question means he is ready to hear the whole story. Preparing a turkey dinner with all the trimmings in response to a request for a cookie would be just as inappropriate and unhelpful.

It is not easy to be honest with ourselves. Until we come to grips with answers to our own questions, we cannot be very helpful to a child. It may be difficult to accept as truth that not all couples who engage in premarital intercourse feel remorse or guilt. Many girls have been promiscuous and have neither contracted a venereal disease nor become pregnant. We may fear that to admit these as true would express our sanction. In reality, a child is more likely to be guided by our opinion when he knows we can face facts which do not represent our own attitudes. Every child must, as we did, decide for himself what is proper and acceptable for him. To pound our own viewpoint home may result in silencing the child rather than converting him.

The child's own life experiences may add to our difficulty in sex education. Eva Burmeister in her book, *The Professional Houseparent*, writes:

> Poor adult behavior often puts a stigma on the subject of sex, with the implication that the relationship between the sexes is something to be hidden, to be ashamed of, and which causes parents to fight, separate, and divorce. The child often may need reeducation rather than new knowledge, to be freed first of the troublesome attitudes which he may have absorbed, the information he has picked up, and the anxieties and feelings which have developed as a result, before he is ready to understand and accept on a new and fresh basis.[25]

The institution itself is an important factor which may influence our approach. Some Homes care for only one sex and social contacts with the opposite sex are limited or closely supervised. My own experience reveals that campuses with only boys or girls generate just as many questions and feelings about sex among the children, but the attitudes are more elementary.

The constant changing of the group composition indicates there will be varying levels of interest and knowledge. Sex education must be geared accordingly. Dating policies, even a policy forbidding dates, contribute substantially to how children perceive that the Home feels about the boy-girl relationship. Unfortunately, most dating policies seem to underscore our mistrust of children and make them feel they could not make proper choices in managing themselves around dating.

Sex education is for everyone, not just for teenagers. The content and approach will vary with the age of your group, but sex education should be begun as soon as the child arrives in your care.

I once believed it was sufficient to wait for the child's questions to determine when sex information should be offered. I am convinced this is too passive and the adult must take the initiative. If for no other reason, it signals to the child that you recognize he has questions even though he has not asked them of

25. Eva Burmeister, *The Professional Houseparent* (New York: Columbia University Press, 1960), pp. 142–43.

you. It also indicates your readiness and willingness to bring the topic out in the open.

Perhaps an easier approach for you will be first to bring books into the cottage. The books will be needed anyway. If you feel uneasy discussing the subject it often is helpful to admit this to your group. You may be amazed and reassured to see how they understand. Unfortunately, we are having to pry ourselves out from under generations of guilt and shame about sex where the good and wholesome aspects of sex were forgotten or denied.

It is important to think of sex education as an integral part of your total job, and as an integral part of a child's responsibility for learning. Sex information is not something to be brought out only at widely spaced intervals. The most effective teaching takes place when the child has indicated interest.

You must be prepared with facts and be expert to cope with feelings about sex. Especially with children under ten, your own feelings about sex information are more important than the facts, for you reveal whether the topic is safe and welcome or dirty and forbidden. When children sense the latter attitude, you are saying you cannot be a resource person in this area. Each response you give, verbal and nonverbal, conveys some of your attitudes.

Sex information is really easy to teach when we recognize there is information we can give to any age, for a child of any age has questions about it. These questions can assist in telling us when a child is ready to have information as well as how much he already knows. There are many excellent books available, some written for adults, some written for a child or young person, some you both can read and discuss together. I particularly recommend a recent book entitled *The Stork Is Dead* by Charlie W. Shedd. This book is especially helpful to adolescents and, as with any book in your cottage, you should be familiar with it.

Before planning an approach to sex education for your cottage, we can learn from the inadequacies of similar programs. Many are edited to avoid offending anyone and come out useless. Most fail to equip the adult with a glossary of terms which young people use and this hinders communication. For example, how many of you would know what a child might be describing if he used the term "making out," "sixty-nine," "cornhole," "cruising," or "balling"? Many sex education programs ignore the fact that sexual intercourse is a means of pleasure in itself. The emphasis upon reproduction leaves the impression that sexual intercourse is practiced solely for the purpose of producing a child, not even mentioning the fact that many babies are conceived accidentally.

Of special interest to the child care worker is the sad fact that most books and audiovisual materials assume the child is living with his parents in a family where love is ever-present. It is possible to describe reproduction factually without making value judgments of the parents. Children in care are actually aware that something in the parental relationship has gone awry, but sexual feelings and expression remain.

Finally, it may help to announce to your group that you have neglected sex education in the past and wish to do something about this. You might find them quite helpful with suggestions, after they are convinced you seriously want to be of help.

If your home is like most, sex information has found expression primarily in the bathroom, boiler room, behind the gym, or in other "secret" places. I hope you will in some way let the children know that sex education is a topic which belongs in the living room and around the dining-room table. They are ready to place it there if you are.

## 9 ❧ Celebrating Victory
*From an address to the Chapel Hill*
*Workshop Reports, 1973*
### ALAN KEITH-LUCAS

A child is born, and immediately he starts to learn—how to do things, what to do, what things work and what things don't, what gives in this incredibly complex world into which he has been thrust. For some things he has to wait—for most things, as a matter of fact—until his muscles coordinate better, until he understands how things are done, but at the same time he does not just learn by waiting. He learns by doing, by working at his problem, by trial and error, by wanting to be able to do something. Sometimes he gets frustrated when what he wants is more than what he can do at this time. I can recall the despair and anger that my small granddaughter showed in those difficult weeks when she could get up on all fours but could not as yet progress in that position—how she stormed and wept and struggled and finally fell forward each time on her nose. And if the task is too hard, a child can, of course, give up and decide that it is not worth putting out all that energy and feeling to achieve what he set out to do.

A good deal will depend on the reactions of the people around him. For the baby is not alone in this world. He or she is urged on or frustrated, laughed at, ignored, appreciated, starved, doped (that is, has his body chemistry changed), rewarded, punished, loved, or rejected by the adults around him. Whether he wants to learn and what he wants to learn are deeply affected by how his parents interpret his actions. The pride, the deep sense of accomplishment, and the desire to learn more come perhaps most readily when a child can share his victories, when they are celebrated as important things.

I do not mean just being praised or rewarded. Celebration is something more than praise. It is something two people do together, not something one does to another. For that is the child's chief problem. The adults in his world are all too often not cocelebrants of his victories or consolers of his defeats, but people who want to do things to him, to make him good, to keep him quiet, to stop him doing things, to teach him this or that, to guide him in the way he should go. Still more, they are people with needs of their own who demand of him that he love or respect them, or minister to their pride, or be someone they can boss, or cuddle, or show off or be amused by, or whatever it is they like to do to children. Too many of them accept without thinking a responsibility to mold, to rear a child, with their eyes on the future, to worry about what kind of adult he will be, instead of relating to him as he is, a struggling, acting, living, and doing person who happens to be not a middle-aged matron or a senior citizen but a child or an adolescent.

So we force the child to go to school, and we advise houseparents to parcel out rewards and punishments, which, when we want to get very professional, we call behavior modification, and talk about it all too often as if it were the ultimate solution to all the problems of growing up. It is not, of course. It is our own way of imposing our will on children in certain aspects of their behavior and we assume that our will is a good one and ought to be imposed—a proposition one could argue about. I would not doubt that there are behaviors we would want to impose on children. There are acceptable and unacceptable actions which a child needs to learn if he is to get along in this world. Teaching these to children is part of our job. It is not the whole of it. There are other important goals, such as helping a child grow up with confidence, helping him develop close and meaningful relations with people, helping him solve for himself what he really wants to be, and why, and, many of us would say, helping him have that openness to the heart of things that we call religion. And these things are not the result of behavior modification—which was, after all, derived from studies of rats who did not, through their learning, develop any essential qualities of rathood in the process.

But behavior modification, once it became scientific, did at least one very great thing. It pointed out, as a matter of fact and not of opinion, that positive reinforcements (that is, praise and reward) were far more effective in changing behavior than were negative reinforcements (blame and punishment). It also made clear that exemplary punishment (that is, trying to scare others away from some kind of behavior by being absolutely sure that anyone who commits it is punished severely) is virtually useless. As historians have pointed out, the public execution of pickpockets was one of the most fruitful harvest times for the pickpockets who operated in the crowd. It appears to be human nature to believe that what happens to other people is not going to happen to oneself.

How we as a people came to believe that we should not reward people for being good but should punish them for being bad is something of a mystery. Some ascribe it to Calvinist theology which held that all evil was man's fault, and therefore, to be punished, and all good God's doing and therefore no credit to us, but if so it shows very little understanding of how difficult it is for most of us to be good. It may have come from a time when the duty of a child, or of the lower classes, was very simple and consisted largely in obeying the Ten Commandments, with emphasis on the fifth, and with the substitution of the word "obey" for "honor," whereas the inventiveness of evil was illimitable. But wherever it came from it is a sad commentary on human nature and has caused untold misery to generations of children, slaves, and poor people. Try this as an exercise. Write down, for one full day, all the things you have said to children. Unless you are quite exceptional, 80 percent of them will be negative or corrective— "Brush your hair," "Don't make so much noise," "Why can't you realize that?" Very few show either appreciation or praise.

But it is appreciation rather than praise that I want to talk about. There is always something a little condescending about praise. It is something one does *to* another person, not something one does *with* him. Let me start by taking a look at some of the things most of our children have gone through before they come to us.

In the first place they lack self-confidence. They do not think in their hearts that they are worth anything. Most of them know that they have not been loved as children ought to be loved. They are apt to blame themselves for what has happened to them. Far from being encouraged in life, they have been ignored or rejected. No one has ever cared enough to celebrate life with them.

Second, most of them have had a tremendous struggle to keep their end up where they have been. They have lied, fought, stolen, and rioted, not because they are liars or thieves or rowdies by nature, not because no one has told them that these things are not acceptable, not even because they have not been punished harshly enough for doing them, but because these were the only ways they could keep their heads above water. In their world, their family, their community, these things worked. They got the food or the attention or the status a child needs to survive. Good behavior did not produce results. Nice guys finish last. Some of these things even became second nature to them; that is, they were no longer under conscious control, but became so natural that the child turned instinctively to them without thinking. This is particularly true of things that affect their whole relationship to people, such as manipulation of others rather than responses to them, so-called compulsive lying or stealing, the use of sex (sometimes the only weapon they have) to dominate others, the need to escape reality through daydreaming, masturbation, liquor or drugs, or the use of violence to gain their ends.

Third, they have lost trust in the adult world, which has let them down, exploited them, frustrated them, blamed them, punished them, often capriciously and without rhyme or reason, or has been so unconcerned, so manipulable, or so hypocritical and inconsistent that they have quite reasonably lost all respect for it. Add to this fact that the modern child is well informed, is getting signals from all sorts of different directions, and is facing a world which is confused in its values and incredibly complex, and remembering that we are talking about a child without a wealth of practical experience, without the right to opt out of the system, frustrated in many of his endeavors by his own powerlessness, culturally kept in subjection even when physically he is an adult with strong desires of his own, and at adolescence at least swayed by bewildering physiochemical changes, and we can see that it is going to be very difficult for him to learn more productive and more acceptable ways of coping with life. He certainly will not do so because we tell him he ought to. The trouble with trying to punish him into changing is that although punishment may make bad behavior not worth the cost, nothing is substituted in its place. It does not make acceptable behavior more attractive except in the very negative sense of being less likely to bring bad results. And I for one am not willing to settle for a life that sees good as only the avoidance of unpleasantness. Life, if it is to mean anything, something to be lived joyously and abundantly, must not be at very best only something that is not too bad.

How do we try to help him learn? We often start by labelling him as disturbed, sick, in need of treatment or correction, or as having problems. We work on things he does wrong. We decide that he needs discipline. We pay very little attention to what he does right and have little sense of what he is up against. The very word "disturbance" troubles us. We see it as a deviation. We try to calm it, to reduce it. But let me say here and now, that much of what we call disturbance is not a sickness. It is a sign that the child has not given up, is still trying, maybe wrong-headedly, but still actively, to deal with his situation.

This is where celebration comes in. For celebration adds joy to finding a new and better way. It reinforces the child's own pride. It reverses the too-common situation in which a child's only way of getting attention, of having someone single him out, listen to him, become concerned about him, is to do something unacceptable—and the more spectacular the better. A great deal of children's bad behavior is, as we know, a cry for recognition. "This is me! This isn't a problem child, or one of the group, but me." One of my pet aversions is the phrase, "He's only doing it for attention." Only? How can a child ask any less of those who care for him?

To be a true celebrant does, however, need skill and discernment. I hope I have made clear the distinction between celebration and, say, false reassurance or a hearty back-slapping, "Let's-not-look-on-the-negative" point of view. Celebration needs to be for the things a child wants to celebrate. It is wise to remember that what may seem to us a victory may be for a child a dangerous self-exposure to adult expectation. Because he has done this once he may be expected to do it again and again, feeling like a failure when he cannot. Or it may be something which he knows will bring him praise, but for the wrong reasons, not for something he really cares about, as a child pointed out when he said, "Mother loves me for getting As but she doesn't love me for myself." Whether you learn the true meaning of a child's act by asking him how he feels about it, or whether you learn it through nonverbal communication, it is wise to be sure that you and the child are in tune about it. False reassurance and back-slapping are things you do to a child, not things you do with him. And the other side of celebration is consolation in defeat.

What needs celebrating, too, is not always success. It is often the courage, the effort, the plugging away at something that did not quite come off. And sometimes I think one needs to celebrate in a quiet way, "just between the two of us," just the very fact of being together, or the fact that your eyes are blue.

Let me give three examples of what I mean by celebration. One is a very disturbed, frightened, withdrawing child I know. She creeps, she shrinks, she acts bizarrely, and lately she has become much worse. Yet she has new, young houseparents, much more intelligent than the rather childish woman who preceded them. In pondering this rather strange fact, it occurred to me to reflect on how Amy was spoken of in my presence. The new houseparents center on Amy's problems. They are deeply and properly concerned about her nail biting, her lies, her inappropriate remarks. The former, less discerning houseparent introduced her to me as "our artist" and immediately asked her to show me some of her work. She does draw extremely well. And, thinking back, the last time I saw Amy's face light up and a little peace come into it was over a drawing. Of late I never heard of Amy's art—only of Amy's disturbance.

The second is a boy in a Home where one of the standard penalties is what the children call the "chain-gang," an involuntary Saturday afternoon working detail. Clyde was a chronic chain-ganger. He had been on it eight weeks in a row. Then, as he recounted it to me, he got fed up and made a tremendous effort. For three whole weeks he did his work well, was nice and well-mannered, obeyed all the rules, and for three weeks he was off the gang. The fourth week he slipped, and as he reported, the supervisor, calling his name, added the words, "As usual." As Clyde said, "What's the use? No one even noticed. Why work like I did to keep off the gang when you don't get any encouragement?"

The third was a boy with a school phobia. He could get himself to school in the morning but by ten or half-past the classroom began to feel like a prison; he was shaking all over, he had to have air, and he left. Though the mental health clinic was trying to help him find out what irrational association or memory was triggering his fear, the Home had asked the school to report his leaving, and he was required to do extra homework to compensate for every hour of school he missed. It was not until someone suggested that the Home keep a record of how many hours he had managed to stay in school each week that he came back, white and shaken, one day and announced, "I made it—a whole day," and the whole cottage celebrated. I do not mean to say that there were not relapses, but these were handled with understanding and in time his attendance became quite normal.

The ultimate human emotions are love and joy—or joy and love. It is hard to say which comes first. One has to be loved to be joyous, but one also has to be joyous to love. I am distressed sometimes at the lack of joy, of rejoicing, in our handling of children, especially when we become more professional. We often disperse rewards and punishments as if they were pills. We talk about being "warm" and "accepting." What tepid words these are! Cannot we sometimes glory in what a child has done, rejoice with him, celebrate the grade that goes up, the habit less frequently indulged in, the well-made bed, the happy day, putting less emphasis on the defeat? The children who come to us are only too accustomed to defeat.

# ✻✻D

# In the Area of Group Living

## 10✻ Group Process: The Key to Helping in Residential Care

*Paper given to the Southeastern Group Child Care Association, 1974*

MARJORIE L. FARADAY

The use of group process in residential child care seldom gets major attention in workshops or meetings. It is ironic that this is so, since the development of group child care has led us directly to the recognition that the group living experience is what it is all about, really.

If we take away the group living experience from the residential group care program, the whole structure collapses for lack of purpose. All of the other services we provide—food, clothing, shelter, medical care, education, spiritual training, case-work and group work services, recreation, specialized therapy of many kinds—any or all of these can be provided for the child in his own home or a foster family or to young people in independent living situations; none of them is unique to residential group care. Only in the group setting can we offer children the experience of group living. Since this is our unique service, it is appropriate that we analyze it, recognizing what is unique about it and why it is the best way to serve some children who cannot remain with their own families.

Currently, there are an estimated 360,000 children who are unable to live with their own parents and are in some kind of alternate care. About three-fourths of these children are in foster families, and some 90,000 are in some form of residential group care. One of the first questions we usually ask is "Why are they in care?" That question really embodies two questions or interpretations, and our failure to distinguish these has a strong impact on how we serve the children for whom we accept responsibility.

The first question or interpretation is really, "Why can't these children stay with their own families?" Robert Geiser, in *The Illusion of Caring*,[26] one of the most exciting and compelling works in the field of child care, reports on studies which identified five reasons for placement of children. Geiser points out that in only 15 percent of the cases are the child's own problems the reason for placement. Only 15 percent of the children needed to be placed because their own personal or emotional problems made them unmanageable or unacceptable to their parents and/or the community.

In 85 percent of the cases, placement was necessary because of the breakdown of the family unit or the malfunctioning of the family. Eighty-five percent of the children in placement, then, could not remain in their own families because of the inability of adults to care either for themselves or for the children in a mature way.

This very significant point tells us that in 85 percent of the cases, the major problems which necessitated placement rest not in the children, on whom we have traditionally concentrated our service efforts, but in the families, with whom we have dealt minimally, if at all. By some spurious reasoning, we have surmised that removing the children from the problem situation and working with them was all that was needed to correct the difficulties.

What has happened, of course, is that either the family

26. Robert Geiser, *The Illusion of Caring* (Boston: Beacon Press, 1973).

disruption has been solidified to the point that the children remain "forever ours," "orphans of the living," "children in limbo," or we have returned the children at some point to the situations from which we rescued them earlier, apparently believing that some magic has occurred while we were "working on the children" so that the problems of the parents have disappeared.

But let us return to the children themselves.

Does the fact that only 15 percent of the children in care are there because of their own problems mean that the other 85 percent do not have problems, that they are sweet-tempered, well-behaved, adequately functioning children? Certainly not. But it does begin to tell us something about what these children are like and what they need in the way of help.

We know, for example, that children who are placed away from their own families are ridden with feelings of grief, rage, despair, intense anger, rejection, indignation, hopelessness, guilt, helplessness, anxiety, and confusion, even when placement is not the children's fault. They see themselves as worthless and unlovable, as unable to cope with life, as belonging to no one, or as having no one to be like, to care for, and be cared for by. They have little or no sense of self-worth, self-competence, or self-identity.

We also know that children act out their feelings, that their behavior and their relationships with others reflect the breadth and depth of the feelings that absorb them. We can expect, then, that children who are overwhelmed by enormous negative feelings will generally behave in fairly negative ways and that the behavior is not likely to change just with a change of setting.

We know further that parents who have been inadequate or neglectful and perhaps abusive have their own problems and have not been able to give their children the opportunities and help necessary for the children to develop positive ways of using their capacities and strengths. Since we know that relationships are reciprocal, we know that children who are part of a distorted parent-child relationship will have had to develop distorted ways of relating to adults and probably to their peers.

# Group Child Care as a Family Service

The inferences we draw from this knowledge, then, destroy any hope that most of the children will be easy to live with and help. We have confirmed what our daily observations tell us. As long ago as 1955, Gisela Konopka told us, "The population in our children's institutions is becoming a more and more difficult one. . . . This means that the impact of the group living relationship becomes even stronger and is charged with greater tensions, more outbursts, more problem situations."[27]

Even though this information about the children in placement suggests that our jobs will not be easy, it leads us directly to the second half of the question, "Why are the children in placement?" What can we do about, for, and with these hurt, angry, pain-ridden children? We can give them what they need. Their first and greatest need is defined by the knowledge we have about the family situations from which they came and about the feelings which engulf them and pour out in their behavior. These children need to have their basic needs met in ways that will promote positive feelings about themselves and their world and will support their normal, healthy development. Along with this, they may need corrective help to deal with the delays, distortions, and blocks in their normal developmental journey. Often in our dealing with children who have problems we forget that their greatest need is still one common to all children: continued help and support in their growth and development.

The resources for satisfying a child's basic needs are found in his primary life relationships. Here the child receives the care and nurturing appropriate to each stage of his development. Here he finds support and encouragement in his strivings toward independence and self-management. Here are the roots of his sense of self-worth, his feelings of self-competence, his sense of identity. Here he learns who and what he is, whether he is worth anything, and what kind of a person he can hope to become.

To be in a primary group means to belong, to be accepted, to have opportunities for self-expression, achievement, and recognition. In his primary life experiences, the child struggles to

27. Gisela Konopka, "The Role of the Group in Residential Treatment," *American Journal of Orthopsychiatry* 28, no. 4 (1955), p. 679.

find the important balance between freedom and limitations. A primary group also provides means for healing hurts, enhancing strengths, and clarifying and resolving conflicts and problems. In the give-and-take of primary group experiences, the individual deals directly with life's concerns, tests out his own responses, discovers the natural consequences of his behavior, and experiments with interpersonal relationships. Here he learns ways of dealing with his own feelings. Primary groups have been labeled "the springs of life," "the marketplace of ego development." All human beings need what these groups have to offer.

The family is one kind of primary group, and it is the first and most continuing primary life experience for most children. When we intervene in this primary relationship and remove the child, temporarily or permanently, from his family, his healthy development requires that we provide for him another primary life experience in which his needs can be met. For some children, group living provides an alternative kind of primary experience.

It is not the purpose of this paper to describe children for whom group care is the appropriate choice or the basis on which the choice is made. We must make it very clear, however, that family care and group living are two different kinds of primary life experiences and that they cannot be used interchangeably or indiscriminately to meet the needs of individual children.

Our failure to make these distinctions has inhibited greatly our capacity to understand and to use group living responsibly. We have tried to make residential group care an imitation of family living, and the resulting confusion means that children get the full benefits of neither and, frequently, the shortcomings of both.

I cannot stress too strongly the implications of our confusion. The agency is often named or referred to as "The Home." We urge the child to think of this as his home—at least during his stay there—and to think of the living group as a family. We may feel disappointed or angry when he is careless or destructive and does not take care of "his home." We may feel betrayed when he is reluctant to join our pretense, when he does not want people to know he is "one of our family" and lives in "our home." We are disturbed by his disloyalty and lack of appreciation.

Do we really fool ourselves into thinking that any of the following are characteristic of home and family in our society?

1. A large number of unrelated children residing in an isolated setting with several adults, none of whom is related to the children (and perhaps none to each other), but all of whom share reponsibility for the children;

2. The potential that a new child (and one who is not a baby) will come into the family suddenly, often without any warning or preparation;

3. The possibility that tomorrow some of the children in "the family" across the road will move into the house next door, while some of those children will move into this house and others will go home;

4. The chance that at any time some of the adults in these "families" will exchange places or just leave;

5. Periods of time when the adults take time off from caring for the children in "this home and family"—time which they may spend at home with their families;

6. The promise that if the children behave "here at home in this family" they will get to go home to their families.

Children know there is a difference between home and family on the one hand, and what we provide for them in group care. They are puzzled when the adults in the setting do not seem to know the difference.

Children are angry when adults who do know the difference insist on carrying on the pretense or trying to invest the group care setting with bonds and loyalties which belong to other people and places in the children's lives.

Children resent it when we do not accept the adage "Home is where the heart is" or recognize that the heart of the child separated from his family is not with us but with them, where he desperately wants to be.

Children are very wise in knowing that sometimes "the home" they have in the group setting is the kind best described as, "Home is where you go when there's nothing else open," or,

"Home is where when you go there they have to take you in." I urge continuing effort to make our group settings as attractive, as comfortable, as filled with opportunities for normal, enriching life experiences as possible, but we must be clear about what they are and what they are not.

If any primary life experience is to be meaningful, it must be authentic. If the arena in which the child does his learning and growing is phony, whatever knowledge and skills and capacities he develops will not serve him well when he puts them to use in the world outside. These children have not had an authentic, constructive primary life experience before they reached us. Will we perpetuate that deprivation? Neither the child nor the staff will be able to recognize and use fully the unique values in the group living situation until we come to grips with the fact that family living and group living are not, cannot, and should not be the same.

What, then, are some of the characteristics of group living which distinguish it from family care and make it an effective form of primary life experience for some children?

One essential aspect is that the group constellation has not been brought about by the accident of birth but can be consciously arranged in accordance with the needs of the individual child.

In the group living situation, moreover, the essential nurturing experiences are consistently and systematically provided through the processes of daily living. The child's dependency is accepted and met through orderly provision of the necessities of life, rather than in a direct, parent-child kind of relationship. Whether he receives the essential care and nurturing is not left to chance, as it may have been in previous situations.

In the group living situation, the child has a structured context for developing the primary relationships every human needs. He is given new primary caring persons whose involvement with him is governed by his own needs, readiness, and capacities rather than by the traditional expectations of the parent-child relationship or by the adult's needs. Because he has little or no basis for trusting adults, he will be allowed to move slowly into relationships with them as he develops the capacity to interact effectively with other members of the group.

Not only does group living offer him the opportunity for the diluted kind of relationships with adults which may be all he can manage, but it gives him many adults from among whom he can select his models and toward whom he can make his tentative moves toward more personalized relationships as he wishes to and can. In the group setting, moreover, he is freed from the demand to relate to anyone immediately if he is not ready or able. Schulze reminds us that the "touch-starved children, like those that are food-starved, need to be fed frequent small doses."[28]

In the group living situation, the child does not need to mask his feelings and distort his reactions. He is allowed—and expected—to experience the pain that comes with facing the realities about the separation from his family, to grapple with the confusing and frightening feelings about the family who has let him down, to bring into the open his fears about what is going to happen to him now and in the future. Facing the realities of life is essential in learning how to deal adequately and constructively with them.

Learning to live through confrontation with his peers is one of the most potent virtues of the group experience. In these interactions he learns that others have feelings similar to his own and that they can take help and support from one another. He can discover that he is not so alone, so without help and hope, as he had thought.

In group interaction, the child can discover ways in which his behavior and values differ from those of others, and what impact this has on his acceptance by and his happiness in the group. This kind of experiencing of the consequences of his own behavior is reality testing on the front line. It gives the child the basis for making the important choices about which of his differences he will give up in favor of something he needs and wants more—acceptance and mutual caring, for example—and which

28. Susanne Schulze, *Creative Group Living in a Children's Institution* (New York: Association Press, 1951), p. 8.

he will retain and reaffirm and use as channels for finding joy and satisfaction in life.

In the group living experience, the child can develop and test out new and different ways of coping with his feelings and his conflicts, and in the process he can learn to experience the pleasurable sensations of self-expression, achievement, and self-mastery.

The process by which the child does all these in the group living situation takes place in a structure which assures that he will have whatever external controls he needs at different points in his development, and it offers fewer controls and greater freedom as his own inner controls and capacity for self-mastery are strengthened.

In essence, the group living situation is a socially engineered, structured, purposeful primary life experience in which the child is provided with the human and material resources to meet his basic needs, to experience the consequences to himself and others of his patterns of dealing with the realities of life, to learn more effective ways of coping, and to develop the self-identity and ego-adequacy necessary for growing into an adequate, independent, self-fulfilled—and perhaps even a happy—adult. Through the group process in group living, he can learn to be a real person who can live in a real world with real people.

Therapeutic group living, as Alt and Grossbard point out, is not merely "indiscriminate exposure of youngsters to good, wholesome experiences and activities." It is, rather, "controlled and regulated flexibility—the ability to expand and contract the breadth and depth of the experience in accordance with the needs of the child."[29]

The uniqueness of the group living experience and the key to its special value, then, lie not in its purpose or goals but in its method. The group living experience does not differ from the family experience in what it aims to do, but in how it goes about doing it. In the family living experience, the child's development

29. Herschel Alt and Hyman Grossbard, "Professional Issues in the Institutional Treatment of Delinquent Children," *American Journal of Orthopsychiatry* 19, no. 2 (1949), p. 282.

is rooted in and conditioned by his relationship with mature adults who are able to carry their responsibilities in meeting the total constellation of the child's basic needs. As the child grows and moves out into ever-widening circles of life experiences, he can meet and cope effectively with the relationships and experiences he encounters because of the capacities he has developed, tested, and refined in an adequate parent-child relationship.

In the group living experience, he develops his basic capacity for relationships and for coping effectively with the realities of life, not through the adult-child relationship, but through interchange with a group of his peers. We might say that the order is reversed in the two kinds of primary life situations: in the family we see development beginning with the adult-child relationship and moving on to peer-group relationships; in group living, relationships are developed first with peers and then with adults. The first might be seen as a natural sequence, the second as a corrective one which is necessary for those children whose early experiences in relationships have been inadequate, distorted, or unproductive.

The implications of this vital difference are enormous. I cannot attempt to deal with very many of them here, but I want to make reference to a few.

Constructive group process requires a structured, appropriately balanced group to provide the collective strengths and weaknesses, the individuality and mutuality, the variety of experience in succeeding and failing which are necessary ingredients for learning and testing in encounters with reality. The art of group composition is a specialized subject that deserves its own paper. We cannot create an effective arena for the process of group living by pulling names out of a hat or assigning children to the cottage at random or on the basis of where the empty beds are.

I also want to underscore the importance of well-thought-out, prepared admission of children to the cottage group. Recognizing the need for this in terms of the individual child, I want to draw attention here to the impact on the group process of a new child's coming into the group. The group process—our primary tool in helping children in group living—suffers greatly when a new child is introduced into the group without careful consideration of what happens to the group at that point and what will happen when the composition of the group changes. Planning for and receiving the newcomer is in itself an important part of the group process; when it is left out, subsequent process and progress are affected.

At times in the life of a group a painfully earned step forward may be inhibited because of an untimely or unplanned admission. At times a group may be struggling with conflicts and problems which require all of its energies and strengths and has nothing left over to give to the new problems a change in group membership creates. At times a group may emerge from a period of striving and would like to celebrate its victories without the intrusion of a newcomer who has not been part of it struggles. At times it may need to rest before regrouping to deal with new challenges. When we consider the potential admission of a new child into a group, we must look not only at what the group can do for the child, but also at what the child can do for and to the group, and we must be sensitive to timing.

Most of what I have said about admissions to the group also applies to departures from the group. A child's leaving the group means another experience in separation for all of the children, most of whom are still immersed in the grief of previous separations and losses. All of what we know in relation to separation applies here. Recognizing the combination of negative and positive relationships the group experience entails, we can anticipate a resurgence of the sense of loss, the guilt, the anxiety, the anger, and all the other feelings that separation engenders in human beings. Establishing and severing relationships are realities of life with which every individual has to come to terms. He must learn ways to deal with such realities, which will occur again and again in his life, ways which will not leave him devastated and defenseless. The children in our care have not learned these ways in previous life experiences. We cannot control that.

We can control, however, whether we too do the same thing to them or whether we invest these learning experiences with sensitive planning and gentle caring.

Even more damaging is what has been called "the trauma of precipitous discharge." An unplanned, impulsive departure of one member of the group from the primary living group is traumatic to all those who remain as well as to the one who leaves. The trauma is even greater when the departure is a dismissal, a clear rejection and abolishment of the child for something he has said or done. These children have been hurt desperately by the careless, whimsical, vindictive, immature actions of the adults in their lives. Do we dare to recreate those experiences in the name of caring for and serving them?

We must also remember that we cite as some of the healing aspects of group living the promise of continuity, the opportunity to work through feelings, the assurance of caring adults who accept children as they are now while they struggle to become something more. Do we really think children will believe this, when they saw what happened to Johnny last week because he did just what we should have expected he would do in his pain and confusion and inability to cope?

I am aware that changes will be necessary, since some children will not be able to remain in and benefit from the group living experience, but I am concerned about the impact on group process of the precipitous discharge. Children will not be able to make free and full use of the opportunities in group living if they must keep their guards up, if they must be ever alert to the danger that when they need us the most we will prove that we are, indeed, like the other adults they have known who deserted them or sent them away because they were so unacceptable.

The group process is significantly affected by the presence of the child who either should not have been admitted to group care or who no longer needs the special feature of group living and is ready to move into family or independent living. No child can participate fully in or benefit from the group process when his needs and goals are strikingly different from those of others in the group, and no group can implement and benefit from the group process when it must spend energy and effort carrying a nonparticipating member.

I have chosen these examples to illustrate some ways in which the requirements of structure and planning must be met in the use of group process. Each of these examples involves an activity or activities inherent in normal, day-to-day life experience: making and losing friends, establishing and severing other kinds of relationships, struggling with conflicts of interests, dealing with the crises of life, etc. Each of them affords opportunities for planned use of the group process in helping children learn to meet and cope with daily experiences. The same potential exists in every aspect of group living. Effective use of the group process means being alert to and using these experiences to help the child grow and develop. We cannot afford to dismiss as inconsequential any of these opportunities.

The fact that the most meaningful learning experiences in the group living situation will take place in the give-and-take of daily life underscores the need for an appropriate degree of cottage autonomy. As we have added to our knowledge and skill in using the group care setting in the best interests of children, we have narrowed our focus from the overall group to the cottage or living unit group. The three great diseases inherent in institutional life characterize mass care of children: anonymity, standardization, and authoritarianism. All of these mitigate against sound development; the antidotes to them are in the small living group.

## 11 🌂 Group Meetings in the Cottage

*From a panel of child care workers held at the*
*Chapel Hill Workshops, 1968*

DRUSCILLA HARTE

Our agency exists to serve children and parents at a point in which family life is in danger of breaking down. About a year ago we began developing a set of standards of performance for the child care worker, at which time we took a close look at our role and our responsibility. One area that we were all particularly interested in was our role and responsibilities as the leader of our group of children. After we defined our areas of responsibility we ranked them to see if we could arrive at a consensus about which responsibility was the most important. We also had the children rank the areas of responsibility to see what they thought was the most important responsibility of the child care worker. The children and staff were fairly close together in their rankings in all areas except one, and that was the responsibility of counseling with children. The children as a group ranked this responsibility second in importance, whereas our staff gave it a much lower ranking. It did not take a genius to figure that one out and to show us the way in which we as a staff needed to move.

At about this time the consultant from Group Child Care Consultant Services visited our agency and during his week's visit it again became evident that we needed to strengthen our role as group workers. So for the next few months we spent our Tuesday morning sessions examining the role of the group leader. To try out some of the theory we began learning about, we looked at cottage group meetings through the use of role playing. One child care worker would serve as the leader of the group and the other staff members acted as her children in the cottage that she was representing. We began by having some "how-not-do-it" sessions. In this way we quickly learned how a group meeting can be killed if the leader takes too dominant a role. We were also able to see how a meeting can get out of hand if the leader takes too passive a role.

# In the Area of Group Living

When it came time for the child care worker to be the group leader, it was my luck to be chosen first. If you think it is difficult to hold down a bunch of teenaged girls, and to be serious with discussions, you should try to do it with a group of house-mothers, a housefather, and a director of child care. There you really have something. I was scared and nervous. I looked around and they were all staring at me, just as my girls do at times. I thought, "This must be how a monkey feels on a string." Seeing no escape, I decided to carry on to the best of my ability.

The procedure went something like this: "You've been getting on each other's nerves lately, so why don't we get to-gether and see if we can find out what seems to be upsetting you? Let's see if we can't bring this thing out into the open and maybe find a solution to this bickering that has been going on for the past several days. Everyone will have a chance to say what is on his mind, so please let's not all try to talk at the same time. Now, who would like to start it off?" Complete silence was my answer. I again asked, "Who will be the first to speak up?" Still all I got was complete silence. I turned to one of the workers and said, "Cindy, you were the one to come to me yesterday, so why don't you start it off?" "Well, I wish you would make Mary take a bath more often. I room with her and it gets pretty bad sometimes. The truth of the matter is that she stinks." Mary's face turned red at this remark and she replied, "Thank you, I take a bath every day and I can't help it if I don't have some sweet-smelling bath powder like you do." To this Cindy replied, "Why don't you buy some?" Mary remarked, "Well, I'm not on the budget like you are." The discussion really got going then. Mary began taking a pretty good beating, so I realized that I needed to step in. I spoke up and said, "I know Mary takes a bath and uses deodorant too, but I'll see if I can't arrange for her to get some bath powder and a new deodorant. Sometimes a deodorant just doesn't work for some people." Liz spoke up at this time and said, "I know Mary can't help it if she doesn't smell as fresh as a daisy at times, but that's not what's bothering me. The thing that upsets me is the friends these girls bring in sometimes. They look like a bunch of bums and you should see how they act at school. It's really embarrassing." Jan replied, "If you're talking about me, I don't care. At least they're not drunk when they come to school." "Why do you want to blame me?" said Liz. "I'm not blaming it all on you, but you are causing a lot of trouble. It wouldn't be that way if you weren't so wild." Jan replied, "Well, I'll try to do better in the future, but I wish you would all stay off my back once in a while."

As I was listening to all this, I thought how much they sounded like the girls in my cottage. It was comical to us, but to our children, it is serious. We must remember that teenagers are not children. They are the adults of tomorrow. They need to feel they are important to others and that they are cared about. Growing up is like climbing a ladder; the higher you climb, the more you can see. In our role playing we found that the leader of the group has to be very careful not to dominate the meetings. She must let the child have his say and be ready to come to assistance when things get out of control.

After this experience, I felt I was ready to have group discussions in my cottage. So I anxiously waited for the opportunity which I knew would soon come. One night while we were having study hall, the telephone kept ringing. Each time I answered it, a strange boy's voice would ask to speak to one of the girls. After I told the caller we were having study hall and could not be disturbed, he would hang up, saying he would call back later. In just a few minutes the telephone would ring again. Another boy asked to speak to the same girl. One of the girls in the study hall spoke up and said, "I think something should be done about some folks getting so many telephone calls from boys they do not even know. They stay on the phone all the time and the rest of us never get to use it." I thought, "Now is my chance. Now is the time to put some of this theory into practice." So I said, "This telephone situation does seem to have gotten out of hand lately, so why don't we talk about it for a while?" The girls jumped at this chance, and soon they were all chattering. They had a chance to get a lot of their hostility out. The argument began to get hot and some of them acted as though they were ready to come to blows. I felt it was time for me to step in and turn some of the griping to effective use. I called for their attention and then told them that it was pretty apparent that the telephone was creating quite a problem within the cottage. I then asked them what they intended to do about it. I do not think I have ever seen my group more shocked. After a moment of silence, one of the girls asked, "What can we do?" I told her I did not know but thought that if we all worked on it together for a while we could come to some solution. After more discussion, one girl suggested that we form a committee of four and see what they could do.

We ended the meeting for that night and agreed to meet the next night to see what the committee had come up with. There was excitement in the air the rest of the evening. You could see that each girl had really become involved in this decision-making process. The next day the committee came in with the following recommendations: (1) that a time limit be set on the telephone at fifteen minutes per call; (2) that each girl could only receive one call in the afternoon and one call at night; (3) that no calls be permitted after 10:00 P.M., except in case of emergency; (4) that the girls not be allowed to talk to strange boys—a girl must know the boy she talks to. I thought this was a good idea and so did the girls. After each one read it carefully, they all thought it was fair, so they drew up a statement and each one signed it. Needless to say, this has really helped.

I pointed out to the girls just exactly what had happened and congratulated them on solving this problem themselves. I then asked if they would like to have these group discussions more often. To this they all eagerly replied yes. When I asked how often they thought they should have such a meeting, a couple of them spoke up and said they should have one every night. I realized this would be too often, and I explained that if they had the sessions too frequently they would not be meaningful. The girls were able to understand this and after more discussion the group finally settled on a meeting every two weeks unless something came up that needed immediate attention, in which case we would call a special meeting.

Since that time we have had our meetings on a regular

basis and I have been truly amazed at some of the changes that have come about in the cottage. One night the girls began talking about their feelings of "never getting to do anything." They felt that the boys "got to do everything," that they were "always doing something" or going someplace and that the boys were the "pets around campus." They felt that they did all the work and they never got any credit for what they did. One girl said she did not see why the boys could not work in the dining room. Another said she was looking forward to the day she would not have to wash dishes any more. After listening to this discussion I wondered why we could not do something as a group. I expressed this to them and told them that we had some money left in the household budget. I asked what they thought of using it for recreation for the entire group. The vote was unanimous that we would use the money and go to see the movie "Bonnie and Clyde." This we did, and it was thoroughly enjoyed by all. We even had popcorn and drinks. One reason it was enjoyed so much was that it was something the group could do together. They talked about it for days.

Another night we had a meeting in which the subject of sex came up. The discussion was very open and free, and I was sitting back quietly listening to it all, when suddenly one of the girls turned to me and asked, "What is wrong with sex?" This shocked me, but I soon recovered and explained to them that there was nothing wrong with sex in itself, that it was the way we used it that was sometimes wrong. It was not something that we should do just for "kicks." Another girl added, "We must not make mistakes around here, because if you do you've had it."

I thought that here I needed to lend a helping hand, so I told her that we all make mistakes, but learn from experience. It is no shame to make an error. That is part of the learning process. The really important thing is to learn from mistakes we make and not to make the same ones over again.

It is surprising how something like this can help. Each girl is given a voice in the decision-making process, and they also have the responsibility of carrying out decisions made by the group. We have all learned that much disagreement grows out of misunderstanding. Words have different meanings for different people, and sometimes we hear what we want to hear. Group meetings channel the girls' gripes into something constructive, rather than having their gripes simmer for several weeks. As we all know, this can happen if we are not careful.

I have found since we have begun having our group meetings that the girls' hostility and aggressiveness have been greatly reduced. The new approach has helped the griper to become a planner. It has greatly helped with the interpersonal relationships within the cottage, and we have definitely been able to recognize the carryover it has had outside the cottage. It has helped each child build self-confidence. In the beginning several of them were too shy to speak up and give their opinions, but when they heard others speaking up and discussing their problems, they got the courage to do so also. Now the group accepts the isolate more readily and listens to her suggestions, where she was being ignored before. But perhaps the most important thing it has done has been to put me in closer communication with my group of girls. I feel that I know my group much better, and I believe they know me better. It has also helped the children learn to make decisions. Even the youngest in the cottage has a part in this, as she is encouraged not only by me but also by the older girls to express herself at these meetings.

As the adult in the group, I have had to watch myself, because the more I say, the more it seems to encourage them to depend on me to carry the load alone. It is much better to let them speak. When children participate in making decisions they are better satisfied with the choice. And, as a final word, I would say that out of the group's discussions I have learned to trust a child's opinion.

Our discussions are not always serious, for we mix a little folly with our wisdom. A little nonsense is pleasant now and then.

## 12 ❧ Group Process in the Cottage

*From an address to the Chapel Hill*
*Workshops, 1975*

JUANITA PERRY

As a student of child care methods, I am excited about some of the enlightening experiences our cottage has had this past year. I hope that through the sharing of some of these experiences I can communicate to you my enthusiasm for one very basic principle of group care: the child's success in group care depends on his relationship with the group—not with the adult. But before this statement was recognized as truth in my own mind, our cottage had to experience many growing pains.

Because our cottage had been fairly autocratic, it was especially hard for me to make the beginning steps toward autonomy. My husband is employed outside of the home and is away the majority of the time, so we had what amounted to a small matriarchy on our hands. That, combined with my desire to "rescue" the unhappy children of the world, was leading us into a very common trap in child care. We had let's-make-believe-we're-a-family care, instead of helpful, healing group care.

In an effort to lend structure and security to the children's lives, we had made rules for everything: bedtime, bath time, laundry time, play time, etc. Rules were coming out our ears, and they were good and logical rules, too; I know, because I made them. And that is exactly the point; I made them alone, not together with the group. One thing was certain; everyone knew exactly what was expected of him, but no one seemed willing to comply. So my next step was to devise all sorts of consequences, most of which were meaningless and never worked. An example of that would be the time a nine-year-old cussed me out rather colorfully. As that was, of course, against the rules, I sat him down to write one hundred times, "I will talk to Mrs. Perry in a respectful manner." Since he was having trouble with cursive writing, I thought the punishment was particularly apt. He busily began writing, and the result was, one hundred times, "Mrs. Perry, go to hell." Lesson learned.

# In the Area of Group Living

With the system we then had, discipline for the whole group had become an increasing problem. The children were challenging every rule we had, and most of the issues were not important enough to warrant the ensuing battle. We had become trapped in a crime-and-punishment cycle with me the judge, jury, and executioner, and none of us liked it.

So, when I began to learn about the business of group dynamics, and how group process could make life in the cottage more meaningful for all of us, I resolved to try it.

The first step was to call the group together. There, at our first meeting, we talked about what it would mean to begin governing ourselves. Many were too afraid of the responsibility, and voiced the opinion that things were just fine as they were, but luckily we had a few with more independent spirits that latched onto the idea readily, and gradually convinced the others of the benefits.

In the next few meetings, we spent the greater part of our time airing petty grievances and solving puzzling mysteries, such as who stole the last box of cookies out of the pantry. I became confused about my own role and gave up too much authority with some chaotic sessions resulting.

Soon I got the idea of exercising some control of our group time and planting the seeds of ideas, so that the children were making some decisions, but with proper guidance. One of these early meetings was in late November. I gave a rundown of the activites being offered to us by the community that Christmas; then I threw out the notion that it must make people feel very good to do something special for us. Since no one took the bait, the assistant houseparent went a step further and said, "Do you think we would enjoy doing something for someone else this Christmas?"

There followed an enthusiastic response that later resulted in a decision to give a party for some retarded children from a nearby center. One of the boys suggested we have them come to our cottage for refreshments, and then we would all go to the gym to play. Even though we had planted the seed, the children nurtured it and worked to make the idea successful. The next several meetings were spent planning and volunteering for certain duties. Two nine-year-old boys said they would take care of refreshments, giving me a few pretty anxious moments, but as Christmas neared I saw how they intended to solve their acute money problem. As area churches began donating fruit, candy, popcorn, and soft drinks, we divided out a portion to be saved for the party.

This small party was a big step for our cottage, for it was the first time we had done anything as a group with full cooperation from everyone, and with each person adamantly against allowing any outsider to participate. It is hard to describe that evening. The patience and interest our youngsters showed to these children was amazing. Even more amazing was the way everyone pitched in and helped clean up the horrendous mess, both at the gym and the cottage. But most important was the feeling in the air of being needed and trusted by others, and being worthy of that trust.

As the group gained strength, our meetings became more productive and spontaneous; I learned a better balance between the children and myself, with me as a guiding force and influential member of the group with greater ability to compromise. We were tending to cottage business and talking on the surface of each student's needs and goals. At the same time, several strong subgroups were forming, easily combining into a whole that was very close-knit. But, good as it was, I knew we had a long way to go, and I was impatient to get on to bigger and better things. Yet, each time I tried to move our group conversations on to a discussion of feelings, I met with silence. We just had not arrived at that point yet.

In early February, we had several changes in group makeup. Most notable was the addition of a new adolescent girl, whom we brought to the campus with careful planning. First, we sat down as a group and, without violating her privacy with the intimate details, we went over her case and discussed ways we could help her. Before she made her preliminary visits to the campus, her social worker took me on a home visit, where we shared pictures of those living in the cottage and told something of interest about each one.

Bringing a new person into a group so solidly knit is

difficult at best, and so even with the forethought we gave to it, this new child suffered greatly. Initially, she had demonstrated some bizarre behavior patterns, setting herself up to be avoided. None of the girls would volunteer to be her roomate, so I was forced into arbitrarily deciding where she would room. When she came to stay, the girls made an effort to be civil, but this quickly diminished until finally she became the cottage scapegoat. The children found her weakest points and jabbed at them constantly, causing tremendous turmoil in the cottage.

We continued to have fairly good group meetings, now delving a little into feelings and slowly beginning to help each other, but still this one child was excluded.

I became extremely frustrated with the situation, for I wanted them to solve it, rather than me, but as one man said "Don't get discouraged; it's often the last key in the bunch that opens the lock." Soon we had a meeting that was worth having waited for.

We began that evening by talking about the fact that four of our nine children would be leaving in about six weeks. We decided to go around the room and let everyone in the group evaluate the progress these departing four and the remaining ones had made.

The first child was enthusiastic about her accomplishments. She no longer felt it necessary to run when troubles came, dealt less in dope, and had cut down almost completely on a very big shoplifting habit. The next girl said she got along better with others, did her schoolwork some of the time, and worked on her appearance more than ever. One little fellow said he wasn't so grouchy any more, and didn't feel so shy. Our messiest boy proudly pointed out how much better his room looked, and how he was improving at controlling his temper. All of these changes were relative, of course, but it was thrilling to hear the excitement in their voices. Soon everyone was shouting out good things about each other, making sure that nothing was left out—things like "so-and-so doesn't hate her mother any more," and this one cries now instead of holding it all in, while that one cries less, showing more control.

During all this pandemonium, our newest child sat quietly

watching. I asked her what she felt she had accomplished, and before she could begin, the other children started ridiculing her. She let it go for a few seconds, and then said, "I have something to say." They all quieted and waited expectantly, ready to pounce on her the minute she was through. She then covered her face with her hands and said, "I hate my mama, I hate Juanita, I hate this place, and I hate every damn one of you." The quiet deliberateness she gave this statement made it all the more forceful, and stunned the whole group into silence. We waited a moment, and I asked if anyone else had felt the same way. The vigorous yesses and the supportive advice they began to give her made her look up. At that point, one child sat up a little straighter and said, "Hey! I know something you've accomplished! You've never been able to show your anger before without throwing things around or screaming your head off, but this time you did it just right!" Finally we were a complete group.

From that time, our group meetings were helpful times of sharing anxieties, problems, and joys. We were all able to recognize that certain youngsters did not feel free to talk out their problems with me or their social worker, so they talked with other young people in the cottage. One particularly good example would be a thirteen-year-old and eleven-year-old who were roommates. Both girls had had severe communication problems with their mothers. As the thirteen-year-old arrived closer to a place of understanding her mother, she began helping the eleven-year-old. Once the younger girl was given a book by her social worker titled *Dealing with Parents*,[30] and after she read it, she passed it on to the older. This intense, mutual understanding and interdependence could not have happened between myself and either girl, and so this was my first proof that the child's success in group care depends on his relationship with the group, not with the adult.

Another interesting development at about this time was the children's awareness of the negative power of group pressure. This was beautifully learned from an incident one night

30. Jonah Kalb and David Viscott, *What Every Kid Should Know about Dealing with Parents* (Cleveland: American Greetings Corporation, 1974).

after dinner. One boy and girl got into a minor squabble and moved on into name calling and shouted threats. I sent them outside to handle their differences when they got too loud. As I watched from inside the screened porch, out of their sight, it became obvious that neither one was angry enough for violence, but the group was egging them on to fight. They circled round and round in the yard, never taking their eyes off each other. The entire cottage group was instructing the smaller boy to go ahead and beat the older girl, whom they judged to be in the wrong. Soon it progressed to fisticuffs and a bloody nose. Since he was nine and she was fourteen, I was tempted to step in, but coming to the rescue of this particular boy would have made him feel humiliated. He suddenly saw me through the screen and hit on an out for himself. By picking up a broken bottle and threatening her with it, he knew I would have to step in, which I did.

My mind was swimming, making an effort to think of a way to help them all see what had happened. No one made an attempt to leave, so I sat down on the porch with them and asked the two fighters if either one felt that anything had been accomplished. Both said not. I proposed that if they were angry enough to fight, they could use the punching bag. We all watched them throw a few feeble punches, and then our oldest girl, sixteen, got the point.

"They aren't really angry," she said. "We made them fight for our own satisfaction." Others chimed in, and the two boxers saw how they had yielded to group pressure when it would have been better to stand alone to make their own decision. This point was all the more emphatic because they came up with it themselves, never noticing that I had led them into it. This was far more effective than if I had gone out the door, stopped the fight, and lectured the group.

A few days later, we had a group meeting with the main purpose of evaluating our group as a whole. We discussed what a leader was, a follower, isolate, scapegoat, etc., then tried to come up with what our group looked like. The resulting sociogram showed a group with three strong subgroups, one main leader with another in close running, some very strong mutual dependencies, and some very one-sided relationships, particularly with the main leader. The diagram we drew up follows:

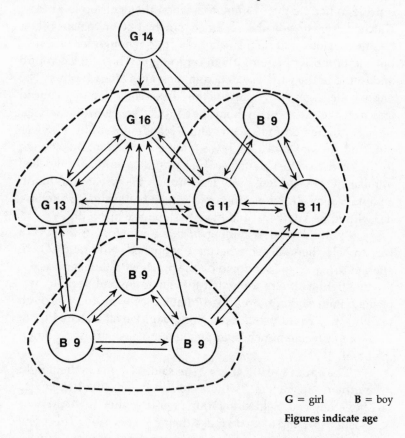

G = girl    B = boy

**Figures indicate age**

In the late spring we planned a trip together to Washington, D.C. This was to be our big final event together, for our group was going to change drastically when school let out. The group planned and schemed until all the details were settled, and off we went. The first few days were joyous. All the film was used, and most of the spending money spent before we got there, but each person was making the best of it. Then, as the group got tired and hot, and nerves were getting frayed, it was interesting to note just how much abuse they were willing to take from each other. Petty bickering would start, but unlike the way it usually went back home, it would stop before any big blow-ups occurred. It was obvious that because we were 450 miles from home and totally dependent on each other, all of us were making a valiant attempt at self-control. We had only one day out of the eight that was bad, and we made a deal to forget it—to scratch Thursday from the trip. An indication of the great effort they had put into being on best behavior came when our youngest, on the way back home, asked sweetly, "When we get back to Charlotte, can we cuss and fight again?"

We learned a great deal on this trip, notably that there are times when we can control our impulses and tempers, which was hard for some to believe of themselves, and that there is a unique comfort in being home, where we can be ourselves, bare our hostilities and faults, and not be afraid others will stop liking us.

After our return, there were just two weeks left for us to get ready for four of the children to leave. Wisely, some started early in the process of separation. We saw a breakdown of the intimate relationship we had shared, and became a looser group. Our farewell party was the perfect ending to a long and difficult year together. We had decorated the den lavishly with crepe paper and balloons and had purchased some silly little hats and horns. At about seven o'clock, the whole cottage went to the grocery store, and the kids went wild. We bought some of every fruit and fruit sherbet they had. When we returned to the cottage, we mixed a really weird punch, fixed the fruit on the table, and passed out some gifts. The noise level was incredible, but shortly we moved into a quieter time. Each person took a turn telling a joke or story, or showing off in some other way, then we went down for a midnight swim at the pool. All of this went without any sign of the sadness I knew some of them felt at the loss of their friends. We returned to the cottage, and all nine children wanted to have a slumber party. It was the last night we would all be together. The next morning I walked out and found them all huddled together on the floor, arms and legs intertwined, sharing two or three blankets among all of them, some lying in a crunch of pilfered cereal. I was part of the group, and they did depend on me for certain things, but I could never be a part of the oneness pictured so beautifully on our den floor.

The story I have shared with you is not intended to give you a picture of a perfect cottage, for that we were a long way from becoming. But it is a picture of children with many emotional weaknesses, who still, if we give them a chance and trust them to have some common sense, can share their many strengths.

When we take children into group care and try to do all the work ourselves, we run into innumerable frustrations and few joys. But when we tap the power that lies within the group, we lessen those frustrations, increase the joys a hundredfold, and are able to send out youngsters who have progressed from dependence to independence, and on to a higher level of human achievement, interdependence.

# ❧❧E

# In the Area of Counseling

## 13❧ Communicating with Children and Young People

*A paper given as one of a series of four Sutherland Self-Help Lectures, Christchurch, New Zealand, 1974*

ALAN KEITH-LUCAS

The person who genuinely wants to communicate with a child or young person—that is, to understand what he or she is feeling or saying and respond appropriately to it—has at least five general problems to overcome. To these can be added, more specifically, a sixth—that many of the children or young people with whom we want to communicate most are already suspicious of adults, partly (but not wholly) because adults' attempts to communicate with them in the past have been clumsy and unproductive.

The first and perhaps most obvious problem, particularly with younger children, is that of disparity in size. Communication is greatly enhanced if it can be on an eye-to-eye level, yet many adults will remain standing when talking to a child and force the child either to crane his neck upwards or to look elsewhere. Small children have even expressed their discomfort in finding that if they kept their eyes level they were observing the one part of an adult's body that they had always been told not to look at. The person who towers over another person inevitably projects an image of dominance and distance. The first rule in talking with children is to get on their level by stooping, or sitting, or, even better, squatting or sitting on the floor.

The second problem has to do with the child's mode of communication. Adults rely almost exclusively on words to convey meaning. They may emphasize their words with gestures, or consciously use certain tones of voice, but words are their principal concern. The child relies much more largely on what is called body language—the way one sits, or holds one's hands, or purses or doesn't purse one's mouth. The preverbal child relies on these signals entirely. The older child uses words but still gets most of his signals from body language. Even teenagers have become very suspicious of words, with some justification, for increasingly in today's world words are being used to conceal feelings, or hide the truth, more than they are to reveal either of them. The Vietnam war provided many examples—the word "liberate" was used to mean "to destroy" and a "protective reaction" meant a punitive raid on civilians.

This fact accounts for two traits of children that many people have observed. One is the frequent futility of preaching morals to them or trying to convince them by verbal arguments. The child rarely follows the logic of our discourse. He is much more interested in how we are talking than in what we are talking about, and he may miss the whole point of the latter.

The other is children's supposed "sixth sense" in detecting when adults are insincere or lying to them. We often say, "You can't fool a child." This is no mysterious or parapsychological gift. It is simply that the child is observing not the words but the accompanying body language, which may be telling an entirely different story.

Children, too, put a great value on confirmatory symbols. A bargain sealed with a kiss or a handshake, according to age, is far more solemn and unbreakable than one that remains purely verbal. Here we have something of an equivalent of the written contract between adults which also carries some aura of greater solemnity and commitment.

Physical nearness or distance also means much to a child. So does actual physical contact. Sometimes an arm around a child is the only way one can convey a sense of support or empathy. In general it is a good rule, when talking to a child, to leave a passage open so that he can touch you or be touched if he wants to. Do not put a desk between you, unless your purpose is not to communicate with him but to control or constrain him. Most young children and some older ones need far more touching than they get. But here again body language—the child's—is important. It is essential to be able to know when the child invites you to touch him and when he or she has had enough and wants to be free again, just as it is important to be able to distinguish, particularly with older youngsters, when touching stops being a request for reassurance or comfort and becomes seduction or aggression. The clues lie not in words but in tense or relaxed muscles, in voice tones, even in heartbeats.

A third problem, more difficult, perhaps, for most adults to solve is the rules of conversation that society imposes on adult-child conversations. It is almost like playing a game under two sets of rules, one for each side. The players must call each other by different parts of their name and children often append some title of respect such as "Sir" or "Ma'am," and this alone makes it hard to talk on equal terms. Involved here is the whole matter of mutual respect. While I am not advocating that children call adults by their first names, adults too often inject demands for respectful titles into the child's every statement, while at the same time feeling free to deny the child even the dignity of a name. This is particularly true in referring to the child or his friends. While he is forbidden to refer to adults as "he" or "that man," he hears himself described as "this little boy" or "that one there."

More important still is the fact that adults are permitted two important licenses that children do not enjoy. An adult considers himself free to criticize a child's dress, or physical attitude, or cleanliness, simply by virtue of being an adult and despite the absence of any responsibility on his part for any of these things. The child can be told to sit up, to wash his hands, to "look me in the face," or to stop smiling. Yet it would cause considerable question if the child reciprocated in kind.

Even worse, from the child's point of view, is the adult's license to ask personal questions, to know the child's age, his school grade, his progress in school, and the reasons for his actions. One of the most frequent questions adults ask children is, "How are you doing in school?" Apart from the fact that this is one of the least productive questions one can ask, for a child to ask an adult how he is doing on his job would seem, to most people, highly impertinent.

Still more fruitless, for the most part, is asking a child, or indeed anyone, why they behave as they do. "Why" is an aggressive word, inviting fanciful justifications. Moreover, it looks to the past and not to the future. And it is something the asker wants to find out, not something the child himself is interested in. Nor, despite some counseling theory, are reasons necessary for coping with behavior problems. Quite apart from the fact that human motivation is generally far too complex to be reduced to simple reasons, the kind of knowledge one is likely to be able to state about one's own actions is so subject to projections, rationalizations, and blocks that it is of little help. It is sometimes good to ask a child if he has any idea why he acts as he does, but not to demand his reasons.

Closely allied to the question of different rules is the inability of many adults to permit children to express two very natural and indeed common emotions, anger and grief. The immediate impulse of most adults is to placate the angry child and reassure the grieving one. The reasons behind this double denial are, one might suggest, a combination of problems number four and five—that is, our preconceptions about childhood and our need to project certain images of ourselves, or of adults, in our dealings with children.

The two most serious misconceptions about childhood are that a child's emotions are transitory and not significant, and, by inference, that what he says and does is "childish prattle" or "play," that he is basically a helpless individual who needs protection from anything harsh or unpleasant. The first gives rise to statements such as, "He will soon forget," "He's too young to understand," or, perhaps worse than any, "He's only doing it for attention," as if to get some attention is not a major human need. Yet all the developmental knowledge we have suggests that a child's emotions are, if anything, more poignant and more lasting in their effect than are adult ones, and that "getting over it" often means repressing the experience, only to have it recrudesce later or to have to drag it from the subconscious before the child can deal with it. Examination of both childish prattle and play also reveals that much of it is extremely purposeful if we would but pay attention to it or learn its language.

What is really at stake here is the child's right to be taken seriously, to be treated as someone with something to say about himself or his environment. As a fifteen-year-old wrote to one of our consultants recently, "What made you so different from most grown-ups was that you seemed to think that what I said was important." Love hurts just as much and probably more at eleven than it does at twenty-one. Death is far more frightening.

The illusion that children cannot face the truth and should be protected from it, and need to live in a world where unpleasant things never happen, or are at least never mentioned, is generally more an accommodation to the adult's fear of having an angry or grieving child on his hands, than it is to the child's real ability to face the truth. Children are, on the whole, very realistic people and it is remarkable how much reality they can endure. Indeed, from observation of practice, I would be hard put to identify any instance in which a child was seriously or in any way permanently scarred by being asked to face the truth about his situation. A great many children have suffered, however, because some nice kind person decided to shield them from the impact of the truth or offered them false reassurance.

Involved here are two principles. The first is that not to know is far harder to bear than to know; the imagined is nearly always worse than the truth. And the second is our fear of a child's becoming "disturbed." Much of what we label "disturbed," with the implicit implication that it is an unhealthy state that somehow has to be alleviated, can be seen more realistically as the child's attempt to overcome a problem. There is real wisdom in the statement of a thirteen-year-old girl who was "disturbed" every time her mother visited, and whom the Home wanted to protect by severely limiting the disturbance-creating visits: "What you don't understand is that this is something I need to get disturbed about."

Our need to project certain images of ourselves or of adults is the fifth obstacle to overcome. The image is not entirely consistent but it usually comprises the elements of rectitude, omniscience, and kindliness. Some people keep a special, sweet voice for talking to children that is recognized by the children as wholly false. It projects a world without anger or dislike in which conditions are always ideal and is a big factor in convincing children that adults are in a conspiracy to cover up the world's unpleasantness. It also tends to glorify the status quo and the world's institutions as they are presently constituted—the church, the school, or the economic system. Adults, in presenting themselves as models of rectitude, also minimize temptations. In "setting a good example" for children they give the impression that good behavior is something easy to attain. There are, of course, good examples that anyone would want to set before children—forgiveness, honesty, perhaps, and courage, especially when these are being demanded of the child. But not to identify with and even enjoy a child's occasional acts of rebellion, or even some of his more scatological interests (providing one is oneself amused by them) is to refuse to enter into the child's world at all. We still suffer from the dichotomous illusion that children are innocent and therefore easily led astray and at the same time basically evil and therefore looking for the least indication of adult permissiveness that will allow them to behave badly. One does not want or need to act like a child or identify with behavior that is likely to become exaggerated or harmful to recognize that we all enjoy and have experienced occasional relaxations from a constant demand for good behavior.

The image of oneself as omniscient, and often omnicompetent, too, is one that many adults would like to maintain. This commonly finds expression in the fear that things "will get out of control" if we do not manage an interview or a group. We also seem to fear that children will lose their trust in adults if they do not have an answer or if the answer is not right. Yet children are often brought near to despair by the knowledge and control of adults. It is often a real asset to the child's image of himself if there are some areas in which an adult is perhaps deliberately ignorant or incompetent. One experience with children illustrated for me the hostility first-graders were experiencing towards a world in which there was so much to learn. Driving a car pool of first-grade children, I maintained a stubborn belief that two and two made five. The children's almost ecstatic pleasure in discovering, even in fantasy, a person who was more stupid than they, and the degree of their also fantasized hostility (which included the most sadistic sanctions such as disembowelment) convinced me of their need to find some antidote to their helplessness.

In the long run, then, communicating with children becomes a matter of respecting them as persons and allowing them to be themselves without constantly regarding them as objects to whom we must always be doing something—towering over them, talking at them, protecting, educating, criticizing, correcting, controlling, or telling them how to feel. This does not mean that education, limits to behavior, example, and even correction are not important, in their place. It is a plea that these necessary things (of which children in institutions usually get enough) not be allowed to permeate all our contacts with them, especially those in which we are trying to learn how they as persons are experiencing life. To use Martin Buber's terms, adults rarely meet or treat children as "Thou" rather than as "it."

## 14❧ Adult Nonverbal Communication with Children

*From a workshop held at the Chapel Hill*
*Workshops, 1972, week 1*

EUGENE WATSON

The development of interpersonal communication skills for staff members in a variety of agencies and institutions working with children has been a continuing commitment of a team in the School of Education at the University of North Carolina at Chapel Hill.

In order to better understand messages that are communicated, the team has worked in public schools with children who are considered to be model children and those considered to be problem children. They have worked with children who are responding to this society in what are labelled as emotionally disturbed modes. In the various settings, team members gradually built trust relationships with some of these children, who ranged in age from early childhood to early adolescence. With a degree of trust established, the children have told the team about behaviors which teachers, administrators, and adults in other positions of authority consistently exhibit that children do not usually speak about, but which are causing problems. The team has found that much of their information from children is about adult nonverbal behavior. Drawing upon that information and several recent publications, the focus here will be upon some basic types of nonverbal behavior and concerns that an adult perhaps should have in regard to his or her nonverbal communication with children.

A discussion of nonverbal behavior and what it may communicate should include not only implications of movement of some part of one's body that children might view and interpret, but also the lack of movement. It also includes how one dresses, which communicates a great deal to some children and adults. In particular, it seems important to consider how one locates himself or herself spatially (proxemics) in relation to children.

There appears to be general agreement among people who are studying human behavior that as much as 90 percent of the messages that people receive are nonverbal. We continuously send potential nonverbal messages, consciously and unconsciously. Ponder that fact in the light of our awareness that many children virtually are begging for information from us and constantly are reading our nonverbal behavior, the behavior over which we have little control. It is possible that most responses of children to us are related to our nonverbal behavior.

As a society, we are somewhat nonverbally illiterate. We have conditioned ourselves to avoid conscious use of our bodies to communicate, especially in professional settings. We try to delude ourselves into thinking that if we do not consciously allow our bodies to communicate—that if we use the spoken or written word—we are being very professional. Yet, we constantly are reading and interpreting the nonverbal behavior of others. We work under the illusion that while another party is sending a wave of nonverbal messages to us which we are interpreting, we are not doing the same in return. Most of us consider ourselves somewhat adept at interpreting nonverbal behavior and spend much time doing so, but are not competent in consciously using our own nonverbal behavior to amplify what we want to say, especially to children. Recently, Rudolph Arnheim, in an article related to his latest book, called us (and this is a generalized "us") the "generation that has lost its senses."[31] We have lost our senses largely because of a preoccupation with the written and spoken word.

In observing teachers and school administrators, it appears that their behavior in the presence of children is often almost that of a robot. However, when they go into the teachers' lounge they become animated, remarkably more animated when they are with their peers than when they are with children. There appears to be a belief that if a person is animated, he or she will lose something in the setting that will make him or her less effective in dealing with children.

In contrast to the reservations so many of us have in using our bodies in the presence of children to try to convey the honest

31. Rudolph Arnheim, *Toward a Psychology of Art* (Los Angeles: University of Southern California, 1972).

messages that they are seeking, children have the capability of using their bodies consciously as sensory equipment. They have not only the capability but often a tremendous drive to use their bodies, until we train them very carefully not to do so. That is accomplished, basically, by late adolescence. We train them not to use their bodies in an expressive sense. They are burdened with strictures and structures, and have muscles that do not respond freely any more because an uninhibited response level is not rewarded in our society. Keep in mind that the child's nonverbal communicative efforts in the earliest years were the basis of his or her first decisions about the nature of trust, affection, and security in this world, including exploring with the hands, rubbing against the mother, feeling the mother's closeness, and grabbing objects. The processing of nonverbal information was the starting point, basically, for trust decisions and it had impact on other decisions the child made or now makes about this world. Yet, some of us work diligently within the child's first fifteen years to limit the use of the equipment from which was derived basic information for dealing with this world.

The interpersonal need theory of William Schutz is helpful in categorizing pressing interpersonal needs to which children seek responses at the nonverbal level as well as the verbal level.[32] Those categories are:

*Inclusion*—in other words, "Do I belong?" "Am I a part of this setting?" "Do I have a continuing relationship with one or several people?"

*Control*—"Do I have some freedom, or don't I?" "Am I supposed to do only as bidden?" "Am I to look constantly for cues as to what is expected of me and always be fearful if I don't get those cues?"

*Affection*—Children constantly are seeking granules of affection. A child starving for affection would like to interpret a casual glance or extended arms as a small token of affection, a movement toward the child. Inclusion, control, and affection are three areas of overwhelming importance to children.

32. William C. Schutz, *The Interpersonal World* (Palo Alto: Science and Behavior Books, Inc., 1966).

# In the Area of Counseling

In considering inclusion, we must emphasize the eyes. Probably most people are tired of the cliché about making good eye contact, but it appears crucial for children to develop the ability to maintain eye contact in our society. One thing the team has been told is that some adults who insist that children make good eye contact also threaten the children through their own staring tendencies. Yet, a person probably cannot receive accurate messages unless he or she is looking frequently at the communicator. When the team goes into public schools, they often watch the principal walk through the halls. Frequently they see him stop and talk with a child. He is trying to be friendly and available. In response, the child often turns his or her head away. This happens most frequently along racial lines. The white principal comes along and the black child turns away. White children often turn away from black principals. They will not make good eye contact. The trust situation remains negative, partly because of the failure to establish and maintain good eye contact.

It is somewhat surprising to find how much some children seem to depend upon the hands for nonverbal cues. It is so easy to extend one's hands and bring people towards one, without even having to come into close proximity with them. One too often displays folded arms, which is a closing-out kind of behavior. It appears defensive, and in a sense offensive, but it also hides one's hands. The hands probably have even more meaning for children, in terms of stroking and loving, than for adults.

Space also becomes an inclusion factor. Some of us are very uncomfortable about getting close to other people, unless there is a contract between us. If one gets within three feet of another person and stands there for several minutes, one is likely to have the impulse either to hug or hit that person. Some writers think such an impulse comes from our animal origins. This can be observed when people get within three feet of one another; watch the arms of at least one participant cross in front. Some questions occur: "Is he afraid of me?" "Do I make him tense?" "Why does he have to ward me off?" Other people put their hands behind their backs and seem to say, "Go ahead and approach me; I'm not afraid." Something about our priorities for the hands dictates that they be seen if relationships are to be considered satisfactory.

In the realm of space, relative heights are important. It is difficult for us to remember how we felt when we were much shorter than the adults around us. Small children frequently have to deal with adults who maintain full, erect posture when interacting with the child. Consider control aspects of that situation for the child—constantly having to look up as one talks, having to appeal to a "higher" source, and trying to make one's message as important "going up" as the adult's message is "coming down." Sometimes children find themselves staring at an adult's genitals or staring right into the breasts. Some of us tell children, directly or indirectly, that they should avoid staring at those regions of the body. The alternatives for the child are to make certain that he or she looks up all the time, which is uncomfortable, or to look away. Keep in mind that the child is, in a sense, in double jeopardy. He or she cannot maintain the eye contact very well, yet cannot continue staring at forbidden areas.

Many of us think it is an affectionate gesture to pat a child on the head as he or she is talking, even when he or she is talking about something very serious. Some children say that this feels more like being beaten about the head and shoulders. Some of the frailer ones say, "You should feel those big paws. I get beaten on the head." Adults seem to like to pull ears or pinch noses. Many—if not all—children hate that. Yet, it is being done today even with children who are in early adolescence. Patting on the head, pinching the nose, and pulling the ears are supposed to be signs of affection, but are often interpreted as signs of aggression.

One simple thing that could be done by adults to avoid some of the above problems and to demonstrate that they are trying to make themselves available is never to carry on a conversation with a child without getting down approximately to his or her eye level. This may frighten him or her at first, because he or she is not used to it, but it may encourage the child to try to maintain good eye contact with adults. When one gets down to the child's eye level, one seems to be saying, "You are worth my being fully available to you." This may help convince the child that you are available psychologically.

Again, all of the preceding points do not hold true for all children, but they are of concern to enough children that we should devote more time to the study of our own nonverbal behavior and its impact on children with whom we attempt to relate. This is especially important for those working with children who have recognizable handicaps or deprivations.

## 15 The Child Care Worker as Counselor and Problem Solver

*From a workshop held at the Chapel Hill Workshops, 1973, week 1*

RAYMOND FANT, *Consultant*
JANET WEDEBROOK, STEVE BAXTER, TIM NICHOLS, *Writing Committee*

Many child care workers have great difficulty describing what they do that is skillful. Breaking down vague generalizations such as "Well, I show them respect," or "Relating is the most important skill in my agency," is essential if child care workers are to be helped to respond in an optimally productive manner. What skills go into forming a positive adult-child relationship? The following skills are suggested as important:

*Listening*—the ability to give full undivided attention to a child who is attempting to verbalize his feelings. Establishing eye contact during the listening process is essential.

*Empathizing*—"getting in the child's skin," letting the child know you are aware of his pain and what he is going through.

*Doing the unexpected*—catching a child off guard in order to cut through defensive mechanisms that have served to keep people away; risking; action rather than reaction.

*Setting limits*—protecting the child from potentially unsafe, unhealthy, immoral situations; saying "No" and meaning it; establishing external controls when the child cannot.

*Curiosity*—letting the child know you want to know more about what is going on through respectful probing, reaching, e.g., "I wonder if . . ."

*Reaching for the negative*—through appropriate questioning trying to reach for hidden feelings or agendas.

*Weather-making*—creating a climate conducive to the task at hand; setting a tone, a mood.

*Postmortem*—taking the initiative to get back to a child after an unpleasant encounter; reviewing the encounter; playing out the alternatives, and reestablishing communication with the child.

*Avoidance of the battle of the wills*—realizing you never win such a battle; presenting and clarifying alternatives to the young person and making a deliberate effort to get out of such a battle; distancing yourself; avoiding pulling rank; putting the problem back on the child; acknowledging with him when you feel the battle is beginning.

*Touching base with oneself*—getting in touch with your own feelings; being aware at that moment what you are feeling; acknowledging your feelings.

*Distancing*—the ability not to take personally a child's behavior or reacting; not overidentifying with the child.

*Modeling*—allowing the child to observe you in a number of different situations, to see how you handle these events as an adult; conveying values through actions; presenting a positive adult life-style and image.

*Decoding*—the ability to decipher the verbal and nonverbal behavior of a child; to interpret what the child is really saying in his own often pathetic way; picking up clues; asking yourself, "What is really happening here?"

# ᎒᎒F

# In the Area of Therapy

16᎒ Integrating Psychotherapy into the Services
of a Children's Home

JOHN Y. POWELL

A violent thunderstorm toppled the historic weathered wooden
cross from St. Mary's Chapel on the abandoned grounds of
Thompson Orphanage. It was rescued and now stands proudly
by the door of the administration building on the modern campus
of Thompson Children's Home. The old cross's durability symbolizes in many ways the church's continuing need over the years
to serve children and families who are in trouble. The acceptance
of that cross in its new home suggests that we must keep the
reason for our existence ever before us yet adapting methods as
we pursue excellence in service.

When Thompson was organized in 1887 there was a need
for long-term orphanage care. Out of this tradition a paternalistic
child-centered philosophy emerged, and until recently it lingered
as a hidden, guiding force. Today we are called upon to serve
families in trouble because of emotional problems, divorce, alcoholism, or perhaps something as simple as being unable to
cope with modern stresses of life in the 1970s. Our focus has

changed from being child-centered to being family-centered as we involve parents from the beginning even if they are in prison, or have been written off by the community as unfit. However, most of our parents are ordinary people who are good citizens in the community and have become overwhelmed and unable to function adequately as a family. A divorced mother of a teenaged girl recently told us, "Coming here was like having a new start— getting away from the daily fights and the tensions has given both of us a chance to think things out in a new way." Both the girl and her mother have made a new beginning and are planning to resume their life together at the end of the school year.

Before any discussion is begun about placement of a child outside his home, we help the families to ask these questions: "What is our situation? What are the alternatives available to us? Are other resources more relevant to our needs? What is your help like? Can we use your help?" This initial exploration with families is in effect crisis intervention. If the family and the social worker feel that placement in one of our residential programs should be considered, the family's request is referred to a planning committee of our agency. The decision may be for the family to enter into a helping process with a direct service unit, to refer the family to a more appropriate agency, or to offer counseling while the child functions in his own home.

Regardless of where a child may be placed—campus, group home, or foster home—we help both the parent and child to set goals for placement. Periodically, every three to six months, we have a review of those goals to determine our progress. Are we, the professionals, providing the kind of support that we promised in the beginning? Has the family moved toward the goals identified in the written contract which charted the purpose of placement? Has the child begun to deal with his problems so that he might return home with a better way of performing in school, in the community, and at home? These are the questions and plans that we make with people. We have been pleasantly astonished with the results. Placements are now a part of a helping process. Families feel that they can handle and are given some choices for self-determination. Our entire staff, not only our social workers, is family-oriented and involved in helping both parent and child to learn new ways of coping with life. While many imperfections are still present in our planning with families, we believe that we are proceeding in the right direction. Both parents and children seem generally to know why they have sought help from us and what point they have reached in the helping process. They understand that we are planning together for the time when Thompson is not needed or when our help will be inappropriate. Planning with families is built upon a family-centered approach, a goal-oriented process, and reality testing of these goals.

In the 1970s the number of emotionally damaged and troubled children referred to us is increasing. Unlike our growth in working with families, our work with disturbed children became an increasing burden. The threats or crime-and-punishment approaches of the past no longer would do. Simple solutions and gimmicks had a hollow ring as we began to recognize the trauma and emptiness of the newly referred children. Some early success with a few disturbed children increased our referrals and put even more pressure on our already overtaxed staff.

Our weakness was in providing appropriate group care and therapy for disturbed children. However, we could not, as a multifunction, family-service agency, fail to offer services to children who are troubled in themselves as well as in their relationships with their families. Not all the children we see can be so described, but an increasing number could.

Our child caring staff members were uncertain of their ability to meet the needs of disturbed children in the cottages. Professional staff felt unsure in assessing the degree of disturbance in many children. With this self-doubt, we sought the services of a psychiatric consultant. The consultant began more than two years ago with consultation of only a few hours per week. His work has since developed into an integral part of our program encompassing one day weekly.

In retrospect our involvement with a psychiatric consultant was characterized by ambivalence which is generic to any process of change. I knew we had to change to meet the needs of more disturbed children, but I had a strong resistance to our becoming a typical psychiatric facility. It seemed that we ought to be able to combine the best of family-oriented work and psychotherapy. Some programs have developed fine psychotherapeutic help for children only to ignore the families, and others have placed an overreliance on the professionals' judgement about the patients' symptoms. I personally like the idea of Thompson's being chiefly a family-service agency. This means that we are serving clients in a way that recognizes that they have something important to say about themselves. If we are not careful, it is possible to slip back into the old orphanage days, with the superintendent as a substitute parent who wishes to perpetuate care as a benevolent autocrat. We needed to move from thinking of the children as patients or as being ours with controlling and permanent relationships over them. I had a rather stereotyped view of the psychiatrist as having the last word. At Thompson I had dreams of our doing things differently, and perhaps in my subconscious mind I was afraid that our psychiatrist might direct us toward a medical model. If this had been the case, the cost of such a program would have relegated us to an inferior quality of service. We could not hope to offer the fine programs that are a part of teaching hospitals. I was afraid for our psychiatrist to dabble in the everyday affairs of Thompson. How much of this thinking reflected my own ego and how much of it arose from a wish to protect a professional theory I believed in, I am not sure. I know both elements were there. Of course, I knew the theory and had helped people through the universal tendency to resist change, but I could not see myself going through this process until later.

In retrospect I can see that I was protecting my own turf and was controlling in my relationships with the psychiatrist. Our psychiatrist continued to be a separate entity and was assigned certain children to see both for evaluation and therapy. We too often expected him to solve behavioral emergencies and to give ready answers to complex situations. Our relationship tended to reach a plateau with our psychiatrist restricted to offering invaluable help to individual children and to staff in crisis situations, but not becoming involved in the agency's program as a whole. Somehow I failed to recognize the extent of his negative feelings about being isolated in that role.

It was not until an open conflict developed that the two of us sat down and talked about the anger and mistrust that each of us felt. There were no final answers, but it did seem that this was a milestone in our relationship. From that time, I have been able to trust him in a new way, not feeling threatened that he was trying to take over my work.

The introduction of psychiatry into a group child care program is a continuing process. Mutual trust is necessary before psychotherapy can truly become a component of child care; it was and continues to be an enriching experience for me, other staff members, and, most importantly, for the families and children we serve.

One historical note needs to be made about change and our general tendency to resist it. Thompson Children's Home, prior to the introduction of social work, was a typical children's institution that offered long-term custodial care. Children felt that they had been adopted by Thompson Ophanage. There was little family involvement and almost no attempt to return children to their homes. Families had to make conscious and deliberate efforts to be involved. The administrator was convinced that more opportunities were available here for children than with their families. This was part of our inherited philosophy in the fantasy that a church Children's Home was better than a "sinful family that had failed." Some twelve years ago social work was introduced to our agency, along with a progressive administration. Social workers positively changed the program. Children were staying for shorter periods of time. Families were welcomed into the process of helping their children. To illustrate that all people resist change, the social work professionals in our agency, like those in other agencies across the nation, came to see themselves as protecting children in a special and unique way. For example, as recently as three years ago, only our "professional staff" read case records. The professional staff was meant to include administrators and social workers. We worked through that phase of our development into one of sharing our records and materials with all staff.

Psychotherapy is a special relationship that can be identified separately from the planning and caring roles of the agency. These three functions are offered to our client system by personnel with differing specialties. Staff in each area of service require special training, with the psychotherapist having the most extensive education and experience. Yet in a helping team all ingredients—caring, planning, and therapy—are mutually dependent if troubled children and their equally upset families are to be helped. The caring person, while he or she may lack the academic background of the therapist or social worker, must have special skills that the therapist or planner may be able to do without. Some therapists admit that they would make poor houseparents. Usually they mean that good houseparents have nurturing abilities that can be sustained over a period of hours or days without long breaks. While the roles cannot be divided so easily in practice, the social worker or planner might be thought of as the person with the road map helping the family and child chart a course through the process of making choices, using help, and breaking away from the helping agency. The caring personnel might be considered the provider of emotional as well as physical nourishment so vital to children who have experienced deprivations, traumas, separations, and uncertainties. They are the ones who provide continuing group and individual process for children while seeing that the basic needs of food, clothing, privacy, comfort, health, play, peer interaction, and individual time for each are provided. The therapist is the special person who can more sharply focus upon the ghostly fears of the past, the uncertainties of the present, and the hope and dreams for the future. Psychotherapy affords an opportunity to heal emotional wounds of the past, to find acceptance of feelings that have been repressed during vital developmental stages, and to go beyond superficial promises of change to basic alterations in one's feelings and self-image. Individually each task—caring, planning, and therapy—is important, but in harmony these elements together multiply the strength that is available to our client system.

Earlier attempts at staff training utilizing our psychiatrist were not successful. Some of the reasons were: (1) the sessions were tightly structured and academic, (2) the staff members at that time were too concerned with their own needs, (3) the administrator was fearful of trusting the psychiatrist, and (4) the agency had not established its own philosophy for its rapidly changing population. From the viewpoint of the consulting psychiatrist, some of the difficulties that need to be overcome are:

1. Staff who react in one of three ways:

a. Those who would regard the psychiatrist as the answer to all the agency's (and sometimes personal) problems.

b. Those who become very defensive and want no part of this "hocus-pocus."

c. Those who adopt a "maybe" or "wait-and-see" attitude.

2. The houseparent who tampers with the child-therapist relationship by:

a. Interrogating the child after individual sessions to find out what was talked about.

b. Viewing the child-therapist relationship as a competitive one and contributing to appointments that are missed by causing "errors" in scheduling.

c. Seeing the therapeutic relationship as an indication that someone feels the houseparent is not doing an effective job; the houseparent thus tries to become an "instant" psychiatrist by holding long, extractive sessions with the child.

d. Misusing general information revealed by the therapist at case conferences by talking openly about it before other children or by confronting the child with such a statement as "Dr. Blank said that you said so and so."

3. The staff member who feels his good ideas are not being heard and who tries to form an alliance or coalition with a consultant in opposition to the administrative offices.

4. The child who feels stigmatized because he is seeing a psychiatrist; he may feel that seeing a psychiatrist means that

"I am crazy." This is reinforced sometimes by other fearful children and unwittingly by staff members.

5. The administrator who asks for ideas but when they are presented has the uneasy feeling that he should have thought of them himself. This sometimes brings about rejection of good ideas or an inordinate delay while the idea becomes ego-syntonic for the administrator.

6. The consultant who oversteps his bounds, trying directly and indirectly to take over some administrative functions, with resulting resentment by administrations and further confusion of staff.

As these points of conflict began to be resolved, another attempt was made to establish ongoing staff training. Our Friday morning coffees began for the campus division and developed into rotating discussions that floated weekly from cottage to cottage. No set agenda was developed. One week the subject might be the rights of children to privacy; the next week we might discuss religious needs and the need for adolescents to rebel against the church. There has developed a nearly unanimous feeling that these sessions have fostered cohesiveness, ventilation of feelings, professional growth, empathy for differing staff functions, and a sense of the needs of troubled children and their families.

While these sessions are not designed as group therapy for staff, they have in some way served that function. Our psychiatrist has not aligned himself with any subgroup, a situation which has enhanced the group's effectiveness. The gap between administrative personnel and child caring staff has lessened as he has held out for the elements in any discussion that may benefit the children and families served by Thompson.

The beginning sessions were times of testing. Would people listen to child caring staff who often feel inferior and ignored? One housemother said that she felt more powerful with our psychiatrist there. Another acknowledged she needed verification that negative feelings and self-doubts were acceptable to our psychiatrist, social workers, and administrative staff. In these sessions, all staff seemed better able to lay aside their various roles and to become freer and more empathetic with one another. No magic or quick solutions have emerged from the several months of experience, but a contagion of hope has developed.

These informal meetings have not directly dealt with psychotherapy or specific details of mental health. However, they have helped to build a foundation for therapy. Our staff has found new ways of observing and interpreting behavior. More attention is given to why certain behavior occurs and how we can helpfully respond rather than making use of the more common "bad and good" philosophy that prevailed in the past. At one time, we were concerned about children's missing appointments with our psychiatrist. This rarely occurs now, and the merging of psychotherapy with total staff may have caused this positive change. The staff's previous fears have subsided. For example, there used to be a fear of revealing incidents that staff members felt reflected unprofessional behavior on their part. Hearing someone else risk himself in telling of an event that was handled poorly has helped inhibited or fearful staff members to feel a comradeship in the complex area of helping troubled people.

Our Friday morning sessions have been limited to the campus team, to maintain the intimacy and sharing that give them vitality. However, we have begun a series of monthly training sessions that encompass the entire multifunction agency. Topics such as theories of child development, emotional health, psychological immunization for children, and needs of adolescents have been selected by this larger group for discussion. These staff training sessions will utilize educators, child caring personnel, social workers, psychiatrists, and others for leadership and discussion.

Psychotherapy has been so well accepted in recent months that children are making self-referrals in addition to the referrals made through staff channels. While social workers carrying the family planning role provide therapy as a part of their job descriptions for the children and parents they serve, our experience indicates that in certain cases a special person not directly aligned to the planning and caring functions of the agency has an advantage as a therapist.

A social worker with extensive experience in psychotherapy has been employed part-time to expand our therapy capacity. Intrastaff referrals are made to these therapists for specialized, time-limited, and intensive help. An example of such a referral is a troubled adolescent who needs to work through his emotional distance from his compulsive parents. By having a therapist who does not work with his overbearing parents, he makes good use of this special relationship. The parents, on the other hand, are helped by the planning social worker to understand the son's growing need for independence.

One problem we are experiencing is in ending psychotherapeutic relationships. With many students needing such services, it is imperative to give help to those who are in greatest need. Frequently at the time when this intensive help is no longer essential, the students desire continued contact with their psychotherapist. We are planning to experiment with an open hour, a special time available to students who wish to drop in to see the therapist without appointment. We shall be interested to observe the number of students who make use of this unscheduled time and how they will choose to use it. Will they come in individually for a few minutes or will an informal group develop among these students?

We chose a psychiatrist specializing in children and adolescents as our first consultant-therapist. It was felt that he would bring both an extensive knowledge of mental and emotional processes and a physician's broad knowledge of physical health. Our expectations have been satisfied. Subtle signs of illnesses are noted and referred to our pediatricians and other specialists. His medical knowledge has been shared with staff in formal and informal ways. For example, he taught a seminar on drug abuse, and we now better understand how certain drugs affect the central nervous system. In a ripple effect, this knowledge was shared by staff with our students and their families. The psychiatrist's knowledge of medicine has proved an asset in numerous situations, for instance in treating an acute hysterical reaction, interpretation of and preparation for medical examinations and procedures, consulting with our pediatricians about psychiatric medications, and screening children for possible neurological examinations.

This two-year account of how psychotherapy has become a vital part of Thompson Children's Home is an unending story. Where are we now? Is psychotherapy a component that is added? In programs that attempt to provide a climate fostering mental health, psychotherapy must become part of the spirit of the agency, with recognition that every individual has both conscious and subconscious mental and feeling processes. While specially trained staff provide therapy, the total staff must be imbued with the art of helping, so that we might get beyond cause and effect to offer a climate in which therapy can flourish.

# 17 ⚘ Three Children and a Family— Some Instances of Psychotherapy
## Douglas Powers, m.d.

The four cases presented below are examples of how psychotherapy may be of assistance to a child or a family in carrying out family plans. The situations are quite different: the children are, in turn, a girl with a very low self-concept, and little ability to control herself; an apparently successful boy who responded to pressure by developing crippling headaches; and a child who was experiencing chronic depression. This third case is particularly interesting in that the child was not actually in care at the time psychotherapy was begun. The fouth case shows the use of the psychotherapist to help a family actualize its desire to be reunited.

All four of these cases are from the files of Thompson Children's Home, Charlotte, North Carolina (see the preceding article "Integrating Psychotherapy into the Services of a Children's Home"). In each case the situation as seen by the administration of the Home is presented in the first paragraph or two, and the psychiatrist's account of the therapy follows. In introducing the material it is assumed that the first and foremost goal of any therapeutic effort in a children's program is to help the child understand as much as possible about himself, the origins of his behavior and the consequences of such behavior; and also to provide him with a setting where he can experiment with and find other methods of relating and other ways of behaving which will be more gratifying and productive for him and will not be destructive of himself or whatever part of the society at large in which he will live eventually.

### Abbie

"I ain't going to live with those honkies," protested fourteen-year-old Abbie to the Department of Social Services. That was two years ago when she and her brothers and sister came to Thompson. Abbie was enuretic, obese, and seemed to think of herself as a black mass without form or meaning. Her brother led a protest against remaining at our agency, but both he and Abbie were frightened of forming relationships here and even more fearful of life away from Thompson. Eventually the brother was helped to complete successfully a survival training program and then to enter a Job Corps camp. Abbie was a part of our effort to help him. She made several trips to the Job Corps Center, and apparently she learned that we had a genuine desire to help. Unfortunately, she lived through several changes in cottage houseparents which compounded the earlier loss of her mother and the trauma of previous placements in foster homes which had failed before she came to Thompson. Prior to psychotherapy Abbie was helped to begin working through the need to live away from her family, to develop some school success, to learn to form relationships with adults, to find ways of compromising and sharing with peers, and to begin planning for her future.

These gains were not enough. It was as if we were helping her to dress up her outward self, only to see deep-seated emotions erupt from the subconscious when she was under stress. She remained emotionally naked and vulnerable.

Abbie's involvement in psychotherapy resulted from the intervention of her capable young housemother, who, along with her social worker, wanted to talk with the psychiatrist about how the housemother could help Abbie.

Reportedly, Abbie had wet her bed every night during her two years of residence; yet she would let no one see her bed or have anything to do with changing the linen. It had been pretty much accepted by the parade of houseparents during this time that no mention was to be made of the problem. To do so resulted in explosive anger and name-calling. The severity of the enuretic problem was later revealed when Abbie asked her housemother if she could possibly have a new mattress. The mattress was decomposed from continual soaking with urine to the extent that she was practically sleeping on the springs. The housemother promptly helped her get rid of the old and replaced it with a new mattress.

Also, Abbie was described as having an uncontrollable, ravenous appetite, with a penchant for sweets and copious quantities of soft drinks before bedtime.

At the conference it was proposed that Abbie be asked if she would visit the psychiatrist, to see whether he could suggest how we could be of help to her. The housemother agreed to propose this to Abbie, but doubted that she would accept it. The same idea had apparently been proposed by other houseparents but had been rejected with a great display of anger.

To everyone's surprise, Abbie agreed and kept her first appointment. She was quite anxious and fearful, but revealed that she had asked a boy who had been involved in therapy for several months what it was like to see a psychiatrist, and he had helped her decide to come. Somewhat hesitantly she agreed to come back the following week and an appointment was made. She kept that and every subsequent appointment.

Early she began verbalizing that she did not like herself and did not know if anyone else really liked her. She talked at length with feeling about the loss of her mother and the feeling of abandonment when her father began living with another woman and the children were sent to various places. She resented the material things which her father provided for the new woman. She worried over whether the many siblings were well cared for.

A great many feelings were expressed, and she said one day, "I have been mad ever since before I came here, and tried to hold it all inside, but it explodes so often."

Nearly six months have passed and several important things have happened with Abbie. She has taken renewed interest in cosmetology, which she is studying in the high school, and will help represent her school in a statewide cosmetology competition. These efforts and interests show every day in her grooming. She has also limited her food intake somewhat, though with difficulty, and has changed her pattern of eating. She now eats breakfast and a moderate lunch and does not gorge herself in the evening.

Her housemother has arranged for herself and Abbie to exercise regularly at a spa. This, with her diet control, has resulted in considerable weight loss which everyone is aware of. At the same time her housemother has gained needed weight on the exercise program.

Arrangements have been made for her to visit her brothers and sisters more frequently, and they have been to see her on campus. On some of the visits she and her sister (also a resident at Thompson) drive an agency car with the older girl at the wheel. One weekend recently she could not go and Abbie went by bus, which she had been afraid to do before.

Now Abbie is working at "getting up enough nerve" to find a part-time job. This girl comments in her sessions with the psychiatrist that she is not nearly so angry as she used to be. She can say that she likes herself much more than she did earlier. Further, her bedwetting has diminished in frequency by half and she has hopes that this will soon disappear.

There has been much progress, but there is still work to be done. But she feels and functions better, and the chronic low image she had of herself has lifted considerably.

## Brock

"Come quick! Brock can't see. He says he's going blind!" was the message from the houseparent. When a supervisor arrived

Brock was staggering about his bedroom gripping his head and moaning. For many years this handsome boy had suffered from migraine headaches. The onset of this attack came as he was being required to move off campus for the summer between his junior and senior years. A few days earlier, he had voluntarily withdrawn from an outdoor survival camping program. If one saw Brock casually, one would think of him in superlatives. He is an outstanding athlete, a fine-looking young man, a dependable and trustworthy person, and a student who is well liked and admired by his peers.

Brock, however, is vulnerable and easily depressed. The details of his early life are cloudy, but his mother gave him up for unofficial adoption at birth. The adoptive mother died when he was five and the adoptive father had been married several times since. The adoptive father has a severe drinking problem, resulting in Brock's being placed here four years ago. These tremendous losses, the ambivalent feeling towards his adoptive father, and the uncertainty of who he is genetically and culturally have created a climate for severe depressions and self-doubt.

The day that Brock became incoherent and unable to see created panic among our staff. He was first taken to our pediatrician, who recommended psychiatric help. Our psychiatrist came and stayed with him throughout the evening. He skillfully helped him back to reality with both verbal and touching responses. From that experience psychotherapy was initiated with Brock.

Brock had experienced a dissociative reaction in the face of the threat of his dependency by the outdoor survival experience and the off-campus move, two events occurring in rapid succession. Both had been designed to give him experience in becoming independent. However, he reported that he had gone to survival camp under pressure. Then, when this experience was aborted and he had to begin looking for an apartment immediately on return to campus, he viewed the series of events as rejection by campus authorities.

Emotionally he was a little boy again and the experience was reminiscent of many he recalled as a young boy, moving precipitously from house to house and town to town with his father to escape the law when rent was due or something else had gone wrong. He recounted tearfully his anxiety, fear, and shame from childhood: middle-of-the-night moves; being cold, hungry, and dirty; ragged clothes; the taunts of other children in strange schools; the scorn of teachers; being sent to the corner grocery store for wine for his father; the fear that his father was dying in an alcoholic stupor; stealing food from the grocery; and hiding out in abandoned buildings to escape the police when he was truant from school to avoid the humiliation he experienced there.

As time went on Brock talked about his headaches, which had been present since early school years. He described them as nearly always occurring under stress and how sometimes he would use a headache to escape unpleasant situations. In fact, on careful and extensive questioning the headache pattern did not sound like that of the classic description of migraine headache.

There was much ambivalence about his father, but he had felt that he must return after graduation from high school to take care of him. Gradually this view began to change as he talked and he modified his statement, saying that he thought he could be of more help to his family by continuing his schooling, getting a job, and contributing to his welfare by financial as well as emotional support.

Without undue pressure Brock began to make his own plans regarding independence—finding a job, moving off campus, and talking of his future. The actualization of these plans has been slow, but he has moved forward and is now working part-time as a construction worker in his senior year in high school, and with another boy his age has found an apartment where he is living the second semester of his senior year, preparatory to leaving the agency in June.

It is interesting that Brock said during his few months in psychotherapy that he had been unable to talk about these feelings before, but had kept them locked inside. A year and a half later, although he has experienced occasional headaches, there have been none of the incapacitating episodes he had experienced so often in the past.

# In the Area of Therapy

To a limited extent Brock is steering his own ship now and one can take hope that his rudimentary navigational skills will continue to improve.

## Patricia

As she entered adolescence, Patricia witnessed excessive drinking and family discord which led to the separation and divorce of her parents by her thirteenth birthday. The mother's feelings were so intense toward the divorced father that she threatened to throw Patricia out if she attended the father's wedding to his new bride. On the eve of the wedding she was thrust into a new life-style, with a compulsive stepmother who expected complete obedience, struggling with the strange dynamics of living with a younger stepsister, and faced with the realization that her father was emotionally indebted to and frequently controlled by his new wife. These events occurred at a stage of her life when she was naturally seeking emancipation. With the intense pressures of these multiple forces bearing upon her, Patricia became severely depressed.

This teenaged girl, just fifteen, was very distressed, almost in panic on her first visit to the agency. She had left her mother's place, with the angry edict that if she went to her father's wedding she need never come back. She had done so and tried living in the mobile home with her new stepmother and father. But this had not worked. There was much conflict among the three, and often it focused around the young stepsister, over whom Patricia had intense feelings of jealousy and sibling rivalry. Matters had gone from bad to worse and Patricia had acted out some of her conflict in the community. Now her father and stepmother had said that they could not make the marriage work with Patricia in the family.

At least they were trying to find a place for her somewhere. She was quite depressed on that first visit, but pleading for admission, saying with tears streaming down her face that she had to have help and had to change her ways.

We considered the need for her to be away from the family

an urgent matter, but no space would be available for a few weeks. What support could we offer meanwhile? Patricia and the family were informed immediately that she would be admitted when there was room for her. Also, a plan was made for her to ride the bus to Thompson on each Friday, have a regular out-patient appointment with the psychiatrist, spend Friday night on campus, and return by bus to her home city on Saturday.

This interim plan served a number of useful purposes. It provided some hope and a definite plan. Someone from the agency picked her up at the bus station on Friday and drove her to catch her return bus Saturday. She began to know some of the children in residence and a number of the staff, and the family and Patricia had a brief moratorium from their mounting conflicts.

Knowing that there was a possibility of help gave renewed hope to all concerned and the high level of anxiety and tension decreased to a more manageable level fairly promptly.

In residence Patricia has worked very hard in therapy, and her family has come regularly for consultation. All have expressed the continuing wish to be reunited. Weekend visits have gone pretty well, but during extended visits the tensions mount again. Patricia at first could see no other plan than an early return to be with an intact family, her family, something which she had never experienced. More recently, after extended visits, she has begun to sort out other aspects of the conflicts, namely her father's need to depend on his wife, who in fact is quite a religious person and who in many ways has helped to rehabilitate the father. She is quite perfectionistic and quite critical of the girl if she does not comply with her wishes in nearly every way.

Patricia now sums up her position by saying, "I cannot be perfect; I am Patricia and cannot be just like my mother; I have to be me." This is by way of saying that she is beginning to wonder if she can return to live with them full time. A new baby is due soon and the house will be more crowded. She appears to understand and have dealt with her rivalry feelings pretty well, and she and the younger sister get along well. Yet, she feels that the stepmother relates to her as she does to the young stepsister and gives her no more freedom.

The family is very important to her, and she wants to visit briefly, but now she is talking of a tentative plan to stay at Thompson another year until she will be old enough to get into some vocational training or perhaps become a student nurse.

How the problem will be resolved is still open, but Patricia is no longer so depressed and is thinking quite realistically about herself and the family.

## The Fletchers

Mrs. Fletcher's statement that "you can't live out of a paper bag" was appropriate as we debated how Tom, the oldest child, would fare in living at Thompson an extra semester after the younger siblings returned home. The mother meant that Tom had to identify with one primary residence. Mrs. Fletcher's statement was extraordinary, as this mother had previously refused to come into our campus buildings. She is sometimes psychotic, and she is constantly fearful of people or places that are a part of a mental health center, a psychiatric hospital, or social service agency. Her previous history of psychiatric hospitalizations and of being left alone with the children while the father was in prison kept her on her guard.

The father made great gains upon his discharge from the prison camp. He felt encouragement and our need for his help in rearing his children. Gradually it became obvious that the father could make it with the children, if a way could be found for them to live with the emotionally disturbed mother. Our psychiatrist was helpfully involved in consultation. When asked if he would be willing to be a cotherapist with our social worker in family therapy, he readily agreed.

The plan was for parents, children, social worker, and psychiatrist to come together as a group on a regular basis. The father said he could get his wife to come, but there was considerable doubt before the first meeting that she would be present. The children and the therapists were somewhat apprehensive that first evening as they waited. Though late, the parents arrived. The mother was extremely anxious and contributed little to the first session. This tension began to lessen as the sessions continued, and she saw us more as allies. It was obvious that the entire family wanted to try uniting, and all entered into concrete plans. The father would shoulder most of the responsibility, such as making school arrangements, helping to shop, finding a larger house to rent, and all necessary plans. He spoke openly of the past and of his demonstrated competency in the job he had held since leaving prison. The mother would have her responsibility in the house, where she felt safest, but together they made plans for some extrafamily involvement by visiting in the extended family with the children.

The affection in this family was obvious, and after several months the plans materialized. Assurance was given that the agency would continue to be involved if and when needed and both parents and children liked this idea. During the planning time the parents came to some campus activities such as basketball games in which their sons participated. Now, nearly a year after the children have left the campus, they all return for brief visits from time to time.

Though one would not have anticipated that this mother could ever function in other than a somewhat restricted manner, she is functioning more effectively than she has in many years. Her husband is a great source of strength and understanding, and both provide these attractive children with love and affection.

## 18❧ Family Psychotherapy
*From a paper given at the Fifth Winter Seminar for
Social Workers, offered by Group Child Care
Consultant Services, 1974*

THOMAS E. CURTIS, M.D.

My orientation to work with families causes me to utilize an approach which views the family as a system, or a network of individuals, tied together with bonds of emotional relationship. Those operating within this system are exremely important one to the other. Significant changes in any one component cause an effect on all others throughout the system. It is somewhat like casting a stone into a pool and observing the ripples.

I think of the nuclear family as being formed at marriage and subsequently developing with the birth of children. Members of the nuclear family, particularly the spouses, are in a relationship system also with their own extended families. The strength of the bonds with the extended family continues. Although significant ties persist throughout life, the possibility exists for relative freedom from this earlier grouping. Happenings in both the extended and the nuclear family systems have reverberations throughout. When tensions develop within the sytem, discharge may take place through any one of a number of pathways. Although there are mechanisms for reduction of tension, a tendency for homeostasis exists. The bonds that hold the component members of the system together are strong. They are an overriding consideration, and this tendency for maintained closure may, in fact, generate as much tension as not.

It is common to see, then, that with varying degrees of dysfunction on the part of some members there follow exaggerated or complementary functions in others. The emotional system may be a relatively closed one; that is, the boundaries separating it from other functional systems may be quite strong. On the other hand, the system may be more open, with individual members able to move about within the system in relative freedom and to move in and out of the system and its influences with some ease.

In general, the more closed the system, the more intensely its component members will react emotionally, as opposed to the greater possibilities for freedom, objectivity, and analysis that exist in systems approximating openness. Transactions within the system take place between individual members. However, with some tension in this relationship, one finds the inclusion of a third person. We generally think of the threesome, or the triangular relationship, as the more stable functioning component.

With many family members there are, obviously, possibilities for many sets of triangles and interlocking systems of triangles in which one unit is related to more than one pair. You may note similarities with concepts of group process and general systems theory. Family systems, however, are unique and can be best understood in that frame of reference alone.

I think that it should be obvious to you as I define my meaning of the term "family psychotherapy" that I define the theoretical base from which I operate. The name implies that one is doing something to or with families. What is done may ultimately be regarded as therapeutic, that is, effecting change. If one pushes far enough, of course, the concept of cure gets into the picture. You will appreciate that I get close to falling into the trap of using an illness model. I think that there are some limitations to this point of view in work with families. This is no different from the sort of conceptual question one faces when working with groups, namely, is one treating individuals within a group? I will not dodge this issue completely. I will, however, have to elaborate further on theoretical concepts utilized in my approach. To some extent, my definition will have to be in a negative sense, that is, speaking to what is not subsumed under the term.

I do not deal with the family unit as a primary object for treatment. Others may take this point of view, hence the need for my clarification. In general, I take the family unit and the various dynamic interactions into consideration, but my work at any specific point will be with one individual member of the family system. This includes such concepts as triangles, fusion, differentiation, multigenerational transmission, family mythology, and the varieties of emotional relationships.

In the strictest sense one can do family psychotherapy with only one family member present. Practically speaking, however, there are technical considerations which make it more efficient to work with more than one family member, usually with spouses. Children may be included, particularly in the early phases of the treatment. You will find some family therapists, and Carl Whitaker is an example, who do in fact insist on working at one

time with as many family members as possible. The important
point, however, is not how many people are in the room, but that
we are dealing with these people, not from the standpoint of their
individual psychopathology, but with an understanding of how
people interact in this highly charged emotional relationship system. I think that the vitality of the family therapy approach lies in
its efficiency in bringing about change in individual psychology.

The treatment, or therapeutic work, is based in a family
frame of reference. It deals with various family members and is
focused at any one moment on one individual component of the
system and that person's interactions with others in the family.
Change takes place in the individual and the relationship system
and its various component parts. If we are not to become locked
into a medical model and the treatment of illness, is it possible to
clarify what is being done in family psychology? I find several
lines of thought useful in this regard. As I have said earlier, I
think of the family as a system of individuals functionally and
dynamically interrelated. Dysfunction in one component member
is closely related to conpensatory behavior on the part of another
member. One frequently finds a dominant member operating in
concert with one functioning at a less than optimal level. Attention may come to be focused on a problem within the family
system when one member or another seeks to effect a change in
the dynamic equilibrium. The defined problem may be in terms
of a family crisis recognizing the involvement of more than one
member, or it may emphasize the dysfunction or malfunction of a
single member of the family. An example of the latter occurs
when a family comes in, for instance, because of the problems of
one of the children. Marital problems will be given as the reason
other families will seek help, with an explicit recognition that
more than one person is involved in the problem, although the
finger of blame may be pointed at one or the other, thus at the
same time denying a systems problem.

Practically speaking, the family psychotherapy approach is
one in which we recognize the existence of problems, dysfunctions, and symptoms, without committing ourselves necessarily
to the treatment of those problems. What actually transpires in

family psychotherapy can be viewed as much as an educative process as a therapeutic one. For this reason some workers prefer to speak not of family therapy but rather of family study. A result of successful family work is often the reduction of tension within the system as it becomes more open. At the same time individual members come to be, relatively speaking, more differentiated, more autonomous and less dysfunctional. Symptoms are alleviated and changes do take place within individuals and in their relationship systems. Hence, whether a process is curative may well become academic.

One may legitimately ask: If families come for help with defined problems, will there not be difficulties in responding to their expressed need with an approach that does not emphasize therapy? Furthermore, isn't the difficulty even greater when an individual seeks help for the relief of psychological symptoms? In my own experience, I have been surprised to find how little difficulty there is in using such an approach. In working with families and individuals, there should certainly be an appreciation and recognition of their needs, their problems, and an awareness of where they are hurting. In defining for them what can be expected of a family approach, one can in all honesty state that changes are possible, and this is what is being sought. Nevertheless, misunderstandings do develop. Clarification and explanation are a part of the educative study that is undertaken.

A realistic appreciation of the span of time that will be involved in the family work comes to be quite important. Anyone needing help and coming to an individual or an agency purporting to offer such help will automatically achieve a certain amount of relief when met with confidence and understanding. Change is a slow process, however, no matter what interventions are undertaken. Change that results from family psychotherapy takes place slowly and over a long period of time. Those in family psychotherapy learn a perspective, a method of defining themselves and of understanding relationship systems that will prove useful and applicable throughout life. The family therapist is as much a coach, a teacher, a model as he is a therapist in the more traditional sense. Family psychotherapy does not provide a means for shielding people from life experiences. It is not a refuge. It is a process which should equip the individuals concerned for more effective living.

The number of hours spent in direct work with a family therapist may be relatively small when compared with the time spent on other approaches. Contacts with families may be weekly, or even more frequent during periods of acute crisis. Beyond that, however, much work is done by people in family psychotherapy in the intervals between consultative sessions with the family psychotherapist. It therefore becomes practical to space therapy sessions several weeks apart.

The family therapist comes to be a resource person, an expert who is knowledgeable about how family systems work. To be most useful and to remain in this position he must allow time for the slow process of work and change to take place in the family system. Such change is possible only as a result of the efforts of the family member. If the therapist becomes an integral part of the family system in any other sense, progressive change will not take place. As I have implied, families adapt to this approach if, in fact, the family psychotherapist is an expert. I will have more to say later about how it is possible effectively to utilize a family approach. I will also approach the question, "What are the applications of family psychotherapy to crisis and other situations in which there is a time-limiting variable?"

I would like to comment here briefly on another technical variation that has proved invaluable. This is dealing therapeutically with multiple family units by having spouses from several unrelated family systems meeting in the same setting. It is analogous to one essential ingredient of psychotherapeutic groups. The principle concerned is the ability of one individual to learn from the experiences of another. In family psychotherapy when one is dealing with spouses, part of the time is focused on the relationship system between the two members of the nuclear family. A substantial amount of time, however, is spent in one-to-one communications between family therapist and one spouse. The focus of this work frequently will be on the extended family system of that spouse, with the other essentially serving as audience to that transaction. This affords the observer the opportunity to appreciate more objectively and understand the other in light of their extended family relationship system. It becomes possible for the observer to appreciate that much of what may be projected onto him or her is more a carryover from key past relationships than the here-and-now relationship between spouses. Distortions in the communication and relationship system between spouses thereby are clarified in this setting which is less emotionally charged and less conflict-ridden than that between the spouses. Usually, with time, each spouse has as much opportunity to receive active assistance in the work of defining his own identity and relationship systems upon the one hand, as to act as audience or observer on the other hand. Within certain limitations of time, it is possible to compound this sort of benefit by dealing with, for instance, three couples in the same setting. Each individual member, then, would only be actively involved in participant discussion one sixth of the time. Five sixths of the time, then, is spent as audience observer. Much can be learned in this setting if the participants are able to compare and contrast their own individual experiences. In a like fashion, much can be learned about one's own communication and relationship systems vis-à-vis one's spouse by coming to know similar systems in others. This approach approximates some sorts of group work and is quite different from others; therefore, I refrain from defining it as a therapy group.

What, then, is the usefulness of this approach? What are the implications? I have noticed that as professionals become knowledgeable and appreciative of the ways in which individuals function in a family system, it becomes almost impossible for them to ignore these factors in evaluating the problems of those persons coming into a clinical setting. This is not to say that family psychotherapy is a panacea. I would submit for your consideration, however, that family study, family psychotherapy, and an understanding of how individuals function in the complex relational system that is family does expand our knowledge in a way that can be useful in any setting in which we are obliged to deal with the problem of human existence. I am not convinced that there is any one professional background that would serve as a prerequisite for learning how to work with families. In one sense, family therapists may well be born rather than made. I would emphasize that to work effectively in family therapy one must thoroughly understand family systems. Some training programs try to provide the necessary content and experience to enable one to become an expert in the field. As a teacher, I have found it easier to work with students who want to learn about families than to work with those who have a fixed commitment to an existing professional model.

One of the most catalytic experiences in the learning process is one's work with one's own family. I think in the final analysis one's effectiveness will be severely limited if one does not appreciate the significance and importance of one's self in one's own family system. It certainly is possible for nonprofessionals to learn to work quite successfully with families. Some interesting experiments have taken place in training indigenous community workers to use this approach in a clinical setting. Considerable effort is required on the part of teachers in the early phases of training. To some extent there may be limitations of such workers' ability to operate independently of a supporting system if work is clinically—therapeutically—aimed.

After this paper and papers given by Dr. Seymour L. Halleck and Mrs. Sarah W. Bowen, a number of questions were asked of the three speakers relating family therapy to the Children's Home. Among the answers given were:

1. That in a twenty-two-month period (average time in which children were in care in the questioner's agency) much could be achieved. One suggestion was that therapy be begun while the child was in care, using this period to establish goals, and that it continue after the child's return to his own home. Another was either to have the family stay near the Home or for therapy to be given in the home community with the child returning to his own home for sessions.

2. That there should be separation between the caretaker and therapist roles.

3. That one might plan therapy if only one member of the family was present at first, with others drawn in later, particularly through asking the participating member not to talk about it at home.

4. That family therapy might even be attempted where parents are divorced and remarried.

5. That even in the event the child is never likely to return home, family therapy can be of help in strengthening the part-time parenting, such as on visits.

# ❧❧G

# In the Area of Advocacy

## 19❧ Student Participation in Decisions
*Paper given at the Southeastern Child Care
Association, 1971*

### ALAN KEITH-LUCAS

Not long ago, in a so-called "prophetic" talk, I made the prediction that there would be in the future greater participation of youth (and, I said also, of their families) in the counsels of the Children's Home. I did not say this, then, at least, with any moral imperative attached. I simply said it was going to happen. I had in mind a phenomenon which seemed apparent in this country, and that is the gradual breakdown of a hierarchical system in which one group—the middle class, the middle-aged, the traditionally educated, the so-called establishment—called all the shots for others, and its replacement by something that might be called a participatory democracy. This seems to me obvious in many relationships that are changing as we enter the Age of Aquarius—the relationships between, for instance, white and black, teacher and student, professional and paraprofessional (look at what has happened between social worker and houseparent in the last four or five years), producer and consumer, young and old.

I said also that it was possible and indeed likely that the

movement would go too far at first. This nearly always happens when things begin to change. We generally go too far in the first flush of the reforms we make, just as we went too far, for instance, in trying to return all youngsters to rehabilitated homes or in shortening the time that children spent with us. In this particular change of climate there is the obvious danger of giving too much power to those who have the knowledge, perhaps, but not always the wisdom to exercise it. There is a danger that wisdom and experience may be discounted. But that does not mean that we should not move at all. Indeed, if we do not we are apt to find our job becoming harder and harder and eventually impossible. We have experienced such a thing before, when we have chosen for a time not to be relevant, not to see what is happening around us, and nearly destroyed ourselves in the process.

But this does not mean that change is easy. As I said at the time, in introducing this prophecy, it is one we may not like. Not only is it always difficult to change and give up some of our own power, to share it with others—we all tend to think the world would be better if we were in absolute charge of it—but this particular change in relationship between the young and the old involves a great deal of challenge, not so much to our ideas themselves but to our comfortable illusions about ourselves, about our programs, about youngsters, and about the nature of life around, us. For if the new youth of today has any demands of life, they are, first, "Let us in on things," and second, "Tell it like it is." This forces us to a kind of honesty that most of us find very difficult indeed. As a generation and a people we have tended to sugarcoat life, to protect from rather than to help face, to shut our eyes rather than to acknowledge, and this youth is not willing to let us do this.

We are also to some extent scared of youth's new knowledge and new demands. We are afraid that if we take them into any kind of partnership they will demand the moon, or want to tear down things we feel to be valuable and sound. We may recognize, which is true, that this first TV generation is the most knowledgeable in history—frequently better informed than we are, in fact—but we question both their wisdom and their moderation.

Let me say that this is not my experience of youth. Young people may appear to be revolutionary, or at first they may seem to see the situation as a battle against authority. But when one manages to get with young people on a truly reciprocal basis I am amazed at their good sense, their willingness to accept necessary restraints, and the moderation of their demands.

So the questions I think we need to ask ourselves come out something like this: In what areas, to what extent, and through what structures are we prepared to encourage youth's participation, and what might be some guides and cautions to those attempting it?

I would suggest that there are perhaps five areas or levels of participation. The first is participation of youth in individual planning for themselves. We have long ago recognized that unless a child has some part in the plan for himself, it is not likely to be successful, but we sometimes do not make this recognition explicit. Some Homes are now beginning to do so, both by including the child as a party to the family plan and by specific instruments such as the junior-senior contract for self-support, in which the Home may for instance guarantee both basic support and the opportunity to earn but transfer to the young person responsibility for such things as clothes or spending money. But I would warn here against the use of such plans to extract from the child pious-sounding promises of good conduct. A plan is not a promise; it is, or should be, a clear statement of conditions, including in most cases alternatives. One Home I visited lately is or was having great difficulty with difficult teenagers who were sent there largely as a last resort, and who for the most part were quite aware that if this placement failed the Department of Public Welfare would in all probability throw in the sponge and return them to the families from which they had been taken. It was little wonder that many of these placements failed. The child's interest in the placement, either as an alternative to correctional school or to a situation which he himself could see as impossible was not being enlisted at all. He felt and had no responsibility for the success of his own placement.

The same is true in situations that develop more gradually, which is the real reason for that process that we have called adolescent reassessment, in which a teenager is made an integral partner in his plan. No normal adolescent can stand being planned for and not with. Nor can such planning be a process of making a plan and conning a child into agreeing to it without some real decision or commitment on his part.

The second level of participation is that of taking over certain decisions, within prescribed limits, for certain aspects of group life. Generally such decisions need to be limited to choices that do not involve authority over the actions of others. Thus, it is wise and sensible for youngsters to decide on the form of recreation they want at a particular time, or to accept or refuse an invitation, or to select the decor of a teenage center, or, within practical limits, to determine the time of meals or the use of a cottage budget, but not on their own to determine essential rules or disciplinary measures to be applied either to a group or to an individual. They may and should have an input to make in such matters but youngsters alone should not decide them, nor is it ever fair to grant a decision-making power that one may have to override or one that is only apparently free but actually manipulated by moral suasion. In other words, although youngsters can and should be entrusted with certain decisions, one needs to be very sure that such power is delegated only where the administration is prepared to stand by the decisions that youngsters may make, wise or unwise, without question. If limits have to be set, they should be set beforehand.

The third and fourth areas are those of input and feedback, if you will excuse me for using a systems vocabulary. By input I mean, first, creating structures by which student ideas can reach administration without taking the form of complaints, and second, the solicitation of student reaction. The first is probably best met through some form of student council which is clearly advisory and not decision-making in nature. The purpose is to let administration know of student concerns. It should be open to such questions as "Why can't we?" and "Would it be possible for us to . . . ?" And let me emphasize here the importance of an honest answer to these questions, whether it be, "Our constituency would not stand for it," "We don't have enough money," or even "I'm not quite sure I could trust all of you in that." It is extraordinary how reasonable young people can be if they know the real reason for things, how understanding of our problems and sometimes how resourceful in helping us overcome them. We may feel that in some way we are weakening our authority or our image as administrator if we admit to the constraints that exist on our power, but for the most part we strengthen it, gaining allies and acceptance of reality if we can share them in this way, besides teaching a most important lesson—that we too have to live with constraints—that we are neither omnipotent nor superhuman, that there are two sides to every question, that compromises have to be made.

May I say here, too, that an advisory council should be advisory to those who have the ultimate right to make decisions, which is in many cases the executive, although in a cottage it may be the houseparent. Dealing with an advisory council should not be delegated to an intermediary. Youngsters need to feel that they are being heard at the top by someone who can speak with authority.

Another principle operative here is essential to all good helping knowledge: if you cannot grant all that someone asks of you, you will gain much better acceptance of what you are able or willing to grant if you will work down from what the other really wants to what you are able to give, with full recognition that this falls short of the demand, than if you try to sell what you can allow without exploring the other's real desires. It is curious how often we make this mistake. We would rather not hear the demand in the first place for fear that we will not be able to meet it, for fear of disappointing someone, of losing status in his eyes.

Communication on policy making should take place at various points. Thus a wise administration, having arrived, let us say, at a policy on work and earnings, with or without student help, would submit the proposed policy to a student group before it reaches final form, to catch any unwitting conflicts or bugs that might exist in it, which youngsters can quite often see because they are consumers of whatever the policy may be. I remember one Home feeling that it was doing its students a great favor by taking them to football games, which it had not done before. It also permitted its boys and girls to sit with their dates during games. What it did not know was that a football date at that school traditionally included a hamburger and a Coke at a particular quite acceptable place near the stadium. The Home's staff would have been perfectly willing to pick up the youngsters half an hour after the game if there had been awareness of this. But because the kids were sent for the moment the game was over, a date in that school that did not include the after-game refreshment became known as an "orphan's date."

Feedback is the other side of this coin, and feedback works both ways. When the administration makes a decision based on a good reason, it is often good policy to communicate this reason to youngsters, so as to forestall rumor or misunderstanding of motives. This may be particularly important in disciplinary actions where perhaps two youngsters have been treated differently because of their situations. I remember in one Home after a particularly unpleasant sex episode, the boy, as it happens, was asked to leave because he was in the Home on a special agreement involving his ability to control himself in this way and because an alternative plan was possible for him, but the girl was retained because there was no other good plan for her and it was felt that the Home had in fact played into her problem by making her too dependent on peer approval. Right or wrong as the decision might have been, it could only be accepted by the group, and was prevented from becoming both a source of friction between youngsters and adults and a most punishing experience for the girl, by discussing the reasons for the Home's actions in a small group of student leaders, who, once they understood what had happened, could support it and interpret it to others.

Similarly, a new rule or a policy should be reviewed from time to time to determine how it is working in practice.

The fifth level is that of policy participation before policy is made. Some Homes have even considered (as have some schools and colleges) student participation on boards or standing committees. At the risk of being thought reactionary, I would urge caution in this practice. The issue is not that of wisdom. It is one of responsibility—responsibility not only to the present but to the future of a Home, and responsibility to the various constituencies and systems, in which a Home is involved. However one cuts the pie, a consumer—a student—can and should advise a board but cannot carry this long-range professional or theological responsibility to the child-welfare field, the church, or the community that board members, administrators, and professional staff who are involved in these systems must carry. Student involvement seems to me much more appropriate in task forces or ad hoc committees to arrive at proposed policies which are then reviewed in terms of these responsibilities. But even then I believe it is very important that there be clarity about what students can properly and effectively vote on or decide. Nothing is further from participatory democracy than any form of tokenism or a committee of adults and youngsters which is foreordained to come out with adult-oriented proposals or decisions which claim to be the outcome of student-adult deliberation. Some dating policies, for instance, are formed in this way and are even more obnoxious to students than would be a simple administration policy, which one could openly resent or oppose. It is hard to struggle against something which one has been conned into agreeing to.

There is still a great deal we do not know about how best to bring students into a real partnership in their own plans and those of the group. I am convinced that we need to do it, and I am equally convinced that we cannot solve the problem through the creation of structures. Clear understanding of what students can decide for themselves, contracts, advisory councils, student participation on task forces, and feedback mechanisms are good things to have, but only if we are fully prepared to use them. Otherwise they will backfire, simply waste time, or die on the vine and gradually fade away. A willingness is required on the part of both young people and adults to make them work. We cannot dictate the student input, but we can do something about adult input and can create, if we want to, the kind of atmosphere to which most young people can respond. I would therefore suggest in closing that we are likely to get genuine and useful student input if we can and do:

1. Genuinely respect the concerns of youngsters and take their requests seriously.

2. Tell it like it is.

3. Share the constraints on our own operation.

4. State clearly what students can and cannot decide, and stick to it.

5. Be undefensive about criticism, remembering that young people are often more direct or less practiced in diplomacy than we are.

6. Have the courage to make some necessary decisions on an adult level without apology, but do not be afraid to give up those that adults really do not need to make.

7. Take the trouble to learn something of today's changing customs, modes of expression, and problems.

If we can do these things, I have no doubt that youth will respond.

## 20 ❧ Working with Children from the Poverty Culture
*Address to the Chapel Hill Workshops, 1968*
JACK KIRKLAND

This is a subject both vast and urgent, upon whose resolution depends the very existence of our civilization—the need to learn how to work effectively with children from the poverty culture, our future parents-in-waiting. Should we lose the war on cities and fail to habilitate as well as rehabilitate not only the brick and mortar but also the people concentrated in urban ghettoes or those in rural slums, then truly we will become a dead society.

# In the Area of Advocacy

Jobs with dignity and upward mobility, equal or in many instances unequal educational opportunities to atone for scars of deprivations and availability of fair, adequate, and equal housing are essential if the American dream is to prevail over the nightmare we have sometimes witnessed erupting in the streets. And while we have declared war on poverty, we still have only a small, poorly trained army fighting a guerrilla war on scattered fronts with very light artillery. The War on Poverty, Model Cities, Urban Renewal, and other such programs on the same scope approximate the predicament of someone on a large lake in a small boat with a hole in the bottom and having only a teacup with which to bail out the water.

Many people in this country still are forced to beg for alms—public assistance—which is still viewed as a privilege and not a right. They and their children go to bed hungry. They are the drop-outs, drip-outs, squeezed-outs, pushed-outs, and walled-outs in our society. It is not mere coincidence that they fulfill the prophecy of a society which excludes them. They have few skills, and frequently no work or opportunity to make a living beyond the subsistence level, yet some choose to call them lazy. Our educators admit candidly that they do not know how to teach this population because the educational system is geared to the middle-class child who has had certain specific early life experiences; many people conclude that there is nothing wrong with the system but rather that the poor are less than adequate. Even when we erect legal, social, and economic barriers in housing, some people voice the opinion that the poor are happy and desire to live among their own. Somehow in this illogical nonsense a large segment of our society is able to find justification for its caustic attitudes and behavior.

The Indian, Chicano, Puerto Rican, Afro-American, and the poor white are the minority groups in this country. These groups account for one quarter of the total population and are growing geometrically. Nearly every grossly deprived child who is unreached gives rise to a family of equally handicapped and socially disadvantaged individuals. And yet no group is monolithic. We cannot speak of the poor as an entity, but this population must be seen as many groups. Among the poor are individuals whose values are similar to those of many middle-class persons. This group will make it because its members have a view not only of what is but a vision of what might be, and in the face of discrimination and other tribulations, they hurdle one obstacle after another in spite of events, circumstances, and adversities. These are the economically poor. We know how to work well with this group because in essence they are like us and some of us here have emerged from these ranks.

I do not want to talk with you about this group of poor. I want to engage you in a dialogue about the spiritual and aspirational poor, those deprived of hope, of the will or desire to dream, those who do not have the inner ability to initiate their own inner motivation.

The child who becomes a mother while she is still a child; the boy who at the age of fourteen talks about the good old days; the mother who has to take all of her children to the clinic and spend the whole day there if only one of the children is ill because there is no family doctor; the family that deals only with rehabilitation, seldom with prevention, epitomized by children's having teeth extracted rather than repaired; parents who seek medical help only at the point of severe bodily pain; the child who has little exposure to protein and only knows that he is full of bread and potatoes at the point when his stomach begins to ache; the family living in a cold-water flat where children are bitten by rats and bedbugs, and roaches stalk the kitchen in open daylight; the working man in the family who becomes frustrated because he can train a number of people to become his supervisor while he himself can never hope to achieve such a position; and a society which withdraws assistance from families if the father, who is not working for a host of reasons, attempts to live at home—this population and their pathetic lives are the focus of our discussion.

In many instances, the man takes to drink, vice, and crime. Illegitimate births, delinquency, and vandalism arise from defiance, doubt, despair, and disgust. We ask, "What kind of models do parents present to their children? What is wrong with their values?" And I ask, what is wrong with ours when we systematically, conscientiously, and methodically close avenues of entry into the mainstream of society and thus deny the individual dignity, humanity, and a sense of integrity? However, surprisingly enough, the value system is not different for the poor. The paradox, as well as irony, is that they are the same.

Go to a local movie and see if sex or crime or both are not at the center of the plot. One of the best moneymakers at the cinema in the last few years has been "Bonnie and Clyde." Contrary to our voiced opinion, crime does pay and it pays well. In fact, it seems the bigger the theft, the less the punishment. Serial monogamy is practiced inasmuch as many people have had many different mates. We may claim that this is the case only for a small segment of our middle-class society, yet nevertheless this may be an outsider's perception of the total group. There is a vast discrepancy between what society expresses and what it does. The child in the ghetto quickly discerns the social inequities exemplified in differential justice and that the keeper of the rules can operate outside of them.

Often after a generation of receiving welfare the poor become apathetic and exist from day to day, unable to give to their children because they have received so little. They accept their station in life and see being a ward of the state as an undesirable compromise. They turn their anger inward and come to loathe themselves. Realizing that they are biological parents only, they continue merely to exist while paying the most difficult debt one can pay to sociey—the debt of gratitude. All people of this group do not turn their hatred inward; rather, some, directing it outward, have emerged as black-power advocates and militants in other minority groups. They are saying that if they cannot have what they are constitutionally entitled to, then no one will enjoy in peace that which they have.

How can we successfully work with children from the poverty culture of which I speak? We must work for a basic change in our social structure, to make it all-inclusive, not exclusive. I am tempted to prescribe how to achieve this goal, but such is not the assignment of this paper nor is it the specific task of workers in Children's Homes. However, I believe if this is not done, then what I say to you beyond this point is purely academic. The shame is that too many people do not fit into society because society has no place for them to fit into. Ignoring this frightening truth and the dynamics of poverty in your work with children would be rather like attempting brain surgery with no understanding of the central nervous system.

We must strengthen family life while others are working on the social structure. Children are hungry nutritionally and emotionally. Far too little love is given them for them to learn how to be lovable, and to ask them to be immediately different from their peers and parents is to expect them to give up something of value without pain.

The child who is aspirationally poor needs a basic tutorial approach with protective sequential learning experiences. He must learn how to master his environment, how to discriminate on a material as well as an emotional level, how to understand cause and effect, and to appreciate that he can control the way in which people relate to him by the manner in which he relates. He must find some balance within his inner world or mind with the outer world, his environment. He must learn emotional skills—how to discharge feelings, how to win as well as lose, and when to say what and to whom. He needs to learn social skills, or how to relate in multiple situations or how to respect people and property. He must learn recreational skills or how to play according to the rules while experiencing frustration, anxiety, and defeat. He needs to learn academic skills to take his place vocationally in the world of work. He must learn to share things, opportunities, people, and himself. He must learn to listen, understand, integrate knowledge, and to practice and rehearse it through repetitive behavior, inculcating this new behavior into his personality. Since it took time for him to learn to be as he is, he will not unlearn his old behavior overnight. As a matter of fact, he will go back to his old behavior long after you have thought that he had given it up, because he needs to know if it is as fulfilling now as it was in the past, and he will need your help in evaluating his feelings. The child must come to like himself, to gain a feeling of confidence so that he can later develop social competence.

Admittedly, the child must learn a great deal, and to do this he must have an adequate teacher—one who can mix love and science together so that only the love will show, one who is subjectively objective, one who does not let his feelings get in the way but begets constructive feelings. What must this person be like? Let me describe the social surgeon. The helping person must be kind, friendly, accepting, and limiting. He must be consistent, flexible, just, and concerned. He must be able to innovate, stimulate, interpret, and teach. He must be able to laugh, cry, pray, and play. He must be childlike and not childish. He must be mature enough to say, "Help me," "I don't know," and "Teach me." He must be predictable and, by all means, genuine.

To do this the worker must be able to conduct a dialogue, show interest, involve himself in the life problems of the child, and invest himself in the task of helping the child to heal his hurt. He must know when to ask and when to tell, when to demand and when to request, when to pursue a point and when to retire.

And after all of this, in the final analysis the houseparent cannot motivate the child. All the houseparent can do is to create the climate and opportunity for the child to become motivated.

You all know the old saying, "You can take a horse to water but you can't make him drink." Well, this is true. You see, the trick is to make him thirsty, and then he will drink himself. I challenge you to make your children thirsty—to thirst to become socially adequate, likable, well-rounded, creative, and inquisitive youngsters.

## 21❧  Persons or Nonpersons: The Rights of Children and Their Families

*Address to the Chapel Hill Workshops, 1972*

ALAN KEITH-LUCAS

What I have to say today is quite controversial. I will not please many of you. Some of you will see it as radical; some will feel that I have not gone far enough. I am deliberately throwing it out to you for discussion, but I do want to make clear that in all of it I have a strong feeling for houseparents who have to struggle with changing ideas and may find themselves lost without some of the traditional authority they have felt was theirs in the past.

When people start talking about children's rights a good deal of idealism is engendered. If we mean by rights what a child needs, we all have our pet ideas, our enthusiasms. A child, we say, needs love, or stimulation, or discipline, or freedom, or one strict and one indulgent parent, or time to twiddle his thumbs, or instruction in the Bible, or a chance to express himself, or to make decisions, or whatnot—all important, excellent things, but open to a lot of interpretation, and very hard to enforce, and in any case one could go on forever until one had described some sort of perfect children's paradise to which we would insist that every child had a right.

I do not mean to depreciate such enthusiasm, or the long and devoted struggle many enthusiasts have carried on for a fuller and better life for children, even if I do deplore the habit some of us have of being sure that our ideas are right and that the person who disagrees with us cannot really love children, or at least does not love them as much as we do. But I am going to dicuss here another kind of right—the more or less constitutional rights of the child and of his parents as citizens, as representatives of two more or less oppressed minorities—children, and parents whose rearing of chidren has not been up to community standards. And I do so because there is in this country something of a revolution brewing about how children are being treated, not only by their own parents but by their so-called protectors (which includes you and me). At the same time there is growing insistence on the rights of the poor, the physically and mentally ill, the victims of lack of education, lack of opportunity, and all the other ills of our society, among whom the parents of our children are a significant group. Moreover, there are in many communities citizen groups who take these rights seriously, and are not going to let some of us escape their scrutiny as they sometimes have done in the past. So-called child advocacy groups, with representation from youth and from the parents of our children, will have much to say in the future about what Children's Homes do.

What kind of rights are these groups likely to assert for children and their families—rights which may eventually get written into law in some form? In the case of families, the Supreme Court, as it so often has done, started the business in the *Gault* decision, when it affirmed the right of a child charged with delinquency to have a lawyer. It said, in effect, that a nice, kind, fatherly person, however well intentioned, even if he were a judge, could not take a child away from his parents without due process of law, including the right to cross-examine witnesses, to challenge the evidence, to put the burden of legal proof on the state to show why it must take this drastic action. And if it said that about a judge, think what the implications are for a church or a community group that does such things as refusing to let a child see his parents, or intercepting their mail to him, or refusing to return him to them, on no other basis than a belief that these things are in the child's best interests, and often with no legal sanction at all—not that legal sanction means anything if it is given illegally by a court playing God with no due process of law. I do not mean by this that Homes do not have the right, for example, to set aside convenient times when parents may visit their children, providing these are reasonable, or that they cannot say, "If you want your child to live with us you'll have to abide by certain conditions, or Johnny may be too much for us, or may simply fail to get anything out of what we hope to do for him." But I do mean that it will be more clearly recognized that he is the parents' child and not the Home's, and that the parent has both rights and responsibilities that can only be taken from him on solid and legal evidence.

Specifically, unless it can be shown clearly that there would be specific and lasting harm to the child, not just a period of struggle or so-called disturbance—that word we use to describe any evidence that a child is battling with his feelings or finding our routine or our rules too galling—a parent has the right to correspond freely with his child, and to visit him at reasonable times. How long ago was it that we used to deny visiting in the first thirty days so that the child could get accustomed to us, despite all the evidence that partial separations are much easier to handle than total ones? Above all, the parent has the right to know what is happening to his child, to participate in planning with and for the child, to make important decisions in the child's life, and he has the right at any time to go back to the court if he can show that the reasons for the state's intervention are no longer applicable. He has a right to know what his rights are, to have them explained clearly to him. And he has the right to be treated with respect, as a first-class and not a second-class citizen, and to be, if not welcomed, at least accepted as the child's parent.

Only in such an atmosphere of mutual respect and common action does the state have the right to judge a parent on the way in which he exercises his rights and fulfills his responsibilities while the child is in care. One cannot expect a parent to act responsibly if he is treated as trash. I wonder sometimes if most of us have any idea how hard it is to visit one's child when someone else is caring for him, correcting what we have done wrong or failed to do, giving him things we could not give, competing with us for his affection, and how much worse it must be if we are met with frigid disapproval or a grudging acknowledgment of the necessity to let us claim a bit of him—if we are told where we may take him, how to treat him, warned that he must be brought back at a certain time. No wonder some parents promise and then find their courage failing. No wonder some of them turn to Dutch courage to see them through. No wonder some cannot take it and simply disappear. And of course if the child is with us voluntarily, as far as the parent is concerned, what he has with us is a contract which we are bound to observe. We may not approve of what he does, we may think it better for this child if he behaved differently, we may make it clear to him that this is our opinion, we may even decline to care for his child if his actions do not permit us to do so, but we still have no authority to deny him the normal prerogative of a parent.

Of course there are many rights a family has before it gets to the point of neglect or other breakdown. These are so general that they are becoming matters of national policy. The family has or may soon have the right to adequate housing at a reasonable cost, to medical care, to opportunity for a job, and a decent income if that is not possible, and if we are going to insist that female heads of families work, as we seem to be doing, to adequate day care for children. It is a curious anomaly that a president who has insisted that mothers of poor one-parent families work vetoed a day-care bill on the grounds that providing day care for middle-class families would weaken the family as the primary child-rearing unit. How discriminatory can one get against the poor?

We really do not know today how much the neglect of children, alcoholism, and unwise buying on credit (an escape from reality very much like the use of alcohol or other drugs, and equally pushed by the industry responsible for it) result from almost intolerable conditions and how much they arise from simple human failure, but we do know that the pressures of overcrowding, lack of income, physical debility, and high mobility are associated with human failure, and in particular with that most alarming of all parental actions, child abuse. Child abusers tend to have several or many children, to be cut off from their relatives, poor, in debt, and living in inadequate housing.

What, then can a child's rights be? In this new day it should be clear that they will exist both against his parents and against us, or anyone else who offers to care for him. They will include the right to a guardian of the person if his own parents cannot fulfill the task—someone outside the agency caring for him who can speak for him and for his interests. While some people hope for a sort of general child-advocate, I think it is much more likely there will be a more personal representative. Children at the present time have the right to be cared for adequately physically, yet still do not have the right to have someone who will make big decisions in their lives or generally look after their interests.

The child has the obvious right to be fed a diet that will keep him strong and help him grow, to be educated (and not excluded from school because he is retarded, handicapped, or hard to handle), to be clothed, housed, and provided with medical care. He has a right, it is true, to be protected from certain obvious dangers, including moral ones, but we must be careful here that we are dealing with clear and obvious danger, not just an influence or a style of life of which we do not happen to approve. In fact, whether we like or dislike it, children, older children at least, are developing the right to be persons—not nonpersons, subject to adult whims and prejudice—but persons in a special group for whom some decisions must clearly be made by older persons, but who have some rights and can make some choices of their own.

Children do have a right not to be exploited for any purpose, however good, if it is injurious to them, whether the exploitation is a matter of using them for publicity purposes, demanding unreasonable work, or exploiting their emotions—demanding love or gratitude from them. They obviously have a right to be free from sexual exploitation of all kinds, both physical and psychological, and the basis of this right is the right to respect of one's person. In view of this, many serious thinkers are today raising questions about the rights involved in children's being whipped or beaten, either by their parents or by others. This is, I know, a difficult question. Most of us were reared in a culture where the woodshed was a part of life. Some of us feel that it did not harm us and even may have done us good. Some of us go back to the Old Testament's advice about not spoiling a child. Some of us argue that the children we care for are accustomed to physical punishment and would be lost without it. Yet here are some facts to ponder. Whipping children does not exist in many cultures which have if anything a better-disciplined youth than we have. Despite its biblical sanction, it was not practiced in polite society in Europe until about the fifteenth or sixteenth century, and even then its use meant that children were deliberately equated with the lowest criminal class, or with slaves. Here arose that horrible theory that children are naturally evil, and the object of education became to break a child's will and make him submissive and obedient. Students of child abuse state that cultural acceptance of parents' rights to beat a child is an unconscious justification used by child abusers—it bears, in fact, to child abuse the same relationship as moderate drinking does to alcoholism. The amount of spanking we may do may not hurt us or the child much, but it sets the example for the truly hostile parent. He can justify violence against his children because punishing a child bodily is socially acceptable. Its potential sexual danger has long been documented. There is little evidence that it does any good. A recent writer calls belief in corporal punishment a national sickness and suggests that it has the same sick roots as this country's apparent preoccupation with other kinds of violence.

All in all, I think it is clear that we will need to find other ways in which to discipline children, especially in adolescence. I am still not sure that I am ready to advocate forbidding hand-spanking of young children, which still seems to me an immediate form of nonverbal communication, although I think I may have to change my mind. But adolescents, yes, and paddles or belts, yes, or rather, no. I believe that these will be declared to be violations of a child's right to his body. I also believe that some of you who disagree with me, and I am sure there are many, are likely sooner or later to find yourselves in court. There has been a big increase of such cases the last few years brought by parents and children against workers in Children's Homes. It is a strange and rather alarming fact that the church-connected Children's Home in particular is the last stronghold of the paddle.

Beyond this I think there may be consideration of the right of the child not to be subject to arbitrary or capricious punishment. In the courts fewer children are being convicted of non-crimes such as unruliness or being beyond parental control. I think we may soon move from the courts to the home, and suggest that to punish a child or deprive a child of something he has counted on or could normally expect because of his attitude, or our own exasperation, or for a minor matter of order, is not consistent with respect. I still get a little hot under the collar when I think of a boy I met this year who lost twelve dollars he had expended for tickets for three friends and himself to go to the fair because he was grounded that morning for leaving his jeans on his bed—not that some penalty might not be appropriate, but disruption of the careful and expensive plans of a sixteen-year-old for such a trivial thing, without alternatives, shows very little respect for a youngster. I have the feeling that the child ought to have sued the houseparent for the twelve dollars. While we are looking at the incident, let us look also at some of the so-called privileges we so blithely take away from children; some of them may in fact be rights. I do not think going to the fair is a right, but going to the fair when one has been told one may go may be a right.

Children, if they are not to be nonpersons, have also, under the Constitution, the right to express their opinions as long as they do so in a way that is not abusive or obscene, and does not constitute refusal to obey lawful rules or orders. They have the right to dress or wear their hair in styles within reasonable limits determined by their culture or the occasion. This does not mean that we have no right to counsel them on such matters or set reasonable limits, but we do not have the right to insist that they must do in these things exactly as we would have them do.

Children also have the complementary rights to their families that their families have to them—the right to see and to visit, to receive mail freely, not to be deprived of their families because of the behavior of either their parents or themselves. Whether they have the opposite right—the right *not* to see their parents, is less clear, because a legal relationship exists, and I am tempted to say that legality here must rule. Children certainly have the right to know what is going on, to participate in any planning done for them—not to make final decisions, perhaps, but at least to have input into them and to know why such decisions are made.

The establishment of rights, however, does not imply permissiveness (which is a poor word anyway and usually means either lack of concern or indulgence). Adults still need to set limits, to say, "No, this you must not do," to require reasonable conformity to the kind of order or routine that makes group life possible, to protect on occasion (but only where really necessary), and to punish on occasion (again, if this is the best way of changing behavior, which it rather rarely is). Children for the most part want firmness from adults, but many of the stories that we hear about the child who begs for punishment do not really demonstrate that at all. The child is begging, not for punishment, but for concern, attention, guidance (positive or negative); tragically, for the most part, the only kind he gets is negative.

The adult's right to control is no longer an absolute authority that cannot be questioned, conferred simply by age. It is rather the exercise of a responsibility taken in relation to a child who still needs adult protection and guidance, in a framework of the child's rights. The need for such protection should decrease with the child's age; I would like to see all punishments disappear by adolescence except for those little semiautomatic penalties for breaches of order (comparable to parking tickets or traffic fines for adults), or restitution for damages, for noncriminal acts by children. Guidance, counseling, example, firm limits, honesty about results, concern, a willingness to listen and share—these are the disciplinary tools that count. And maybe if we had used them more often, if we had not relied so much on establishing children as nonpersons, and our own authority as unquestionable and all-pervasive, we might not have the rejecting and rebellious generation of doubters and don't-cares some of us struggle with today.

So we seem to be moving toward a new concept of the rights of the child or young person. Can we live with it, or will our response be to go on insisting that as adults our word is law in all things, with no checks and balances? We have so much taken this for granted in our society that change may be hard. But I do not believe we can put the clock back. I think change is inevitable, and we are faced with the challenge of making it work.

# PART THREE
# Further Reading
# Index

# Further Reading

Most of the books and articles suggested in this statement are of proven worth as reference material in training courses or workshops. Many have been written by persons in active practice such as child care workers, social service staff, executives, and consultants.

No major comprehensive books on Children's Homes have appeared for the past twenty or thirty years. The last was probably that by Cecilia McGovern, *Services to Children in Institutions* (Washington, D.C.: National Conference of Catholic Churches, 1948), although many of us will remember with particular affection Howard W. Hopkirk's work *Institutions Serving Children* (New York: Russell Sage Foundation, 1944). Very little has been written on the management, staffing, or community relationships of such homes. Two useful articles that speak to the problems of the executive are Clayton E. Nordstrom's "Unique Challenges of Institutional Administration" (*Child Welfare*, vol. 45, no. 3, March 1966) and the *Standards of Job Performance for Child Care Administrators* published by the Group Child Care Project (now Group Child Care Consultant Services) of the University of North Carolina in 1967.

A recent article on communication and organization in the group child care agency is the address by that name given to the seventy-first annual meeting of the Southeastern Group Child Care Association in March 1976 by Clifford W. Sanford. A useful guide for boards is *The Guide for Board Organization in Social Agencies*, revised in 1975 by the Child Welfare League of America. Good articles on the philosophy of children's institutions can be found in Alfred Kadushin's book *Child Welfare*

# Further Reading

*Service* (New York: MacMillan, 1967), chapter 2, and in Donnell M. Pappenfort, Dee Morgan, and Robert W. Roberts, eds., *Child Caring: Social Policy and the Institution* (Chicago: Aldine Publishing Co., 1973). There are also a number of useful source books, particularly in the area of the residential treatment of children, of which the best are perhaps James K. Whittaker and Albert E. Treischman, *Children Away from Home* (Chicago: Aldine Alberton, 1972); Morris F. Mayer and Arthur Blum, *Healing Through Living: A Symposium on Residential Treatment* (Springfield, Ill.; Charles C. Thomas, 1971); and Jerome Beker et al., *Critical Incidents in Child Care: A Case Book* (New York: Behavioral Publications, 1972).

The history of Children's Homes has been dealt with largely in general books on child-welfare services such as Dorothy Zeitz, *Child Welfare: Principles and Methods* (New York: John Wiley, 1959); and Arthur E. Fink, *Field of Social Work* (New York: Holt and Rinehart, various editions to 1975; as well as by Rachel Marks in Pappenfort, Morgan, and Roberts, cited above.

For the more distant past, Henry W. Thurston's work *Dependent Child* (New York: Columbia University Press, 1930) is still the most comprehensive. A more recent comprehensive study can be found in Robert W. Bremner, *Children and Youth in America: A Documentary History* (Cambridge, Mass.: Harvard University Press, 1970). For an extrapolated prophecy the reader is referred to Alan Keith-Lucas, "The Church Children's Home in a Changing World" (*Tennessee Public Welfare Record*, vol. 33, no. 4, 1970) or his "Group Child Care without Apology" (Eighteenth Annual Workshop for Personnel in Children's Homes, Austin, Texas, 1976). Basic studies of the child-welfare field that are important to anyone entering this work are Henry Maas and Richard Engler, *Children in Need of Parents* (New York: Columbia University Press, 1959); Robert L. Geiser, *The Illusion of Caring: Children in Foster Care* (Boston: Beacon Press, 1973); and the Child Welfare League's publication *Foster Care in Question*, Helen D. Stone, ed. (New York, 1970). The ideal community structure is described in Alan Keith-Lucas's article "Co-planning and Advocacy in Child Welfare Services" in Felice Perlmutter, ed., *A Design for Social Work Practice* (New York: Columbia University Press, 1974); and some of the general problems of the field, including the public-private question, in his lead article in *Principles and Problems in Child Welfare, Annals of the American Academy of Political and Social Science*, vol. 355, 1964.

Material on the effects of separation of parents and children is plentiful. Most useful are Almeda R. Joloweiz's classic article, "A Foster Child Needs His Own Parents" (*The Child.*, vol. 12, no. 2, 1947); Clarice

# Further Reading

Freud, "Meaning of Separation to Parents and Children as Seen in Child Placement" (*Public Welfare*, vol. 13, no. 1, 1955), both of which have been reprinted for training purposes; Sidney Z. Moss, "How Children Feel about Being Placed Away from Home" (*Children*, vol. 13, no. 4, 1966); Ner Littner's work, "Problems of Separation and Placement" from *Proceedings of the Second Winter Seminar for Social Workers* (Chapel Hill: Group Child Care Consultant Services, University of North Carolina, 1971); and Kenneth W. Watson, "Social Work with Families Divided by Placement" in *Proceedings of the Seventh Winter Seminar*, 1976, as above. The parent's part in separation is highlighted by Shirley Jenkins in "Separation Experiences of Parents Whose Children Are in Foster Care" (*Child Welfare*, vol. 48, no. 2, 1969); Arthur Mandelbaum, "Child-Parent Separation: Its Meaning to Parents" in Whittaker and Treischman, *Children Away from Home* (1972); and an article by Phyllis McAdams, herself a parent of a placed child, "The Parent in the Shadows" (*Child Welfare*, vol. 51, no. 1, 1972). There is little specific material on planning not included in this book, but the basic article is by Alan Keith-Lucas, "Suggested Structures for Planning with Parents and Children" (*Chapel Hill Workshop Reports*, University of North Carolina, 1964, part 2), and more detail is added in the report of Bettie O'Brien's workshop "Specifics of Planning with Families and Children" (1968, part 2).

The importance of parental involvement in planning is stressed by David Fanshel in his "Parental Visiting of Children in Foster Care: Key to Discharge?" (*Social Service Review*, vol. 49, no. 4, 1975) and Mary Ann Jones, Renee Neuman, and Ann W. Rhyne, *A Second Chance for Families* (New York: Child Welfare League, 1976). The results of working or not working with parents are illustrated by Melvin E. Allerhand, Ruth Weber, and Marie Haug in their *Adaptation and Adaptability: The Bellefaire Follow-up Study* (New York: Child Welfare League, 1966) and Delores A. Taylor and Stuart W. Alpert in *Continuity and Support Following Residential Treatment* (New York: Child Welfare League, 1973).

The role of the social worker in planning and in other activities is discussed at length in the *Proceedings of the First Winter Seminar* under the title "The Social Worker in Group Child Care" (Group Child Care Consultant Services, 1970).

The role, qualifications, and training of child care staff have an impressive literature. Perhaps the most useful formulations are found in Howard W. Polsky and Daniel S. Claster, *Dynamics of Residential Treatment: A Social System Analysis* (Chapel Hill: University of North Carolina Press, 1972); Hyman Grossbard, *Cottage Parents: What They Have to Be,*

# Further Reading

*Know and Do* (New York: Child Welfare League, 1960); Eva Burmeister, *The Professional Houseparent* (New York: Columbia University Press, 1960); and Bernard J. Haberlein, *Residential Treatment of Emotionally Disturbed Children* (New York: Behavioral Publications, 1972); Henry W. Maier, in Whittaker and Treischman (1972); William Schwartz, in Morris F. Mayer and Arthur E. Blum, *Healing through Living* (1971); David Birnback, "Some Observations on the Dilemmas and Pressures of the Child Care Job" (*Child Care Quarterly*, vol. 2, no. 2, 1973); and Mary Diggles, "The Child Care Counsellor: New Therapist in Children's Institutions" (*Child Welfare*, vol. 49, no. 9, 1970).

Books of particular use to child care staff in understanding their job include two classics: Morris F. Mayer, *Guide for Child Care Workers* (New York: Child Welfare League, 1958); and Alton M. Broten, *Houseparents in Children's Institutions* (Chapel Hill: University of North Carolina Press, 1958). The Baptist Children's Homes of North Carolina also have a useful pamphlet, *Standards of Performance for Houseparents* (Thomasville, North Carolina, c. 1965).

For supervision, some of the more useful sources are Robert Goldhammer, *Clincial Supervision* (New York: Rinehart and Winston, 1969); and a number of articles including Alfred Kadushin's "Games People Play in Supervision" (*Social Work*, vol. 13, no. 3, 1968) and Charlotte Towle's "The Place of Help in Supervision" (*Social Service Review*, vol. 37, no. 4, 1963); Harry E. Grob and Eric E. Vandoren, "Helping Houseparents Find and Use Their Creativity" (*Children*, vol. 17, no. 3, 1970); Fred Berl, "The Content and Method of Supervisory Teaching" (*Social Casework*, vol. 44, no. 9, 1963); and a report of a workshop for child care supervisors led by Clifford Sanford and George Kolmer (*Chapel Hill Workshop Reports*, part 2, 1967). The point of view of the supervisee is represented by a publication of Group Child Care Consultant Services, *Supervision of Child Care Workers: Viewed by Child Care Workers* (undated, c. 1966). Group supervision is dealt with by Gladys Weinberg in "Dynamics and Content of Group Supervision" (*Child Welfare*, vol. 39, no. 6, 1960); Martin Seitz, "The Use of Group Methods to Train Professional and Child Care Staff" (*Child Welfare*, vol. 45, no. 5, 1966); George S. Getzel, Jack R. Goldberg, and Robert Salmon, "Supervising in Groups as a Model for Today" (*Social Casework*, vol. 53, no. 3, 1971); and Paul A. Abel, " On the Nature of Supervision: The Medium is the Group" (*Child Welfare*, vol. 49, no. 6, 1970). Two behavioral views of supervision are set out in Ned Rosen, *Supervision: A Behavioral View*, and William Wasmuth and George de Lodzie, *Dynamics of Supervision: Organizational Cases and*

# Further Reading

*Intrigues,* published in 1973 and 1974 respectively by Grid, Inc., in Columbus, Ohio. An excellent work on teamwork is by Naomi Brill, *Teamwork: Working Together in Human Services* (Philadelphia: Lippincott, 1976).

Books that relate directly to the caring and educative functions of child care staff include Albert E. Treischman, James K. Whittaker, and Larry K. Bendtro, *The Other 23 Hours: Child Care Work with Emotionally Disturbed Children in a Therapeutic Milieu* (Chicago: Aldine, 1969), which has a behavior-modification base; Lois Barclay Murphy, *Growing Up in Garden Court* (New York: Child Welfare League, 1974); Eva Burmeister, *Tough Times and Tender Moments in Child Care Work* (New York: Columbia University Press, 1967); Draza Kline and Helen-Mary Overstreet, *Foster Care of Children: Nurture and Treatment* (New York: Columbia University Press, 1972); and Jerome Beker, *Critical Incidents in Child Care,* already mentioned. An article not to be missed is Gisela Konopka's "Self Respect: The Basis of Treatment" (*Chapel Hill Workshop Reports,* 1966, part 2).

Not listed here are many books or articles on child development not referring to the child in care which can be found in any curriculum on the subject. These range from works that are primarily psychoanalytic in approach to those that emphasize cognitive or learning theory. Those with particular appeal for workers in the child-welfare field are L. Joseph Stone and Joseph Church, *Childhood and Adolescence* (New York: Random House, 1968), which gives recognition to moral and ethical values; David Elkind, *A Sympathetic Understanding of the Child: Birth to Sixteen* (Boston: Allyn and Bacon, 1974); and W. M. O. Schmidt, *Child Development: The Human Cultural and Educational Context* (New York: Harper and Row, 1973). Of special importance to child care workers are Gisela Konopka, *The Adolescent Girl in Conflict* (Englewood Cliffs, N.J.: Prentice-Hall, 1966) and Leontine Young, *Life Among the Giants* (New York: McGraw-Hill, 1965).

There are again many sources on group construction and management beginning with Suzanne Schulze, *Creative Group Living in a Children's Institution* (New York: Association Press, 1951); and Konopka, *Group Work in the Institution* (New York: Association Press, 1954). Negative evaluations of group behavior can be found in Polsky and Claster, *Dynamics of Residential Treatment*; and in Schwartz's article, both already quoted; while the most extensive analysis of a group is Polsky, *Cottage Six: A Social System of Delinquent Boys in Residential Treatment* (New York: John Wiley, 1962). Good sources for the management of groups are Harry M. Vorrath and Larry K. Bendtro, *Positive Peer Culture* (Chicago: Aldine, 1974); and Dorwin Cartwright and Alvin Zander, *Group Dynam-*

# Further Reading

*ics* (New York: Harper and Row, 1968). Raymond Fant has a useful article in Mayer and Blum, already cited; as does Emanuel Tropp, "The Group: In Life and Social Work" (*Social Casework*, vol. 45, no. 5, 1968). Annabelle Richardson's "Bringing Cohesion to a Cottage Group" (*Child Welfare*, vol. 36, no. 10, 1957) might be read in chronological sequence with the articles also by child care workers, Harte (1968) and Perry (1975) in part 2 of this book, to illustrate progress in the use of groups.

Counseling techniques and methods of working with problems have been presented lately to people largely in terms of specific modalities, such as Reality Therapy, Behavior Modification, Parent Effectiveness Training, and Transactional Analysis. Readers are referred to the popular texts on these methods. Of more general use as a base for interviewing both children and adults are Alan Keith-Lucas's work *Giving and Taking Help* (Chapel Hill: The University of North Carolina Press, 1972); Alfred Benjamin, *The Helping Interview* (Boston: Houghton-Mifflin, 1969); Annette Garrett, *Interviewing* (New York: Family Service Association of America, revised in 1972 by Elinor P. Zane and Margaret M. Mangold); and Naomi Brill, *Working with People* (Philadelphia: J. B. Lippincott Company, 1973).

For direct work with families a useful source related to child care work is *Family Interviewing* from *Proceedings of the Fifth Winter Seminar for Social Workers* (Group Child Care Consultant Services, 1974) jointly led by Seymour L. Halleck, M.D., Thomas E. Curtis, M.D., and Sarah W. Bowen, M.S.W. An early article, still very pertinent, by Herbert Aptekar, is "Casework With the Child's Own Family in Child Placing Agencies," which appeared in a Child Welfare League pamphlet, *Six Papers on Child Welfare Problems*, in 1953.

The place of the therapist in the Children's Home is treated in part 4 of Mayer and Blum, *Healing Through Living*; and in Whittaker and Treischman, *Children Away from Home*, both already cited.

Books dealing with specific psychiatric techniques include one by Harvey H. and Sybil Barten, *Children and Their Parents in Brief Therapy* (New York: Behavioral Publications, 1973); Haim G. Ginott, *Group Psychotherapy with Children* (New York: McGraw-Hill, 1961); *Disturbed Children*, from the Menninger Foundation (San Francisco: Jossey Bass, 1969); Jan Haley and Lynn Hoffman, *Techniques of Family Therapy* (New York: Basic Books, 1967); William Glasser, *Reality Therapy* (New York: Harper and Row, 1965); Anthony M. Graziano, *Behavior Therapy with Children II* (Chicago: Aldine Publishing Co., 1975); and in a panel discussion of psychiatrists, social workers, and executives at the Chapel Hill Workshops

# Further Reading

(*Chapel Hill Workshop Reports*, part 2, 1967); while those who are quick to categorize children as mentally ill or "disturbed" might read Thomas S. Szasz, *Myth of Mental Illness* (New York: Delta Books, 1961).

A fine source of material on the rights of children is by Albert E. Wilkerson, *The Rights of Children: Emergent Concepts in Law and Society* (Philadelphia: Temple University Press, 1973). Readers might also want to consult Milford Barnes, "The Concept of Parental Force" (*Child Welfare*, vol. 46, no. 3, 1967); and Sol Rubin, "Children as Victims of Institutionalization" (*Child Welfare*, vol. 51, no. 1, 1972).

For the legal aspects of state intervention into family life there is no better source than the publication from the U.S. Department of Health, Education, and Welfare, *Standards for Juvenile and Family Courts* (1966), with its clear definition of legal custody and guardianship. Thomas Gill is also helpful in his "Legal Nature of Neglect" (*NPPA Journal*, vol. 6, no. 1, 1960). On children's actual rights in care one might go back to Gisela Konopka, "Re-thinking from the Beginning What is Absolutely Essential in a Child Care Program Today" (*Chapel Hill Workshop Reports*, part 2, 1969); while Martin Gula's little gem, "Dear Mr. Superintendent" (*Child*, vol. 14, no. 2, 1950) should never be forgotten.

# Index

# Index

# Index

# Index

# Index

and rewards, 159, 160; exemplary,
159–60; arbitrary, 253
Purchase of care, 93–94, 95–97

## Q

Question: adult assumption of right
to, 196

## R

Race, 24, 81, 243
Reality: as helping factor, 105–7, 197,
236
Reassurance: false, 44
Referrals, 106; sustained, 43, 91
Regimentation, 24
Religious nurture, 88, 129
Research, 86, 93
Residential treatment center, viii, 8–9,
10, 11, 12, 19, 34; literature on, 260
Respect: for children, 24, 129, 132–33
Restriction, 113–15
Retardation, 133
Rewards, 159–60
Rights: of children, 24, 36, 248–55; of
parents, 249–50
Right to fail, 132–37
Routines, 24–25, 130, 136
Rules, 4, 27, 139, 184; of conversation
with children, 195–96

## S

Savings, 149
Scher, Bernard: quoted, 136
School, 25, 110, 125, 164. See also
Education
Schulze, Suzanne: quoted, 172
Schutz, William C.: theory of, 202
Separation, 8, 124–26, 167; articles on,
260–61
Service, Gresham's Law of, 90
Sex behavior: fear of stimulating, 25
Sex education, 152–57
Sexuality, 34
Shift system, 73
Sibley, Celestine: quoted, 132
Size: as factor in communication,
193–94, 204
Social action, 92, 245–46
Social engineering, 87
Social Security, 95
Social service: as system affecting
Home, 83
Social work education, 67–68, 93

Social workers, 51, 66, 147, 211; first
employed, 10; role in
"child-centered institution," 10–11;
as link between child and family, 11;
as primary planning personnel,
20–21; claim exclusive role as
advocate, 37, 65; availability in early
days of placement, 48;
responsibility at intake, 49–50; used
to screen admissions, 64; as
counselor, 64; as expert, 65; conflict
with child care staff, 65–66;
education of, 67–68, 93; as helping
agents, 104–5; work with parent
and child care worker, 109–20;
conferences with child, 116
Socialization, 26, 130
Sociograms, 189–90
Special education, 25, 130
Specialists, 64, 71, 79
Specialization of function, 88–91
Specificity of plans, 118
Sponsors, 97, 147
Staff training, 214–15. See also Child
care workers, training of
Staffing a Home, 62–71
"Standby" foster homes, 58
Student councils, 238–39
Structure: in planning, 15–16, 43;
administrative, 62–82
Superintendent. See Administrator
Supervision, 75–76; literature on, 262
"Sustained referral," 43, 91
Symbolic actions, 46, 78, 194
Systems affecting Home, 83–94

## T

Table manners, 26
Tables of organization, 62, 71, 72, 73,
79
Talents, 130, 163
Tastes: respect for child's, 23, 24
Teamwork, 16, 80–82, 109–20
Technical colleges, 69
Television, 236
Temper tantrums, 116–17
Ten Commandments, 160
Therapy, 14, 130, 207–34; as helping
method, 18–19, 34–36; not required
by all children, 34; as part of plan,
34–35; and social workers, 35, 67,
216; with family, 35, 225–34;
literature on, 264–65

271

# Index

Touching children, 172, 195, 204
Tradition, 4, 12
"Treatment-oriented": as
  classification of Homes, 12
Treischman, Albert, et al., 19
Trust, 142, 200, 202

### U
Unit system, 73–74, 79, 80
Units: functional, 75
Use-of-care plans, 21, 93, 128

### V
Vacations, 130
Veterans benefits, 95
Vietnam war, 194
Visiting, 47, 51, 128, 250
Voluntary agencies, 85–87, 95–97

### W
Waifs and Strays, 5
Whitaker, Charles, 228

White House Conference on Children
  (1909), 7
"Why?": uselessness of, 144, 196
Wilkerson, Albert E., 36n
Wills: battle of, 206
Wineman, David: quoted, 136
Words: adolescents suspicious of, 194
Work, 27; as a moral duty for poor, 5;
  off-campus, 10, 149–50
Work-earning-responsibility plans,
  56, 93, 145–51
Work supervisors, 71, 146, 149, 150,
  151
Workhouse: as alternative to
  orphanage, 5
Worship, 129

### Y
Youth. *See* Adolescents

### Z
Zinsser, William K.: quoted, 134–35